THE
BATTLE
OF THE
GENERALS

Also by Martin Blumenson

Breakout and Pursuit
The Duel for France
Anzio: The Gamble That Failed
Sicily: Whose Victory?
Eisenhower
Kasserine Pass
Bloody River: The Real Tragedy of the Rapido
Salerno to Cassino
The Patton Papers: 1885–1940
The Patton Papers: 1940–1945
Masters of the Art of Command (with James L. Stokesbury)
Liberation
The Vilde Affair
Mark Clark
Patton: The Man Behind the Legend

THE
BATTLE
OF THE
GENERALS

THE UNTOLD STORY OF THE FALAISE POCKET — THE CAMPAIGN THAT SHOULD HAVE WON WORLD WAR II

Martin Blumenson

WILLIAM MORROW AND COMPANY, INC.
NEW YORK

It is the policy of William Morrow and Company, Inc., and its imprints and affiliates, recognizing the importance of preserving what has been written, to print the books we publish on acid-free paper, and we exert our best efforts to that end.

Library of Congress Cataloging-in-Publication Data

Blumenson, Martin.
    The battle of the generals : the untold story of the Falaise
pocket—the campaign that should have won World War II / Martin
Blumenson.
        p.   cm.
    Includes bibliographical references and index.
    ISBN 0-688-11837-2
    1. Falaise Gap, Battle of, 1944.   I. Title.
D756.5.F34B57   1993
940.54'21—dc20   92-31705
                                                                    CIP

Printed in the United States of America

First Edition

1 2 3 4 5 6 7 8 9 10

BOOK DESIGN BY LYNN DONOFRIO

To the memory of
CHARLES B. MacDONALD
1922–1990

company commander
military historian
inspiring teacher
and, above all,
cherished friend

Contents

Part I. The Setting

Chapter 1. The Problem   15

Chapter 2. The Allied Commanders   25

Chapter 3. The Coalition   41

Chapter 4. The Struggle for Dominance   53

Chapter 5. The Invasion Plan   69

Part II. The Precipitating Action

Chapter 6. The Germans   89

Chapter 7. The Crisis in Command   103

Chapter 8. The July Difficulties   113

Part III. Cobra

Chapter 9. Bombing   129

Chapter 10. Breakthrough   143

Chapter 11. Breakout   153

Part IV. The Encirclement

Chapter 12. The Mortain Counterattack   173

Chapter 13. The Canadian Attack   179

Chapter 14. The Short Hook   187

Chapter 15. The Stop Order   199

Chapter 16. The Second Stop Order   215

Chapter 17. Closing the Pocket   227

8   **CONTENTS**

Part V. The Aftermath
          Chapter 18. The Seine River Crossings   249
          Chapter 19. Reflections   261
Author's Note   275
Select Bibliography   277
Index   279

There are in Europe many good generals, but they see too many
things at once. I see only one thing, namely the enemy's main body.
I try to crush it.
—*Napoleon Bonaparte*

I admire Napoleon less since I know what a coalition is.
—*Marshal Ferdinand Foch*

The only thing worse than having allies is not having them.
—*Winston Churchill*

PART I

THE SETTING

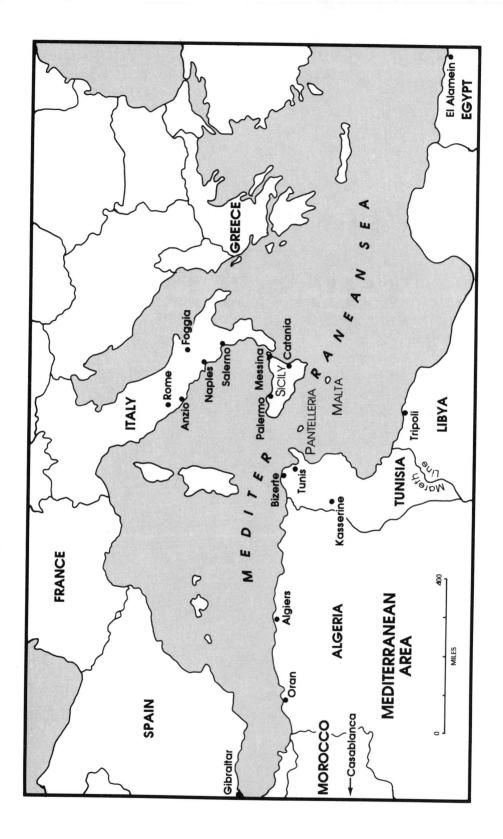

MEDITERRANEAN
AREA

CHAPTER 1

The Problem

EARLY ON A LOVELY August morning, four young army officers, among them Richard McAdoo, rode warily in two jeeps through lush Norman farmland. On the qui vive, they watched for signs of life, listened for suspicious noises. What they dreaded most was to hear the sudden sharp crack of a rifle or whining howl of a bullet.

There was nothing. They met no one. The fields glistened with dew. Cows grazed in pastures dotted with haycocks. The sun was already warm, and the day promised to be hot.

They were traveling north. Eventually, as they expected, the ground rose. The meandering dirt road became a steep grade. They drove uphill to the top of a ridge. There, near an abandoned stone house, they stopped. After a moment, they dismounted. They walked across a small orchard.

The countryside was still and peaceful. Drifting clouds formed patches of shadow on the earth. Bees in the apple trees overhead buzzed around the ripe fruit.

A hedge of brush and saplings marked the end of the property, and the four Americans peered through the natural fence. The ground fell away abruptly. Below them was a broad valley, an open plain crossed by rural lanes. Except for an occasional horse-drawn cart, there was no movement. The main highway, a strip of macadam colored ochre, was empty of traffic. To the left or west was an immense and, to their eyes, impenetrable forest. On the right was a modest village dominated by a square medieval tower. All was calm.

They were elated. They had arrived in good time. Their site was perfect. They had an eagle's view over the territory.

Artillery forward observers, they were the eyes of twelve powerful Long Toms, 155-millimeter guns, in position far behind them. Each piece was massive, weighing fifteen tons. Rolling on ten wheels, towed by an eighteen-ton tractor, each barrel could throw metal and explosive more then fourteen miles. The gunners responded to radio and telephone calls from outposts like the one McAdoo and his party were about to set up. Shooting according to instructions coming from the ridge, they could send their shells to fall on whatever passed along the low ground.

Although aware of their assigned role in the events to come, these artillerymen had little idea of the actual scenes they were about to produce. For they were newcomers and neophytes, and they had reached that place by a relatively uneventful and circuitous route.

After crossing the English Channel the previous month, the men and their pieces settled down temporarily near Cherbourg. Early in August, the soldiers and guns assembled in column for a road march. They found themselves at the rear of a vehicular stream more than twenty miles in length. Moving slowly, almost leisurely, shepherding their heavy equipment through the narrow streets of forlorn habitations battered and ruined by war, the troops traveled to the south.

Proceeding along the coast, the jewel of Mont-St-Michel rising from the water on the right, the unit inched up the long incline into Avranches. On the other side of the damaged town, the organization crossed the small, arched, and miraculously intact Pontaubault bridge, barely wide enough to accommodate the guns. There the outfit bore to the left and southeast.

Fifty miles and several days later, men and equipment were in Laval. Almost due east now, forty miles and three days more, they reached the city of Le Mans. Instead of continuing eastward for another hundred miles to the Seine River and Paris, they changed direction again, this time going left, and started north.

Like those whom they had followed, they had gone around the Germans and were now part of an encircling maneuver. The tempo stepped up, and they hurried ahead through those who had preceded them. Now, near the front of the column, they arrived at the hamlet of Mortrée in the evening. In nearby fields, not far from the celebrated Château d'O, the men set up their guns and prepared for action. They shortly opened fire in slow cadence. Throughout the night, they shelled the small town of Trun, thirteen miles away. On the following morning, McAdoo and his three companions set out for the ridge.

A trap was being closed in Normandy, and the four men at the observation post were in on the kill. To their left, along a line still not altogether solid but extending more than fifty miles through the outskirts of Argentan to the hills around Mortain, thousands of Americans and French whom they could not see were poised to spring upon and crush their opponents. Off to the northwest also out of their sight, a British army was pushing their adversaries toward this area. Somewhere to the northeast, their right, Poles would soon be approaching the looming mass of Mount Ormel. Over the horizon beyond the rise on the other side of the bottomland, Canadians, on their way to the same natural bowl, were heading south to Falaise.

The Allies had almost surrounded the Germans and were now squeezing and compressing the Falaise pocket. The only German escape exit was the Falaise gap, roughly fifteen miles wide. This narrow neck was about to be strangled.

All day long the party on the ridge watched the ground below. Nothing much happened until sundown. A German staff car, its occupants unaware of the eyes upon them, rolled out of the forest of Gouffern on the left, traveled along the main road, and disappeared into the streets of Chambois, the village on the right. Soon afterwards, three German horse-drawn supply wagons emerged sedately from Chambois and went the other way. The Americans requested a fire mission, a few shells, mainly to check and relate range, direction, and timing for accuracy. The rounds delivered exploded harmlessly some distance behind the trotting horses, but they galloped in fright for the cover of Gouffern's trees.

That was the opening salvo of what developed into a fire storm. During the next week, as Germans on foot, in wagons, trucks, and cars streamed eastward across the land, intense excitement built on the high ground. Allied observers yelled instructions into their radios and phoned for gunners to adjust their barrels and hurl exploding metal to pound and devastate the fleeing troops. Officers from other artillery battalions joined the four Americans on the ridge, and the orchard became crowded with men and equipment. Elsewhere, on other knobs overlooking the Falaise pocket and gap, literally hundreds of officers directed thousands of cannons shelling the diminishing corridor of German escape.

All who were present on the heights saw the boiling dust and shreds of smoke, the vehicles careening through the fields and along the roads, many being torn to pieces before crashing or burning. Some observers were too far away to hear the fire of the guns, the roar of the racing motors, the shrieks of the wounded men, the crazed neighing of hurt and panicked horses—even the Allied airplanes bombing off toward the west were soundless, and to the observers it was like watching a silent movie.

During the few short hours of summer darkness, hidden by the night, the Germans worked feverishly not only to flee but also to clear the roads of wreckage and animals impeding and blocking movement. They had to contend with random shells falling in their midst or near them, for the Allies continued to shoot intermittently, the explosions rumbling like sustained thunder, the flashes winking like heat lightning.

The Germans were unable to wait until nightfall to make good their escape. The walls of the pocket were closing in on them. There were too many men, well over 100,000, to stay in concealment throughout the day. Increasing numbers of driven troops pressed into the forest. Groups burst out and raced for safety under the Allied rain of fire. Some blundered into Allied positions and were taken prisoner.

Eventually the melee subsided. Americans fought across the deeply indented ditch of the Dives River into Chambois, most of which was burning, while Poles battled into the town from the opposite direction. The two forces met where the heat from the flames was less intense, at the small open square where the twelfth-century donjon rises. There they closed the pocket.

The Germans were gone. They struggled painfully past the Poles on Mount Ormel, then continued some fifty miles and more to get to and across the Seine River.

When the kaleidoscope was over and the battlefront had moved on, with quiet once again lying over the Falaise pocket, Richard McAdoo drove from Mortrée to the old observation post on the ridge. The orchard, only a few days before packed with excited men and their instruments, was now deserted except for a few soldiers routinely salvaging telephone wire. The stone house was no longer abandoned; a young woman was sweeping the steps at the front door.

Continuing over the top, McAdoo went downhill. Allied troops had cleared the highway between the forest of Gouffern and the town of Chambois, but the strewn debris, tortured remnants of the devastation, defaced the ditches, the fields, and the rural tracks. The smell of death was sweet and sickening under the hot sun.

He proceeded into the cool shade of the woods. Under the trees along both sides of the road, in long rows stood trucks and wagons unable to leave for lack of gasoline or drivers. Parked decorously, all covered with a thin film of dust, they gave the impression of languor after great strain. The silence was brooding.

An American after-action report recorded the "carnage wrought during the final days as the artillery . . . and the massed air forces pounded the ever-shrinking pocket" as being "perhaps the greatest of the war. The roads and fields were littered with thousands of enemy dead and wounded, wrecked and burning vehicles, smashed artillery pieces, carts laden with the loot of France overturned and smoldering, dead horses and cattle swelling in the summer's heat."

A mature officer who was familiar with such scenes in both world wars found nothing to compare with what he saw in the Falaise pocket. "The grass and trees were vividly green as in all Normandy and a surprising number of houses [were] . . . untouched," he wrote a day after viewing the ground. "That rather peaceful setting framed a picture of destruction so great that it cannot be described. It was as if an avenging angel had swept the area bent on destroying all things German.

"I stood on a lane, surrounded by 20 or 30 horses or parts of horses, most of them still hitched to their wagons and carts. . . . As far as my eye could reach . . . on every line of sight, there were . . . vehicles, wagons, tanks, guns, prime movers, sedans, rolling kitchens, etc. in various stages of destruction. . . .

"I walked through a mile or so of lanes where the vehicles had been closely packed. . . . I saw probably 300 field pieces and tanks, mounting large caliber guns that were apparently undamaged.

"I saw no foxholes or any other type of shelter or field fortifications. The Germans were trying to run and had no place to run. They were probably too exhausted to dig. . . . They were probably too tired even to surrender. I left this area," he concluded, "rather regretting I'd seen it."

Another visitor talked of "the acrid smell of burning and burnt-out vehicles. . . . Above the battlefield shimmered a miasma of decay and putrefaction: everything was covered with flies and blue-bottles. In the hot August sun the cattle which had been killed only days before were masses of crawling maggots, and the unburied Germans, swollen to elephantine grossness by the hot sun . . . lay with blackened faces in grotesque positions. . . . Fragments of bodies festooned the trees."

General Dwight D. Eisenhower, the Supreme Allied Commander, came to the area soon afterwards and called it a killing ground, "unquestionably one of the greatest" of the war, "choked with destroyed equipment and with dead men and animals." What he saw, he said, was evidence of an inferno that "could be described only by Dante."

Clearly, at first glance, the Allies had won a great victory, the Germans had suffered a grievous defeat. Less than three months after the D day landings on June 6, 1944, the Allies had swept the Germans opposing them from the field.

Quite literally, encirclement means death. Soldiers trapped in a pocket must fight desperately to break out. If their escape is blocked, they are doomed. They have no recourse but to surrender or die.

Ever since 216 B.C., when Hannibal with about 50,000 men closed around some 80,000 Romans under Varro, destroyed their cohesion, provoked their panic, and overwhelmed them, the battle of Cannae has been, as the military say, the symbol of tactical perfection. In more recent memory, Hindenburg and Ludendorff netted Samsonov's army near Tannenberg in August 1914, Rokossovsky surrounded Paulus's army near Stalingrad in February 1943. All such maneuvers, if conducted with expertise and single-minded concentration, inflict such losses and psychological blows as to be virtually irreparable.

So too in Normandy in August 1944. The Germans had made themselves vulnerable to encirclement, and the major Allied leaders recognized the glittering prize beckoning them. General Sir Bernard L. Montgomery, who headed the Allied ground forces, was very British and understated. Closing the trap, he said, would "put the enemy in the most awkward predicament." General Omar N. Bradley, who led the American combat troops on the Continent, exaggerated, but not by much, when he called Falaise "an opportunity that comes to a commander not more than once in a century." General George S. Patton, Jr., who directed the Third U.S. Army, was unequivocal. "The purpose of the operation," he announced flatly, "is to surround and destroy the German army west of the Seine." In a letter to his wife, he wrote, "I am the only one who realizes how little the enemy can do—he is finished. We may end this [war] in ten days."

The prediction was off the mark. The principal Allied commanders had considerable success forming, compressing, and finally closing the ring. In terms of casualties inflicted, prisoners taken, matériel destroyed, and territory liberated, they gained a spectacular triumph. But the war was far from over in Europe. The conflict would endure for eight more months.

The truth is, a considerable number of Germans evaded the pocket. Most fought their way out as members of their own organized and cohesive units. Some slipped out individually or in small parties. Others coalesced and formed effective ad hoc groups. A few, of course, were picked up by the Allies.

How many were caught, how many escaped, no one knows for sure. Precise figures are lacking and difficult to establish.

Omitting the 50,000 or so in Brittany, there were probably 350,000 Germans west of the Seine River in mid-August. About half of these, or 175,000, were outside the threatened area, on other fronts or in rear-area installations. The rest, about 175,000 men, were potential victims of the closing jaws.

The Allies later improved their counting procedures, but in August, the Graves Registration Units, which buried the bodies, and the military police, which maintained the prisoner-of-war cages, were less than entirely accurate. According to all estimates, Allied and German, somewhere between 6,000 and 10,000 men were killed or had disappeared inside the cauldron. The figures of those captured varied even further. The British announced an overall total of perhaps 25,000 prisoners. The Canadians, unable to distinguish between those who were swept into prisoner-of-war enclosures and those who perished, believed more than 50,000 had been killed and captured. The Americans estimated a probable total of 50,000 taken prisoner. The highest numbers, 10,000 dead and 50,000 captured, indicate the escape of well over 100,000 soldiers of those exposed to encirclement.

Most of the survivors were devoid of their heavy weapons and equipment, which they had left behind. German matériel losses were in the neighborhood of two hundred tanks, three hundred cannons, seven hundred artillery pieces, two thousand wagons, five thousand vehicles, and one thousand eight hundred dead horses.

But most of the German leaders, their headquarters and staffs, together with their cadres, after great exertion and an exhibition of consummate skill, reached safety. Five German corps commanders had been inside the pocket; only one was taken prisoner. Of fifteen German division commanders, merely three were captured. The troops who managed to get out were tired, even exhausted, but they were elated by their escape.

Still another ordeal awaited them: crossing the Seine River while the Allies were at their heels. They traversed the water with relative ease. During the last ten days of the month, approximately 240,000 men, including those who had been outside the pocket, moved from the left to the right bank of the Seine. They soon joined and gave coherence to a line of defenses protecting the approaches to Germany.

How inconclusive the Allied achievement had been was apparent almost at once. In the early days of September, the Germans established a continuous defensive front more than one hundred miles long between the Channel and the Ardennes. Among the twenty divisions holding there, more than half, twelve, had escaped from Normandy. They were understrength and short of matériel, but they were intact and veteran organizations.

More evidence appeared later in the month, when the Allies launched their ill-fated airborne drop and armored drive, code-named Market Garden, and attempted to cross the Lower Rhine River at Arnhem, the Netherlands. Stopping them were units that had fled from Normandy. And finally, in December, in the Ardennes counteroffensive, the battle of the Bulge, survivors of the Falaise pocket in large part manned fifteen of the twenty-five German divisions committed to the attack.

Contributing to the German resurgence was industrial output, which in 1944 was about three times greater than in 1942. Plants turned out, for example, 1,600 tanks per month. The high rate of production reequipped the formations depleted in Normandy. Adolf Hitler needed only a short respite to reconstitute his combat forces, and the Allied supply crisis in September, when the columns ran out of gasoline, gave him time to rebuild.

The fact was, the Allies had had the Germans on the ropes in Normandy and had been unable to administer the knockout blow. As the exhilaration of the moment vanished, optimistic intelligence reports foretelling the imminent collapse of Germany quickly changed in tone and substance.

Prime Minister Winston Churchill, having expected an abundant harvest of prisoners, expressed his disappointment. The Germans, Montgomery conceded, had been able to extricate a substantial number of men. But he minimized their strength and importance.

To Bradley, the Allies had destroyed beyond question the enemy west of the Seine River. Only the mobile elements, he insisted, had escaped, and they had taken such losses as to be unfit for combat.

Patton made no comment.

Eisenhower was candid. "Due to the extraordinary defensive measures taken by the enemy," he wrote, "it is possible that our total bag of prisoners will not be so great as I first anticipated." His explanation was careful and reasoned, and to a large extent true. The Germans had indeed been skillful and adept.

But that was hardly the whole story. Large operations of encirclement are extremely difficult to execute, but the Allies let the chance for an overwhelming victory slip through their fingers. What should have been a finely tuned and well-oiled maneuver was inept and bungled, displaying contradictory impulses. Hesitation, wrangling, and uncertainty marred the venture. The Germans themselves had foolishly pushed their heads into a noose, and the Allies had been unable to pull the string shut. They closed the Falaise pocket too slowly and then failed to trap the fleeing Germans again at the Seine.

There was little bitterness or recrimination in the immediate aftermath, for the campaign produced a quick succession of heady thrills—the liberation of Paris, the pursuit across the Seine, the lightning thrusts toward Germany.

Yet nagging thoughts remained. Why had the Allies been unable to generate a truly cohesive effort and knock Germany out of the war?

The answer lies in the realm of three considerations: the abilities of the Allied commanders, the nature of the Allied coalition, and the weight of the Allied invasion plan.

CHAPTER 2

The Allied Commanders

WHETHER MILITARY ACTIVITY IS a science or an art has long been debated. In actual fact, the occupation partakes of both. A profession like those deriving from the medieval guilds and brotherhoods—clergy, medicine, and law—the military displays the same general characteristics as the others. It renders service to the community. Its members require special education. They engage in full-time employment or active duty for pay. They hold a commission, which is a license to practice. The body follows a prescribed code of behavior, regulates its own procedures, and selects certain individuals for promotion and honor.

What distinguishes the professional from the amateur in all callings is the standard response to a given situation. Physicians facing the same set of symptoms are likely to agree on the malady and to prescribe much the same treatment. So too in the military. The normal solution to a problem is largely the product of knowledge gained by prior learning, training, and experience, all constrained or driven by current doctrine or methodology. To that extent, military operations are scientific. Deviations from the rules are minimal.

On the other hand, individuality has a recognized place in the order, particularly among those on the higher levels of authority. Leaders are different in personality, temperament, and habit. Some are naturally reckless, others prudent. A few are imaginative and out of the ordinary.

Their perceptions are flashes of genius. Their actions may develop into creative flair. This is the artistic side.

Commanders are at the heart of warfare because their decisions shape events in the process of happening. Their judgments, as well as the course of action flowing from them, foreshadow the future. Some reactions come from the gut as instinctual reflexes without conscious thought, instantly expressed and applied. Others emerge deliberately as the result of logic or a conscious weighing of alternatives. Most deal with balancing risk and gain, both of which are unknowns beforehand. At stake are victory and defeat, and the lives of their soldiers.

Complicating the enterprise is the deadly contest in progress. In a clash of arms, the two opposing sides are constantly jockeying for advantage. Each seeks to anticipate what the other will do and attempts to counter with an unexpected move. The fact that professionals act in much the same predictable way in all armies hardly simplifies the situation, for the element of surprise is always present or in the offing.

A commander exercises a double function. He is the source of authority; he is also the repository of responsibility. First, only he has the power to direct whatever takes place and to compel obedience to his wishes. No one else can issue orders except in his name. Secondly, to him alone belongs the credit or the blame of whatever results from the exertions and the endeavors of his subordinate commanders, those under him.

Aiding the commander are staff officers. They are advisers, assistants, specialists, administrators. They collect information, chart progress, run offices and shops, and perform a wide variety of duties. They are accountable for their efficiency and mistakes. They may recommend certain courses of action, but the commander alone decides.

What holds the entire military structure together is the glue of discipline, which buttresses and enhances the omnipotence of command. What keeps the edifice firm is the sacrosanct force of the chain of command, the established hierarchy of command levels or echelons, which denotes the senior and junior status of commanders, from top to bottom, army group, army, corps, division, and so on. Permeating a well-functioning organization are mutual trust and confidence.

All these factors were consequential in the panorama unfolding around Falaise. The glue failed to stick entirely, the chain of command was less than firm, and mutual trust and confidence were often absent.

A good part of the reason for this state of affairs came from the dissimilar personal traits of the principals involved. Eisenhower, Montgomery, Bradley, and Patton were mature professionals. Each had a lifetime of military experience. All had assiduously studied warfare. Yet their habits made it difficult for them to interact in complete harmony.

Eisenhower, short-tempered, exuding charm, chose to be aloof from the everyday concerns of his subordinates. He preferred to be above it all, and, where battle was the subject, had no hard-and-fast rules.

Montgomery, an ascetic and essentially a loner, tended to be cautious. The memory of Britain's enormous losses in the First World War conditioned him, and the diminishing manpower available during the latter part of the Second World War reinforced his conservative outlook. The shortage of men by 1944 compelled officials from time to time to disband existing units in order to use the troops to replace the dead, wounded, and sick who thinned the formations in the field. Montgomery had to be careful in his practice of the art of war.

At the opposite extreme stood Patton, endowed with the seemingly infinite resources of America. A swashbuckling figure compensating for inner anxieties, he was nevertheless shrewd and calculating in his plans. He believed in daring and dash. To him, the small incremental casualties taken by the measured British actions over the long run surpassed the higher short-term expenditures that suited his personality.

Somewhere in the middle was Bradley, who affected humility. He played by the book. Admired for his soundness and dependability, he preferred to take no chances. Bradley, they said, was solid and safe. If he would win no outstanding victory, neither would he suffer a disastrous defeat.

Although Eisenhower was in Normandy much of the time, he took no active role in the affairs leading to and culminating at Falaise. Head of the land, sea, and air forces invading and liberating the Continent, he had temporarily turned over the direction of the ground effort to Montgomery. Having delegated that responsibility, Eisenhower scrupulously refrained from meddling. His headquarters was moving from England to France, its location far to the rear of the front, and Eisenhower felt keenly his lack of the machinery, above all, his staff and signals people, to enable him to influence what was occurring. Without an information system of his own, he visited his subordinates, listened to them, encouraged them, and never interfered.

If Eisenhower never had what the combat leaders call an intuitive feel for the battle, he accurately assessed and frequently reported the situation in his correspondence with his mentor Marshall. When he mentioned operational opportunities open to the Allies, as he often did, he refused to indicate how he thought the advantage ought to be exploited. If he can be faulted for his behavior, he failed to exercise his personal will and mandated authority. He might thus have set right an enterprise going out of kilter. He elected to keep his distance. That was his manner.

According to John Keegan, commanders of national renown wear masks.* They show certain externals to satisfy their culture and countrymen. They hide certain signs running counter to expectations. In short, the leader displays a military ethos in tune with his particular context, the desires of the society he represents.

Eisenhower, Montgomery, Bradley, and Patton all created images of themselves to stir their compatriots. All four, strange to say, were on the periphery of the mainstream as boys—Eisenhower in Kansas, Montgomery in Tasmania, Bradley in Missouri, Patton near Pasadena, California, vague reminders of Napoleon Bonaparte growing up in Corsica. Eisenhower and Bradley related closely to the Americans, Montgomery captured the imagination of the British, Patton was occasionally out of step.

Montgomery wore his commander's mask perfectly for the British people. A graduate of the royal military college, Sandhurst, Montgomery had been a twenty-six-year-old platoon leader when World War I started. He was severely wounded in the opening days and received the Distinguished Service Order for his gallantry. After a long convalescence, he returned to the Western Front in 1916 as a staff officer with a brigade. He was later on the staff of a corps. When the war ended, he was a lieutenant colonel and the chief of staff of the 47th (London) Division.

He had amply demonstrated his excellence, not only as a young commander but also as a staff member, and he had mounted rapidly in rank and responsibility. His duties had provided him with a variety of learning situations on several echelons. His experience gave him a good view of warfare. What impressed him most was the loss of life resulting from frequent amateurishness and consequent incompetence among some of the leaders. The needless sacrifice of young men haunted Montgomery, and he resolved to be, above all, a professional, an expert, a knowledgeable and conscientious soldier whose preparations would be meticulously correct and whose orders would be perfectly clear and thoroughly understood.

During the interwar years, Montgomery zealously pursued his goal. He was a serious student of military art and science. He gained a name within the British army as an effective instructor. He tolerated no foolishness. He learned to be precise in his directives to his subordinates.

---

*See Select Bibliography.

He also mastered the subtle art of showing ambiguity to his superiors, that is, of appearing to be right no matter what the circumstances.

In 1939, at the outbreak of World War II in Europe, in command of a division, about 15,000 men, Montgomery took his outfit to the Continent as part of the British Expeditionary Force. During the eight months of the Phoney War he conducted the normal affairs of a unit in the field, maneuvering, deploying in defense, training. When Hitler struck in May 1940, Montgomery showed his mettle and expertise in battle. He distinguished himself in the fighting in Belgium and northern France. He was outstanding during the Anglo-French defeat and particularly during the withdrawal to and evacuation from Dunkirk.

So well had he functioned that, once he was back, he became head of the Southeastern Command, that part of England most directly threatened by German invasion. He was an exemplary trainer of the British and Canadian troops who defended the area.

The only possible stain on his career was his responsibility, to what extent has never been determined, for planning the unsound and unfortunate Dieppe operation, a landing by Canadians turned back with heavy losses. Montgomery escaped blame or censure by receiving, just days before the Dieppe crossing, the opportunity for another battlefield command. This one came by virtue of a miraculous set of circumstances.

On August 7, 1942, while Montgomery observed a training exercise in Scotland, he had a telephone call informing him of a new appointment. He was to replace General Sir Harold Alexander in the Allied command structure for the invasion of North Africa, landings scheduled for November, three months in the future. Alexander was unavailable because he was going to Cairo, Egypt, to be commander in chief of the British Middle East forces.

Montgomery returned at once to London, where he found instructions to get in touch with Eisenhower, who less than two weeks earlier, had become the Supreme Allied Commander of the North African venture. Montgomery phoned him. Eisenhower, he learned, was expecting Patton, who was also associated with the North African operation, to arrive in London that day for planning discussions. Montgomery agreed to confer with Eisenhower and Patton that afternoon of August 8 to help plan what would be the first Anglo-American amphibious operation on the European side of the war.

Eisenhower and Montgomery had met once before. In the spring, Eisenhower, a new major general, had come from Washington to England with several American officers, among them Mark Clark, on a fact-finding trip for General George C. Marshall, the U.S. Army chief of staff. During their travels, Eisenhower and Clark visited Montgomery's headquarters for a briefing on British training methods.

A lieutenant general and therefore senior to Eisenhower and Clark, Montgomery was hardly pleasant. He delivered his presentation. But he made the Americans feel as though they were intruding on his time and taking him from more important matters. He curtly ordered Eisenhower to snuff out the cigarette he was smoking, and Eisenhower meekly obeyed.

Now, on the morning of August 8, before the conference in London with Eisenhower and Patton scheduled for that afternoon, Montgomery learned of the sudden death of the British Eighth Army commander in Egypt. Instructed to take his place, Montgomery departed at once.

Had he served in French Northwest Africa under Eisenhower, whom he barely knew, Montgomery might well have missed his chance for fame. Instead, under Alexander, with whom he was well acquainted and whom he was able to dominate, Montgomery was in charge of the largest British army in existence and operating against the Italo-German forces under Field Marshal Erwin Rommel, whose astounding exploits had elevated him into a myth, a magician, a demon.

Montgomery made the most of his luck. He transformed his Eighth Army from a virtually defeated body of men into a superb instrument of war. Through discipline, training, and showmanship, he erased the doubts among his troops and created a new mood of self-respect and assurance. Eschewing the romantic, he waged battles with cold-blooded efficiency. He defeated Rommel, and his string of successes at El Alamein, in the long pursuit of Rommel across Libya, and during the final expulsion of the Axis forces from Tunisia, bequeathed to his Eighth Army a legend of invincibility. In the deadly business of tactical warfare, Montgomery was regarded in British circles as without peer. His soldiers adored him.

After the subsequent campaigning in Sicily and in southern Italy, when Montgomery, at the beginning of 1944, departed the Mediterranean area to prepare for the Normandy landings, he was an international star. His personal symbols, the sweater, the beret, and the ascetic mode of living in the field, were well and widely known, appreciated, and beloved. He was, it appeared, the savior of Allied hopes.

"How nice," King George VI said innocently, reflecting widespread British sentiment, "How nice to have Eisenhower in nominal command with Monty at his side"—presumably exercising real command.

Concealed under Montgomery's mask of command were qualities

less than endearing. His egoism, inflexibility, insensitivity, and lust for power and glory were growing into megalomania.

Quite unlike Montgomery, at least on the surface, Omar Bradley was little known before the Normandy invasion. Although Eisenhower, Patton, and Clark were by then household names, Bradley remained quite obscure to the public. As late as February 1944, three months before the Normandy landings, Patton received a letter from a Girl Scout troop in Providence, Rhode Island. It told of their prayers for him, Eisenhower, and Mark Clark. "I am quite sure," Patton replied graciously, "that between the three of us—and not forgetting General Bradley," he added, "—we will eventually secure the victory you want."

Dubbed a "soldier's soldier" by war correspondent Ernie Pyle, Bradley fitted well the American conception of the general officer. He was pragmatic, unruffled, apparently unambitious, somewhat dull, neither flamboyant nor ostentatious, and he never raised hackles as a potential man on horseback. Efficiency and the job at hand drove him. His round, steel-framed, government-issue eyeglasses, his rural manner, and his hayseed expression gave him a homespun look. Underneath the mask was a cold and ruthless mind.

He came from, he said, "plain Missouri farmers, proud, honest, hardworking and poor. Desperately poor," he emphasized. His schoolteacher father died when he was fourteen, and Omar Bradley's ability as a sharpshooter with rifle and slingshot—cartridges were expensive—provided squirrels, rabbits, and quail for the family table. As a young officer, underpaid like his peers, he played poker with his associates, not for the joy of the game, nor for the pleasure of male companionship, but for the chance to win money. He generally won, for he never strayed from the odds. His high school yearbook called him "calculative." Later in life he sought to explain the label on the basis of being good in mathematics.

A West Point classmate of Eisenhower, graduating in 1915, Bradley spent World War I in the United States. His absence from the Western Front, he was sure, had ruined his career. Fortune smiled during the interwar years when he served as an instructor at the Infantry School under George Marshall. He impressed Marshall with his ability.

When Marshall became acting army chief of staff of the U.S. Army in the summer of 1939, he quickly obtained Bradley, who was a member of the War Department General Staff, to be one of his three close assistants. Two years later, Marshall promoted Bradley from lieutenant colonel directly to brigadier general, one of a very few—Mark Clark was another—to skip the grade of colonel. Marshall placed Bradley in command of Fort Benning and the Infantry School and, shortly after Pearl Harbor, elevated him to major general. Bradley activated and trained a division, then took over and straightened out another division plagued by problems. His accomplishments and efficiency shone so well that Marshall was about to give him command of a corps. Instead, in February 1943, he sent Bradley to North Africa in a vaguely defined assignment as Eisenhower's "eyes and ears."

Eisenhower's position in French Northwest Africa was more than a little shaky. He had signed the Darlan Deal with a member of the odious Vichy government to facilitate Allied military operations in Tunisia, and the arrangement outraged American and British public opinion and provoked intense criticism of Eisenhower. His drive to capture Bizerte and Tunis before Axis forces arrived in substantial numbers seemed poorly coordinated and broke down. The inter-Allied command structure on the Tunisian battlefield was chaotic, and Eisenhower, absorbed in political and logistical problems far from the front, was unable to institute order and coherence. The humiliating American defeat at Kasserine Pass was the final blow suggesting Eisenhower's lack of fitness to head the Allied effort. Oblique whispers from British and American sources obliged Marshall to send Eisenhower a troubleshooter, and Marshall selected Bradley.

Bradley reached Eisenhower's headquarters in Algiers as the battle of Kasserine Pass was coming to an end. After reading into the situation and discussing matters with Eisenhower, Bradley set out for Tunisia. He met with American commanders, observed their troops, and wondered how he might help Eisenhower.

The answer came early in March. When Eisenhower decided to replace the American commander in Tunisia, he summoned George Patton from French Morocco, where Patton was planning for the invasion of Sicily. Put in command of the II Corps, the American forces in Tunisia, Patton was overjoyed by the assignment but suspicious of Bradley's presence. Bradley's status was ambiguous. He was a member of Eisenhower's office in Algiers. What was he doing in Tunisia? He seemed to be Eisenhower's "spy" (Patton's word), and Patton objected. To fix Bradley's loyalty to himself, Patton suggested making Bradley his deputy corps commander: Serving under Patton in that capacity would regularize his standing. If Patton eventually returned to Morocco to complete his preparations for Sicily, and if Bradley proved to be capable as Patton's understudy, Patton further suggested, Bradley was to get the corps upon Patton's departure. Eisenhower agreed.

Learning much from Patton, Bradley flourished in his introduction to combat. When Patton left, as contemplated, in mid-April, Bradley took over the II Corps. He led it well in the final push of the campaign. As the British and French entered Tunis, Bradley and the Americans captured Bizerte. The expulsion of Axis forces from North Africa and the capture of 250,000 prisoners of war led to Allied euphoria and restored confidence in Eisenhower. Thus did Bradley contribute to Eisenhower's well-being.

Under Patton again in Sicily, Bradley commanded the II Corps in Patton's Seventh Army with conspicuous success. He also showed complete loyalty to his boss after Patton slapped two sick soldiers who he thought were malingering. When Bradley received a medical report detailing and protesting Patton's abuse of the two hospitalized soldiers, Bradley locked the papers in his safe and said nothing. The medical authorities then carried their complaint directly to Eisenhower, who reproved Patton discreetly.

Patton's inexcusable behavior catapulted Bradley to his next post. After the Sicilian campaign and before the invasion of southern Italy, Marshall instructed Eisenhower to send a high-ranking officer to England to prepare the American forces for the Normandy landings. This person, whomever Eisenhower chose, was to activate, form, and organize not only an army headquarters but also an army group headquarters and to train their staffs and subordinate units for the invasion. As Eisenhower mulled over his options, he thought immediately of Patton, who was the obvious candidate. Patton had commanded an army in Sicily. He had more combat experience than any other American commander of high rank. He was ready to step up and handle an army group. Unfortunately, his conduct toward the sick soldiers had disqualified him, for he seemed too quick to lose his temper.

Eisenhower then inclined toward Mark Clark. He had commanded an army for eight months, although not in battle. He had very favorably impressed the British, particularly Winston Churchill. He had the requisite intelligence, knowledge, drive, and flair for a position of such sensitivity and importance. Unfortunately, Clark was about to lead his Fifth Army into Italy via the invasion at Salerno.

Although Eisenhower briefly considered substituting Bradley for Clark at the head of the Fifth Army, thereby making Clark available for the appointment to England, in the end he selected Bradley.

Thus Bradley in September 1943 found himself in England, where he created the headquarters of both the First U.S. Army and what would later be called the 12th Army Group. Apart from his inexperience at those levels of command, he had a rather strange problem. Sometime after leading the First Army ashore in Normandy, Bradley was to relinquish control of the army and move up to command the 12th Army Group. In that position he would direct two armies, the First Army, now under his replacement, Courtney Hodges, and the Third Army, under Patton.

Hodges and Patton would be Bradley's direct subordinates, although both were older and more senior to him. They also had more combat experience than he. So impressed was Bradley by their stature that he tended to think of them and occasionally to address them as "Sir," the customary mark of respect for a superior that becomes a matter of habit in the military. When the word slipped out in conversation, Bradley, it seemed to some observers, felt like biting his tongue.

Growing up in Georgia, Courtney Hodges entered West Point with Patton. Hodges flunked mathematics and resigned after his plebe year. He then enlisted in the Army. In 1909, he was commissioned from the ranks. After serving in Mexico with Pershing, he fought in France as a battalion commander, later as a regimental commander. He received a Distinguished Service Cross, as well as other recognition, for gallantry in action. He was a genuine war hero, and Bradley admired him and looked up to him with some awe.

It was Hodges whom Bradley had succeeded at Fort Benning, and Hodges had moved to Washington to be the chief of infantry, a prestigious post. After a series of command positions, including a corps, Hodges headed the Third Army in Texas. He brought the army headquarters overseas to England early in 1944, passed it to Patton, and prepared to take over from Bradley at the First Army in Normandy at some future and still undetermined date.

Bradley, it would turn out, would have no trouble with Hodges, a soft-spoken, handsome, white-haired gentleman, distinguished in appearance. He was unassuming and self-effacing. Bradley called him "unostentatious and retiring," words perhaps slightly pejorative. Without flair or originality, Hodges disliked "the uncertain business" of "tricky maneuver" and thought it "safer, sounder, and in the end quicker to keep smashing ahead." Such a course required little imagination. Performing his duties matter-of-factly, Hodges sought no publicity, and the newsmen paid him little attention. He posed no threat to Bradley.

Patton was something else. Patton intimidated Bradley. By his lifestyle and professional assurance, Patton made Bradley feel inferior, in effect, like a poor country hick.

Along with Eisenhower, Bradley, Hodges, Clark, and others, Patton was a Marshall man, that is, one who owed his rank and standing to the U.S Army chief of staff. Patton had impressed Marshall in France during the First World War and again in the United States during the early years of the second conflict. As Marshall did with all his protégés, those whom he believed were exceptionally well qualified professionally and personally for high command, Marshall nurtured and advanced Patton.

Descended on his father's side from a prominent Virginia family, among them a governor and numerous Confederate officers, including his grandfather, and on his mother's side from a pioneer California heritage, Patton combined the elegance of a Southern gentleman and the roughness of an outlaw cowboy. He exhibited each as the occasion warranted. His marriage to a wealthy and cultured Bostonian with international entrée endowed him with an international flavor. He hobnobbed with the rich and the famous and, paradoxically, had an extraordinary rapport with soldiers.

His exhibitions at horse shows, participation in horse races, and ferocious polo playing attracted widespread attention, not always entirely favorable. His competition in the 1912 Olympic games and his navigation of the Pacific Ocean to Hawaii, later back, in a relatively small yacht with an amateur crew, created satisfying publicity. He was afflicted with dyslexia, a reading disability, and, except for his spelling, which remained quaint and sometimes comical, he overcame the handicap by extremely hard work. He was a multifaceted figure who wrote poetry and diligently studied military history. An eccentric, a showman, he was a patrician in the style of Douglas MacArthur and a thoroughly sound and innovative military professional.

A year at the Virginia Military Institute reinforced Patton's Southern roots. At West Point he had to repeat his first year, thus spending five instead of the normal four years at the Military Academy, graduating in 1909. Accompanying Pershing in Mexico, he became a national hero for about two weeks—his photo appeared in newspapers across the country—after carrying out the very first American motorized combat action.

With Pershing in France, he activated and trained the first American light tank brigade, then led his men and machines in battle at St-Mihiel and during the first day, until he was wounded, of the Meuse-Argonne offensive. The recipient of the Distinguished Service Cross for gallantry in action and of the Distinguished Service Medal for outstanding achievement in a position of high responsibility, Patton returned to the United States an authentic war hero.

He soon regained his status in World War II. Once again with tanks, he commanded an armored division, then an armored corps. He drew newsmen like a magnet, and stories about him filled papers and magazines, as well as the radio air waves. He landed near Casablanca during the invasion of North Africa, battled the French, and became, without question, the greatest American fighting general of the war.

Patton wore a mask of his own creation. The centerpiece was his scowling face. He exuded ruggedness and masculinity tempered by courtesy and charm. His uniforms were impeccably tailored. His ivory-handled pistols were conspicuously in view. His profanity, occasionally vulgar, rarely obscene, never irreligious, was a trademark. Widely admired for his energy, unorthodoxy, and redoubtable will to win, Patton refused to hide his mercurial temperament, his violent ups and downs, his hint of inner instability. For some Americans, he was too tough in his appearance and language, and he inspired doubts among them and made them uncomfortable with his posture and demeanor.

He was at Fort Benning training his armored division when Bradley assumed command of the post. In their duties, both officers had a close relationship, and each came to appreciate the other's strengths. Shortly after Patton left, he wrote a letter to Bradley. "Dear Omar," he said, "During our service together I never was associated with anyone who more whole-heartedly and generously cooperated with everything we worked on together."

Their stint at the II Corps in Tunisia was equally pleasant. In letters to his wife and in his diary, Patton recorded his impressions. Bradley "is good," and it was "a great comfort" to have Bradley around. Soon after his departure from Tunisia, Patton wrote to Bradley, "Please accept my most sincere congratulations on your magnificent work."

After the Tunisian campaign, Patton remarked to his wife, "Omar did a swell job." To Bradley he wrote, "I want to repeat that I never enjoyed service with anyone as much as with you and trust that some day we can complete our warlike operations." When Bradley rejoined Patton, the latter met Bradley's plane with a guard of honor, hosted a champagne luncheon for him, and toasted him as "the conqueror of Bizerte."

The harmony continued as they prepared for Sicily. Bradley, Patton noted in his diary, "grows on me as a very sound and extremely loyal soldier." Afterwards, Patton wrote to Bradley "to make," he said, "a permanent record of my frequently expressed admiration for and appreciation of the magnificent loyalty and superior tactical ability you have evinced throughout the campaign of Sicily."

What destroyed the closeness was news of Bradley's appointment to go to England and head the American forces in the Normandy landings.

Patton was disappointed and hurt. He wrote in his diary, mildly for him, "I had thought that possibly I might get this command." He had, as a matter of fact, ached for the assignment. All his combat achievements pointed to this culminating point in his career—to be, immediately under Eisenhower, the head of all the American ground combat forces on the European continent in the decisive campaign of the war.

As gloom enveloped Patton, he recalled and reviewed his relationship with Bradley and reversed some of his earlier judgments. "Bradley," he said in his diary, "is a man of great mediocrity." Patton went on to record several instances of Bradley's hesitation and timidity in Tunisia and Sicily and Bradley's objections to operations he had deemed to be "too dangerous." At the end of his reflections, Patton concluded, "I consider him [to be] among our better generals." Whether this was a sincere tribute to Bradley or a sideswiping aspersion on all the American general officers, only Patton knew, and probably he was far from certain.

What stood revealed in absolute clarity was Patton's humiliation. He had introduced Bradley to combat, had brought him up and taught him the business, and now this younger and less experienced subordinate had surpassed Patton and would, in Normandy, be over Patton and command him. The thought was galling. Were they, whoever they were, trying to get him to resign? Or to say, as he put it in his diary, "What the hell! Stick it up your ass, and I will go home."

He swallowed his pride. If serving under Bradley was a fact of life, Patton would accept it. He would do his duty to the best of his ability as a faithful soldier. He could do no less than to obey Bradley's instructions and directions to the fullest measure in the interest not only of winning the war but also of gaining the fame that Patton pursued with all his might.

In Normandy, both men would be uncomfortable with each other. Their new roles, the reversal of authority, took some getting used to. In addition, to Patton, Bradley seemed tentative in his decisions. To Bradley, Patton's manner set his teeth on edge. "Had it been left up to me," Bradley later said, "frankly I would not have chosen Patton."

Any high-ranking and well-known military figure who is regarded as having gained success in his profession and who is comfortable with his attainments customarily mellows in his later years. He prefers to remain silent or evasive on controversial issues. He generally refuses to divulge information damaging to a colleague or contemporary. He likes to smooth over disagreements, skip over quarrels or differences of opinion. For the good of the service, he has convinced himself, he paints a picture of all-pervasive harmony.

Contrary to this stereotype, Bradley, all his life, made no secret of what Carlo D'Este has called "a deep personal dislike of Patton the man and a professional disdain for Patton the soldier." In postwar commentaries, Bradley surprisingly revealed, openly and candidly, his distaste for Patton, who was, Bradley thought, "a rather shallow commander." According to Bradley, who had been bred in the infantry, Patton, brought up in the cavalry, had a rudimentary conception of tactics. Patton followed, Bradley said, "simply a process of bulling ahead. Never seemed to think out a campaign."

Bradley was "more and more outraged by Patton's childlike histrionics . . . his fantasies . . . his hopeless inability to run an efficient army headquarters." Bradley "disliked the way he worked," and his methods "sickened me and soured me on Patton." Bradley confessed, "If it had been up to me in Sicily"—he was referring to the slapping incidents—"I would have relieved him instantly and would have had nothing more to do with him."

Unfortunately for both, Eisenhower deemed them to be necessary for the operations in Normandy, Patton to exhibit his know-how and will to win, Bradley to keep a tight rein over Patton's presumed eccentricities.

Although discussion and debate in the military are permitted before a commander reaches his decision, once he has made up his mind, further talk is prohibited. All subordinates must carry out their commander's wishes. Patton would follow this precept strictly. When Bradley was searching for a solution in order to make a decision, Patton offered suggestions. He toned down his natural exuberance, did his utmost to be diplomatic, tried to make his ideas come out as though Bradley had originated them. Sometimes Bradley accepted Patton's good sense, sometimes not. And when Bradley issued his orders, Patton obeyed.

Yet once when Patton was importuning Bradley to take a particular course of action, Bradley flared angrily in his low-key manner. "George," he told Patton in an ice-cold voice, "you must remember that I did not ask for you."

It was Eisenhower who had insisted on having Patton as a member of the Allied team in Normandy, and Marshall had strongly backed him. Despite Patton's supposed indiscretions, despite his seeming potential for flying out of control, they needed him. He was indispensable for the success of the venture. No one else could exert such pressure on the enemy. No one could drive his troops with such inspiration and relentlessness. No one else had his intuitive grasp of what was possible on the battlefield. Despite his faults, he was brilliant and a proved winner.

In comparison, Bradley and Hodges were merely workmanlike.

Montgomery, Bradley, and Patton would shape the events at the Falaise pocket. Other figures, among them Sir Miles Dempsey and Henry Crerar, respectively the British and Canadian army commanders, Jacques Leclerc, the French division commander, and Hodges, playing lesser roles, would contribute to the disjointed nature of the operation. But the three principals would carry the major responsibility. Their relationship was far from happy. They suffered too from a burden imposed by the coalition.

CHAPTER 3

The Coalition

ALTHOUGH BRADLEY AND PATTON were temperamentally unlike, suffered from their reversal of roles, and tended to have conflicting views, they were together and steadfast on one point: their commitment to their national outlook. They were American, solidly so, and Montgomery was outside the pale. In public, they scrupulously respected the chain of command, which descended from Eisenhower to Montgomery to Bradley to Patton. In private, they resented and belittled Montgomery, who stood at the head of the Allied ground forces.

To some extent, Bradley's and Patton's feelings stemmed from differences in British and American doctrine and training, which emerged out of dissimilar geography, history, and tradition. To some extent, the ill will came from the friction engendered by the enforced close association of two distinct peoples.

As George Bernard Shaw said, the British and the Americans are separated by a common language. It was natural for each side to disparage the characteristics of the other. The American gum-chewing, coffee breaks, and boisterous back-slapping seemed strange and often repugnant to the British, while their customary afternoon tea and excessive reserve turned off Americans. To the British, the American soldiers were "overpaid, oversexed, and over here," and their presence prompted some British misgivings. In a sense, misunderstandings flowed from stereotyped images of Limey and Yank.

Friction arising out of physical proximity was hardly serious. It was even amusing, and letting off steam by griping was usually harmless. Yet discomfort and disdain impeded harmony and cohesion.

Eisenhower kept himself free from bias. He consciously and conspicuously tried to be statesmanlike and an Allied, rather than simply an American, leader. Unlike Douglas MacArthur, who, in the Pacific with Australian, British, and Dutch allies and later in Korea at the head of the United Nations forces, operated out of a normal U.S. Army type of headquarters, Eisenhower created a new and inter-Allied instrument, with British and Americans sharing approximately equal representation and power. Even though officers in different uniforms first approached each other like, in Eisenhower's words, "a bulldog meeting a tomcat," he insisted on mutual respect between the nationalities, and he dismissed an American staff officer for calling his counterpart a *British* son of a bitch.

So far did Eisenhower go in promoting Allied good will that some Americans accused him of selling out to the British, and some British suspected him to be acting disingenuously. Criticism appeared in conversations among close friends, in diaries, and in letters home. Patton, for example, was perturbed, as he wrote to his wife, because Eisenhower "spoke of lunch as 'tiffin,' of gasoline as 'petrol,' and of antiaircraft as 'flack.' I truly fear that London has conquered Abilene."

Eisenhower "was determined," in John J. Sullivan's words, "to go the last mile" to achieve Allied cooperation. He was "loyal to his subordinates to a fault, especially to those who were British." Most Americans "believed he held them to a higher standard than he did their British counterparts." What truly bothered Patton and some of his contemporaries was Eisenhower's propensity, they thought, to espouse a British line, that is, to make decisions conforming to British desires.

In his behavior, Eisenhower was mirroring the close association of President Franklin D. Roosevelt and Prime Minister Winston Churchill. Each directed the affairs of his country. Together they directed the course of the war.

They genuinely liked and esteemed each other. To a large extent, each understood and sympathized with the other's problems and point of view. Half American because of his mother, Churchill was, as John Eisenhower has said, all British. A certain deference marked his dealings with Roosevelt, and he was sometimes ingratiating, for Roosevelt was both the chief of state and the head of government, while Churchill occupied only the latter seat. In addition, the potential power of the United States far exceeded that of Britain. Churchill did not hesitate to argue with Roosevelt, but he could never risk an open break. As for Roosevelt, his focus was on the future, on how to organize a new method of keeping the peace in the postwar world, and he paid scant attention to the traditional balance-of-power politics and paid but lip service to the former glory of the British empire.

Communicating often by transatlantic cable and telephone, they met several times during the war and thereby fostered a remarkable unity in the coalition. Yet however cordial the two men were in their relationship, their own national interests were never far from their thoughts. They had different preoccupations.

The Anglo-American alliance in World War II was probably the most successful alliance in history. Born in a time of danger, when each state individually was too weak to challenge the enemy alone, the association had as its fundamental aim the defeat of the Axis powers. This common purpose led each country to put aside temporarily purely national considerations in order to proceed together. But the agreements reached on how to prosecute the war were compromises, satisfying some of the wishes of each partner, yet failing to meet the desires of both entirely.

Major L. F. Ellis put the situation into exact perspective. "In the conduct of a world war," he wrote, "the widely separated standpoints of two such differently circumstanced countries as Great Britain and the United States must inevitably make it difficult for their political and military leaders always to find a mutually acceptable policy, and it is neither surprising nor disturbing that British and American views did not always coincide, that, indeed, they differed radically at various times. What is more impressive is the fact that their leaders so often saw alike, and that even when prolonged discussions failed to reconcile opinions, agreed decisions were none the less arrived at and, once reached, were loyally observed."

What is lacking in this description is the tension below the surface. Beneath the delicate balance of the coalition simmered, and sometimes seethed, not only discord, as William H. McNeill has said, but also jealousy, suspicion, and a constant jockeying for place, position, and prominence in the partnership. As the approach of victory seemed about to overcome the peril originally producing the union, the marriage became increasingly fragile, ready to dissolve, as both states fell back on their own individual concerns.

At the beginning, the menace of Nazi Germany was frightening and real. A rearmed country geared for offensive warfare and in the hands of a totalitarian regime pursued a renegade role in international affairs and violated treaties and diplomatic conventions, threatening not only peace but also democratic values and institutions. A program of genocide, so brutal as to be incredible at first, gathered momentum and flamed into the Holocaust. Germany spread fear, annexed adjoining states, then invaded Poland to start the war in Europe. The incomparable power and mobility of blitzkrieg—the combination of tanks, motorized infantry, self-propelled artillery, and closely supporting aircraft—astonished the world. Victory swiftly followed, and Poland, divided between Germany and the Soviet Union, once again vanished from the map. The German occupation of the conquered territory degraded human dignity and the quality of life.

When Great Britain and France entered the war against Germany in September 1939, the United States could only look on. Suspicion of Old World conflicts, disillusionment after the First World War, pacifism and antimilitarism, plus the protection afforded by the breadth of the Atlantic and Pacific oceans, created a sense of isolationism. Neutrality acts specifically prohibited American intervention. Furthermore, the American military establishment was incapable of significant action; comparable to Portugal's, it ranked about seventeenth in size and modernity among the world's forces in existence.

President Roosevelt, sensitive always to American public opinion, privately and circumspectly, yet clearly, indicated where his sympathies lay. On September 11, he wrote to Prime Minister Neville Chamberlain, saying elliptically, "I hope you will at all times feel free to write me personally and outside of diplomatic procedures about any problems as they arise." To Winston Churchill, then first lord of the admiralty, he said, "I shall at all times welcome it if you will keep me in touch personally with anything you want me to know about." More to the point, Roosevelt assigned eighty ships to patrol duty off the shores of the Western Hemisphere, and the vessels regularly informed the British of German naval movements in those waters.

The scope of the war enlarged as the Soviet Union invaded Finland in November and as Germany seized Denmark and Norway in April 1940. On May 10, Germany ended the Phoney War and struck western Europe.

On the same day, Churchill became Prime Minister. He wrote to Roosevelt, saying, "Although I have changed my office, I am sure you would not wish me to discontinue our intimate private correspondence." The exchanges proceeded and flourished.

In comparison with Germany, which had 140 divisions and more than two million men under arms, the United States had 80,000 soldiers and a total of five understrength divisions. The air service consisted of 260 American pilots, 160 pursuit planes, and 52 heavy bombers. The danger overseas prompted Roosevelt to request the Congress to appropriate more than a billion dollars for defense. The response voted more than was asked and authorized U.S. military expansion.

When Britain and France in May asked for planes, antiaircraft guns, ammunition, destroyers, and steel, Roosevelt declared World War I weapons to be surplus to American needs and shipped them to England. He was unable to do more without jeopardizing the start of the American military buildup, without violating the neutrality laws, and without antagonizing public opinion.

The entry into the war beside Germany of Benito Mussolini's rather less efficient Fascist Italy, the rapid military defeat of Britain and France, the evacuation of nearly half a million British and French soldiers from the Continent to England, and the shocking surrender of France raised the question of whether Britain, now alone, save for the Commonwealth countries, could survive. The addition of one hundred Italian submarines to Germany's fifty-five strengthened Axis control of the western European coast from Norway to Spain, while the loss of almost half of the British home destroyer force compromised Britain's ability to turn back an invasion and to protect vital trade in food and arms.

As the battle of Britain raged in the air and as Hitler assembled barges for cross-Channel landings in England, Churchill appealed to Roosevelt for help. He asked for the gift or the sale of fifty or sixty old and over-age American destroyers as "a matter of life and death." Britain needed these ships to remain alive during the next three or four months.

In August, with the approval of the Congress, Roosevelt transferred fifty destroyers, twenty torpedo boats, and ten modern planes to Britain in exchange for the American purchase or lease of naval and air bases in seven of Britain's Western Hemisphere possessions. This transaction, in effect, as Robert Dallek has noted, ended American neutrality.

American military authorities deemed a one-million-man army necessary for security, and Roosevelt in September called the National Guard to federal service and instituted selective service. In October, sixteen million young men between the ages of twenty-one and thirty-five registered for the draft.

By then, although Britain's survival was no longer in doubt, for Hitler had apparently postponed and perhaps canceled his invasion, Britain's future, militarily and financially, looked grim. In contrast, the

Axis stood triumphant on the Continent, occupying the states overrun, and Germany was starting to organize its conquered satellites into a European "New Order."

After the 1940 elections in November, Roosevelt pondered how to keep Britain in the war despite Britain's near-bankruptcy. How could the United States send ships, planes, and ammunition without hope of receiving payment for the goods? The solution was Lend-Lease, approved early in 1941. The President received authority to sell, transfer, exchange, lease, lend, or give defense items to any country whose strength he deemed to be vital to American security. Furthermore, he could decide how the United States was to be reimbursed, whether in kind, in property, in direct or indirect benefit, or not at all. By this action, the United States extended to Britain all assistance short of war.

The scope of the war escalated in dramatic fashion late in June 1941, when Germany invaded and seemed about to overwhelm the Soviet Union. Roosevelt included the Russians in Lend-Lease. He also sent 4,000 Marines to free a British division guarding Iceland.

Roosevelt and Churchill met for three days in August at Placentia Bay, Newfoundland. They enunciated and issued what was called the Atlantic Charter, a declaration of broad general aims. But the most important result was the encounter itself. The two men came to know each other and to enjoy each other's company. Roosevelt had been assistant secretary of the navy for eight years under Woodrow Wilson, Churchill had been the first lord of the admiralty in both world wars, and their views on naval matters were complementary.

Roosevelt had already enlarged the scope of American activity in the war. Declaring Greenland and the Azores to be vital to security, the president authorized air and naval patrols to search for German sea raiders and to report their locations to the British. He had U.S. Navy vessels join the convoys crossing the Atlantic on escort duty. He had U.S. merchant ships armed for defense against attack. The United States thus entered into an undeclared war against the Axis.

If the British government and people were grateful for American generosity enabling Britain to survive, American military planners harbored a general hostility toward the British. Sending American goods to Britain had competed with and impaired the buildup of the American armed forces. If the military leaders seemed to be shortsighted and appeared to misunderstand the advantages of keeping Britain, as well as the Soviet Union, in the war, they were, with good reason and ample justification, apprehensive over the unpreparedness of their own military services for combat.

The Japanese bombing of Hawaii's Pearl Harbor in December 1941, which catapulted the United States into war against Japan, unified the American nation and made isolationism irrelevant. The American people clamored for action, but the military establishment of small, untrained, and ill-equipped forces was hardly ready for commitment or able to undertake an immediate and consequential prosecution of the war. Almost at once, Germany and Italy declared war on the United States, thereby regularizing hostilities in the Atlantic. When Churchill telephoned to confirm the news of Pearl Harbor, he heard Roosevelt say, "We are all in the same boat now."

Four days later, Churchill proposed traveling to Washington to meet with Roosevelt. If the two states were in fact now partners openly arrayed against the Axis, a momentous question required answer: how should the Allies vanquish their enemies? Roosevelt was amenable to Churchill's suggestion, and he welcomed the prime minister's visit.

In large part, the guideline had already been set, although it was less than binding. As early as June 1940, American military men responsible for drafting war plans had agreed to consult with British officers on general strategic options. Informal meetings in London and Washington during August 1940 and unofficial staff conferences in Washington during February and March 1941 considered methods of how to proceed if the United States became a belligerent involved in both the Atlantic and Pacific regions. The solution emerging from the talks was a Europe First strategy.

As projected, the United States was to make its initial main effort against Germany in order to defeat the most dangerous foe before turning in strength to the Pacific. As developed, Britain and America were to employ economic blockade, air attack, and peripheral harassment, especially in the Mediterranean basin, before mounting an eventual direct strike against Germany. Essentially a British concept, the program remained in place throughout much of the war despite American and Russian pressure to hurry the final step.

The prime minister spent three weeks in the United States, from December 22, 1941, to January 14, 1942, and during discussions with the President, the Allies uncovered some areas of difference—divergent views on India, China, France, colonialism, imperialism, and other issues threatening to hamper the unity desired by both political chiefs. Putting these matters aside for the moment, seeing them as having little importance in the near future, they reached agreement on two significant points.

Despite some reservations, especially among U.S. Navy officials who preferred to strike as soon as possible in the Pacific, the Allies accepted the Europe First strategy. Europe and the Atlantic were to be "the decisive theater" of operations, Germany was to be "the prime enemy," the defeat of Germany was to be the "key to victory," and "only the minimum of force" was to be diverted elsewhere. The Allied leaders also created a machinery to be headquartered in Washington—the site upset some British members—in order to provide for a central direction of the war.

In erecting their new organization, the Allies drew upon their experience in World War I. Very late during that conflict, toward the end of March 1918, the French and the British, quickly joined by the Americans, elevated Marshal Ferdinand Foch to be the Supreme Allied Commander. His task was to coordinate the efforts of the three national armies on the Western Front. Foch had little actual authority or power to command. He worked out of a small French headquarters. But he carried out his role by suggesting and persuading rather than by directing. The system was rudimentary but successful. On that fragile foundation, the Allies in World War II built a solid and sophisticated structure.

General Marshall, who had been in France during the previous war and was aware of Foch's difficulties, argued strongly to extend and to strengthen Foch's prerogatives. He wished to establish a real unity of command in Anglo-American operations. Leadership vested in a single individual conformed better with American theory and practice. The British had their own method of exercising command. They relied more on executive action in conference, and they preferred their own command by committee. A compromise combined the best features of both.

At the top of the chain of command stood the political leaders, Roosevelt and Churchill, with coequal authority over Allied matters. Because Churchill had his Chiefs of Staff, the heads of the three armed services, plus his military representative, serving him directly on military affairs, the Americans formed the same organization: the Joint Chiefs of Staff, together with the president's military representative, came into being. Both groups sitting together as a single Anglo-American board became the Combined Chiefs of Staff, the corporate Allied military mind.

Two men within the system soon emerged as the leading and opposing proponents of the body. One was George Marshall, the U.S. Army chief of staff. A graduate of the Virginia Military Institute, he served as a young officer in the Philippines, then made his reputation in France in 1918 as the principal planner of the St-Mihiel and Meuse-Argonne offensives. Closely associated with John J. Pershing, he commanded an infantry brigade in the late 1930s. Apparently too junior in rank to be considered for the top army position, he was ready to retire when he attracted Roosevelt's notice and received the appointment.

Austere and forbidding, Marshall was formal in his manner. He permitted no familiarity. Even the president, who was on easy terms with his close associates, dared not call him "George." Tall and imposing, principled and selfless, Marshall was undeniably American in his point of view, yet global in his outlook. He regarded the war in Europe as of primary importance to the U.S. Army, and the Pacific as having the most meaning to the U.S. Navy, although he kept his eyes and authority firmly focused on the war against Japan. His favorite subordinate was Eisenhower, who was then serving as head of War Plans, later renamed the Operations Division, Marshall's small planning group in the War Department.

Because the president saw his military advisers about once a week and remained aloof from the detailed military planning, Marshall became the driving force in the Joint Chiefs of Staff. In subsequent meetings of the Combined Chiefs, Marshall usually presented the American position.

The other prominent member was General Sir Alan F. Brooke, chief of the Imperial General Staff. Marshall's counterpart as head of the army, Brooke had just assumed the post about the time of Pearl Harbor and was absent from the meetings in Washington. An artilleryman in World War I, the director of military training in the mid-1930s, the acknowledged mechanization expert before World War II, Brooke gained fame in the ill-fated campaign of 1940. He distinguished himself as corps commander during the British withdrawal from the Continent, took command of the British Expeditionary Force in England, then served as the commander in chief of the Home Forces. The subordinate in whom he had the most confidence was Montgomery, who had been a fellow instructor at the staff college, Camberley, who had led a division under Brooke in France, and who was then training troops in England.

Physically unprepossessing, with narrow shoulders, spindly legs, and a seemingly crooked mustache, Brooke was icy and condescending, precise and methodical. He had a sharp tongue. An avid hunter and bird-watcher, avocations he practiced for recreation, he had the ability not only to keep the prime minister's vivid imagination in check but also to stand up to Churchill, who took far more interest in the military than Roosevelt and who usually made the British case in the working sessions of the Combined Chiefs.

After less than six months in his position, Brooke was the acknowledged leader of the British Chiefs of Staff. Neither modest nor optimistic, he was no friend of the United States. He saw Europe as fundamentally a British theater, the Pacific as an American region. In the Atlantic-European setting, the Americans to him were "still only beginners," and in his mind they always remained so.

The first time Brooke met Marshall, he judged the American to be "overfilled with his own importance" but endowed with a certain charm too. Later, as they came to know each other, mutual respect rather than cordiality marked their relationship. Precluding friendship were their divergent national interests and concerns.

The Combined Chiefs of Staff acted for the president and prime minister, advising them, translating their wishes into military directives, allocating assets to the various Allied areas, and supervising operations in the Allied theaters of war. They were, in effect, the fount of authority for the Supreme Allied Commanders in the field, each of whom, whether British or American, directed the national forces of both countries in a designated geographical sphere.

Putting the organizational edifice together and in place was an important accomplishment. No less significant was deciding how to prosecute the war. The Allies agreed on some generalities. They would close the ring around Germany, sustain the Russians, support resistance movements in the states occupied by Germany, and increase the air bombardment of German targets. These were mainly British concerns, and the Americans were glad to acquiesce in these objectives.

What the British offered the alliance was experience. Having already been in the war more than two years, having fought the enemy on the ground, in the air, and on the sea, the British claimed to be and were indeed competent, particularly when compared to the Americans, who were novices. Additionally, the trained and available British military forces outnumbered the American contingent. At the outset then, the British took the lead in the coalition.

What the Americans contributed were potential resources. Raising and training a huge military body, manufacturing and distributing an immense stock of weapons and equipment, both at an accelerating pace, the Americans were at first content to follow the British initiatives. Later, as American strength grew, the Americans would challenge the British for dominance.

Leadership in the partnership conferred the ability to choose the progressive next steps in the unfolding strategy. At issue were not only how to defeat the Axis but also how to shape the postwar world, for the method of gaining victory would in large part determine the realities of the future. On these large questions the Allies were divided. Their wartime equilibrium was thus precarious, disturbed from time to time

by the constant, if usually muted and often concealed, clash for prominence. If the United States seemed foreordained to assume the influential
role by virtue of its increasing power, Britain was loath to accept either
the premise or the eventual fact. This fundamental struggle permeated
the whole structure of the alliance, from the making of policy and strategy
at the top to the personal grousing on the lower levels.

The inter-Allied tug of war would blemish the maneuvers around
Falaise.

CHAPTER 4

The Struggle for Dominance

THE AMERICAN CHALLENGE TOOK form early in 1942, when General Marshall asked his assistant to draw an outline plan on how the Allies ought to fight the war. Eisenhower took as his central thesis the need to defeat Germany quickly, thereby allowing full force afterwards against Japan. The best way to attain the first step was to concentrate in England for a descent upon the European continent as soon as possible, then to confront and overwhelm the main German armies on the most direct approaches to Germany.

Marshall approved the concept, and a power thrust scheduled and executed according to a definite timetable came to be the basic American position. The course was at the moment unrealistic because of insufficient assets.

The British, less favored in manpower reserves and matériel, looked to victory by an indirect method. Essentially opportunistic, they opposed firm commitments to the distant future. They preferred to maintain sea blockade, intensified air bombardment, and naval raids, to encourage Resistance sabotage and terrorism in the German-occupied countries, to establish short land fronts around the periphery of Europe in order to stretch the Axis defenses, and to await the proper moment for the final blow. With Gibraltar and Malta their bastions, they saw the Mediterranean, the sea route to the Suez Canal, which led to the Middle East and India, as the prime area for military endeavor.

In line with this notion, Churchill had already, when in Washington, proposed an Allied expedition to seize French Northwest Africa. The advantages were considerable. No Axis troops were in French Morocco, Algeria, and Tunisia, for the armistice signed with Germany and Italy in 1940 pledged France to defend the territories against invasion. The French forces, about 100,000 men, were concerned mainly with pacifying the native peoples. If they opposed landings, they would furnish the untried American soldiers with valuable combat experience. Against them, the Americans would certainly be successful. The result might persuade the French in North Africa to come over to the Allied side. An Allied presence in Northwest Africa would threaten Libya and the rear of Rommel's Italo-German army facing the British in Egypt.

Roosevelt was noncommittal in his reaction to Churchill's suggestion, yet he was eager to initiate an effort somewhere in the Atlantic-European theater. In the interest of the Europe First strategy, he wished to divert the American public from their clamor for action in the Pacific. In April, he sent his assistant Harry Hopkins and General Marshall to London to discuss what the Allies might do in the months to come. Because American formations were already arriving in the United Kingdom to prepare for an eventual cross-Channel operation, Marshall suggested small-scale landings in France.

In such a venture, the British, it was obvious, would have to furnish the bulk of the resources. They rejected the idea.

Nigel Hamilton has given a striking, if somewhat exaggerated, picture of the British attitude toward American temerity. How could the former colonials dare to advance their design for victory? "Britain's once-reluctant Allies," Hamilton wrote, "were now hot to wage war in Europe, yet without the remotest strategical conception of how to do so or the problems involved." A parochial reaction, the view perhaps represented an unpleasant anticipation of the inevitable growth in American power.

Churchill was in the United States again in June visiting with Roosevelt when Rommel gained a crushing success in Libya. News of the fall of Tobruk was especially disconcerting to the prime minister. Roosevelt at once offered to ship three hundred American tanks and one hundred self-propelled guns to the British forces in Egypt. Churchill gratefully accepted before hurrying back to England to deal with the crisis.

In July, Roosevelt again sent Marshall and Hopkins to London. He instructed them to reach agreement on an Allied operation in 1942. The Americans tried to persuade the British to undertake landings in western

Europe. The British refused. The Allied assets on hand, they maintained, were too sparse, and the opposition on the beaches was likely to be too strong. Invading France, they said, might be feasible in 1943, but only Northwest Africa was possible in 1942.

Unable to reconcile the views, Marshall and Hopkins reported this fact to Roosevelt. He decided on Northwest Africa, as much in the interest of Allied unity as of American domestic politics. He thus set in motion the first Anglo-American offensive operation of the war.

The Allies thought it best to put an American face on the enterprise. Anti-British sentiment pervaded the French, animosity deriving from mutual recriminations during the campaign of 1940, from the British attacks on French warships after the armistice, and from strife in Syria. British troops arriving on French soil in Africa were sure to provoke an extremely hostile reaction, whereas the traditional Franco-American friendship would perhaps incline the French to welcome American soldiers. To this end, the three landings eventually planned were to be, and also to appear conspicuously to be, American in composition. Near Casablanca, Morocco, there was to be an all-American show under Patton. Two task forces composed of British and Americans and heading for Oran and Algiers in Algeria were to put the Americans ashore first. Furthermore, the overall commander was to be an American.

Appointed to this function, Eisenhower was then in England as the Commanding General, European Theater of Operations, U.S. Army. He had previously commanded tanks preparing for battle near Gettysburg, Pennsylvania, in 1918 and an infantry battalion in training at Fort Lewis, Washington, in 1940. Eisenhower's inexperience in command and his lack of participation in combat appalled many British. But the venture needed to look American, and besides, the British figured, the larger the American stake in North Africa and Europe, the more distantly would recede the ever-present possibility of an American departure in strength to the Pacific.

Two weeks after Montgomery scored a striking triumph over Rommel at El Alamein, Egypt, the Allies under Eisenhower came ashore in French Northwest Africa early in November. Although the Allies had hoped to complete their conquest by the end of the year, operations bogged down. Bad weather, supply difficulties, and command friction among British, French, and Americans hampered the effort. Most of all, the Axis had poured a substantial number of Germans and Italians from Sicily and southern Italy into the northeastern corner of Tunisia, and they held Bizerte and Tunis stubbornly. At the other end of the North

African littoral, Rommel withdrew his forces slowly westward across Libya toward southern Tunisia. Montgomery followed but was unable to trap or destroy him.

Planners in Washington and London had over the past few months studied where the Allies might seize the initiative after winning all of North Africa. The British wished to continue the momentum in the Mediterranean area. The Americans saw additional Mediterranean undertakings as draining resources from and postponing a cross-Channel effort.

To resolve the impasse, as well as to discuss a wide range of global subjects, Roosevelt and Churchill, accompanied by their chief advisers, met in Casablanca, French Morocco, in January 1943. The British attending the conference were well prepared and presented a united front and a consistent policy. The Americans were in some disarray, with internal dissensions diluting a firm outlook. Although disagreements were downplayed, Marshall later remarked on the "very decided difference . . . between the American and British point of view." During at least one session, the exchanges became so heated that the participants declared the proceedings in camera, and no notes were taken.

Compromise eventually emerged on the European problems. The Americans agreed to invade Sicily after the Tunisian campaign was over. The British, fearing an American decision to turn abruptly from Europe to the Pacific, accepted landing in France in August or September 1943. As a nod to British competence and also to guarantee continuing British interest, the Combined Chiefs of Staff appointed General Sir Frederick Morgan to head an Allied staff charged with planning for a cross-Channel operation code-named Overlord.

Because Rommel was entering southern Tunisia with Montgomery still in pursuit, the Allies at Casablanca decided to place the British Eighth Army into the Allied command framework. Although the British outnumbered the Americans in Tunisia, the Allies retained Eisenhower in overall charge, in part to ensure American commitment to the Mediterranean area, in part to avoid offending those French who had come over to the Allied side and were reluctant to serve under the British.

The new organization was to have Sir Harold Alexander, coming from Cairo, as Eisenhower's deputy and commander of the Allied ground forces, Sir Arthur Tedder as head of the Allied air, and Sir John Cunningham as director of the Allied naval components. Eisenhower's principal subordinates were thus to be three British officers, all of whom outranked him and had considerably more combat experience.

The British seemed to have had their way. Not only had they secured assent on Sicily; they had also imposed a committee-type command in North Africa. To a disgruntled American who had participated in the conference, these results were shameful. He said, we came, we saw, we were conquered.

Churchill was pleased. "I love these Americans," he said. "They have behaved so generously."

Brooke confided his thoughts to his diary. "At one time," he wrote, "I began to despair of our arriving at any sort of agreement. Now we have got practically all we hoped to get when we came here." Sure that Eisenhower lacked the tactical and strategic background required for so high a position, Brooke was happy to have helped push him "up into the stratosphere and rarified atmosphere" of the Supreme Allied Command. There he could devote his attention to political and other problems while British commanders dealt with the military situation and provided the drive and coordination they felt had formerly been absent.

Alexander arrived in Tunisia at the height of the Kasserine battle. Going immediately to the front, he was horrified by what he saw in the American sector. The situation was disorganized and confused. Many troops lacked proficiency in handling their weapons, displayed a lack of steadiness under fire, tended to be unduly alarmed and to break and run, while many units were unaware of even the simplest combat requirements, such as maintaining firm contact with adjacent formations.

What saved the day was the firm stance of the British. Backing the Americans at the Kasserine Pass and the French and Americans at the Sbiba Pass, they strengthened the defenses to the point where Rommel abandoned his attack.

"Broadly speaking," Alexander informed Churchill, "Americans require experience." To Brooke he was more candid. "They simply do not know their jobs as soldiers," he wrote. They "were soft, green and quite untrained." The problems were "very serious indeed." What made things worse, "there is no policy and no plan . . . no firm direction or centralized control from above." The Americans were likely to be "quite useless" in subsequent operations.

From Montgomery's perspective, Eisenhower's theater appeared to be ill-managed because an amateur was in command. Intelligence was badly gathered and disseminated, and air cooperation was poor. The trouble was, the Americans had too few first-class chaps. As he said, "The real trouble with the Americans is that the soldiers won't fight. . . . The reason they won't fight is that they have no confidence in their Generals." In his diary he wrote, "The Americans were complete amateurs at fighting." They "do not know how to fight the battle."

The American failure at Kasserine was a direct result of the interwar years of military neglect. The Regular Army had suffered from poverty. Pitifully small numbers and obsolete equipment prevented realistic training. Antiaircraft gunners, for example, had had little practice firing against planes. No firm doctrine existed in a variety of matters—for one, how to employ the new tank destroyers.

As George Marshall had warned, it took time to raise and modernize an army, but the United States began seriously to mobilize and to train in 1940, much too late. The interval between preparation for and commitment to battle was simply too short. The deficiencies and shortcomings at Kasserine arose from the hasty attempt to be ready.

After Kasserine, the British were contemptuous of the American soldiers, judging them to be inferior, second-class, and incapable of meeting the Germans with any sort of equality. If the war was to be won, the Allies would have to rely on the British.

The Americans resented the patronizing attitude of the British. Criticism of American leadership and battlefield proficiency stung.

What the British overlooked was the resilience of the Americans. They would display a surprisingly quick aptitude to learn from their mistakes. But this, of course, would become evident only later.

Eisenhower visited Montgomery at his command post in southern Tunisia at the end of March and stayed overnight. This was their second meeting, and both men were outwardly courteous. Eisenhower refrained from smoking in Montgomery's presence. He retired early. Montgomery impressed him as "conceited" but "unquestionably an able tactician and organizer."

Montgomery recorded in his diary that he thought less of Eisenhower. "He knows practically nothing about how to make war and definitely nothing about how to fight battles." In a letter to Alexander he said, "I liked Eisenhower . . . but he obviously knows nothing whatever about fighting." To Brooke on the following day, Montgomery called Eisenhower "a very nice chap," then repeated his remark—"he knows nothing whatever about how to make war or to fight battles." He added: "He should be kept away from all that business if we want to win this war."

Early in April, Alexander warned Montgomery about the Americans and gave him some advice: "One has to deal very carefully with them," he wrote, "because they are not one of us."

The final part of the Tunisian campaign was virtually an all-British show. Alexander was the director, Montgomery the star. Patton's II Corps, to his mortification, received a small and subsidiary mission designed to keep the presumably less efficient Americans from fumbling. Eisenhower seemed oblivious to the treatment, as if unaware of how the British were shutting out the Americans. If Patton, seconded by Bradley, had not complained and protested to Eisenhower, who finally urged Alexander to give the II Corps a more substantial role, the Americans under Bradley would have had little to do.

Already planning to invade Sicily in the summer of 1943, the Allies had no firm understanding on what to do afterwards. Hoping for full-scale landings in France, the Americans wished to close down or diminish Mediterranean operations after Sicily. The British saw Sicily as a stepping stone to the Italian mainland, which in turn was to be a preliminary for a cross-Adriatic strike into the Balkans. The Allies had failed to resolve this basic divergence at Casablanca, and they tried again in Washington in May, when Roosevelt and Churchill and their main advisers met in what was called the Trident Conference.

As before, the British came well prepared. This time the Americans were unified too. They were suspicious of British diplomatic smoothness, alert to the possibility of being hoodwinked or tricked into supporting and extending British empire and influence. They were also in the ascendent.

Churchill called for canceling the Channel operation in the autumn of 1943 and going instead for Italy. Entering Italy, the Americans feared, would postpone Overlord indefinitely and perhaps annul it completely. Yet they recognized the impossibility of mounting an overwhelming thrust into northwest Europe in 1943, and they tried to get the British firmly committed to Overlord in the spring of 1944.

Some arguments were vehement, even acrimonious, but the Allies finally came to a settlement. They would invade Sicily in July with a view to knocking Italy out of the war. They set May 1, 1944, as the target date for Overlord.

Uncomfortable with the results of the Trident meetings, Churchill, accompanied by Marshall and Brooke, traveled to Algiers to enlist Eisenhower's support. Eisenhower seemed to favor going to the Italian mainland after Sicily, and Churchill tempted him with the prospect of gaining Italian capitulation, then jumping the front at once to the Po River valley, perhaps even to the Alps. Marshall staved off a final decision. Until the Sicilian campaign was over, Eisenhower was to plan a variety of amphibious expeditions, to Sardinia, Corsica, the Italian toe and heel, and then recommend to the Combined Chiefs of Staff the operation he preferred and thought had the best chance of success.

Churchill returned to London in better spirits. "With a little patience," he reported, "we British, being all agreed, will probably obtain the desired solutions." He may have been whistling in the dark.

The planning for Sicily was strange and almost dreamlike. Eisenhower remained aloof from the process. Because no one else had the authority to coordinate the Allied land, sea, and air forces, each of which had its own point of view, methods, and desires, the services failed to mesh their activities into a synchronized effort. Alexander, ostensibly directing the ground operations, proved to be vacillating, unable to reconcile either set of conflicting wishes and demands, those separating the British and Americans and those pulling apart the ground, sea, and air commanders. In this power vacuum, Montgomery took charge. He submitted his own blueprint for the landings and, over American objections, as well as over naval and air force arguments, pushed his concept to acceptance. One glaring deficiency existed. There was no scheme on how to develop the campaign once the Allies were ashore.

Patton's Seventh U.S. Army and Montgomery's British Eighth Army came in around the southeastern corner of the island. Montgomery was on the east coast and had the shortest and most direct route to the city of Messina in the northeastern tip. Messina was the only objective of any meaning, for its seizure would cut off the Axis forces and prevent them from departing Sicily. As Montgomery started north toward Messina, Patton had the secondary mission of protecting Montgomery's rear and flank. To the British, this was a suitable role for inferior troops. To Patton, it was an intolerable humiliation.

Exercising cunning, concealing his motives from Alexander, Patton dashed to Palermo. The city was militarily meaningless, but taking it gained Patton sensational newspaper headlines, secured a port for supplying the American forces, and, most importantly, put Patton on the northern side of Sicily. Now Patton could advance eastward toward Messina and complement Montgomery's movement to the north.

Montgomery's drive had by then bogged down, held up by strong Axis defenses around Catania and by an outbreak of malaria among his troops. The fatigue of his soldiers, together with his reluctance to put additional pressure on them, gave little hope of reaching Messina swiftly. Montgomery decided to share the burden with Patton. Whatever force Patton exerted on the Axis would divert and lighten the opposition facing Montgomery and therefore speed Montgomery's progress. For the sake of form, Montgomery notified Alexander.

Alexander responded by directing Patton to see him and Montgomery at the latter's headquarters in Syracuse. Patton arrived ahead of Alexander, and, without waiting, Montgomery explained the purpose of the meeting. Inviting Patton to head for Messina too, Montgomery suggested two highways for the advance, not only the coastal route but also a parallel road about twenty miles inland that was reserved for British use. Patton was at first startled, then suspicious. "I felt something was wrong," he later wrote in his diary, "but have not found it yet." When Alexander showed up, Montgomery told him what he had done, and Alexander, with some annoyance, approved.

The Montgomery-Patton conference between two prima donnas was remarkable for its quiet candor. Patton's whirlwind movement to Palermo had impressed Montgomery with its speed, mobility, boldness, and determination and had given Montgomery respect for Patton's expertise and energy. Patton knew his tactical business. Where the battlefield was concerned, Montgomery felt, the two generals saw eye to eye. As army commanders working on the same level, they could be rivals and at the same time find mutually acceptable solutions to problems.

A year later in Normandy, Montgomery would make a similar decision in a similar situation. Unfortunately, Patton would then be serving two steps below Montgomery in the chain of command. This being the case, there was no opportunity for them to have mutually frank exchanges on a purely professional basis. Patton would have to work through Bradley, and so would Montgomery.

On the northern shore of Sicily, Patton drove his units to Messina with ruthless determination. He reached the city several hours before the British appeared on the scene. Personally gratifying to Patton because of the newspaper headlines, the exploit fulfilled a larger aim. He had demonstrated the merit of American troops. He had proved their ability to excel in combat. They were at least as good as the British and could no longer be regarded as second-rate.

There was one great disappointment. Patton's and Montgomery's converging jaws closing on Messina failed to trap the bulk of the German and Italian soldiers. Substantial Axis elements crossed the Strait of Messina to the mainland and escaped.

The event foreshadowed the Falaise pocket exactly twelve months afterwards. The Allied air and naval forces missed the opportunity to eliminate a good portion of their adversaries in Sicily. They did the same in Normandy.

The Sicilian campaign produced fresh bad blood between the Allies. Soldiers of both countries listened to the British Broadcasting Corporation news on the radio. Americans were at first astonished, then angered by what they heard. According to the BBC, the British were doing all the fighting. The Americans were living the life of Riley. They had "nothing

to do except walk through Sicily, eating melons and drinking wine,"
swimming in the sea and picking grapes. Whether the remarks were
simply insensitive or quite deliberate, Eisenhower felt obliged to register
a sharp protest.

One dramatic achievement was King Victor Emmanuel III's removal
of Mussolini from power. In the weeks following the Allied conquest of
Sicily, Italian emissaries secretly made contact with the Allies and
offered to surrender.

Although the Allies differed on the terms, for example, whether to
retain the monarchy or to replace it with a republic, they compromised
and accepted the capitulation and later Italian cobelligerency. The immediate consequence was the necessity for the Allies, as Churchill had
anticipated, to enter the Italian mainland in force.

President and prime minister, together with the Combined Chiefs
of Staff, met again in Quebec for ten days in August and reargued the
old strategic issues. Churchill wished to delay Overlord in favor of
expanding Mediterranean operations, but the Americans were adamant.
They insisted on priority for Overlord over whatever the Allies undertook
in the Mediterranean. To them, this course was the quickest way of
ending the war. To make the intention absolutely clear, to shift the
focus squarely to western Europe, the Americans compelled British
acquiescence on still another point—as a matter of fact, on two additional
points. Mediterranean theater resources were to furnish Overlord with
seven divisions, a fair amount of aircraft, and other units, all scheduled
to depart for England late that year and early next. Furthermore, there
was to be an invasion of southern France to complement and support
Overlord. Assets for the Riviera landings were to come also from the
Mediterranean theater to the tune of ten divisions. With these losses in
assets, whatever Mediterranean operations were then in progress would
be so weakened as to become distinctly subsidiary in importance.

Brooke recorded his disappointment. "I am not really satisfied with
the results," he wrote in his diary. "We have not really arrived at the
best strategy but I suppose that when working with Allies compromises
with all their evils become inevitable."

Until the Allies executed their decisions in 1944, they invaded
southern Italy in September 1943. As Alexander directed the ground
operations, Montgomery's Eighth Army crossed the Strait of Messina
from Sicily to the Italian toe, then made slow progress in mountainous
terrain against skillful opposition. A British division was ferried to the
heel, where Italians helped the soldiers disembark. Clark's Fifth U.S.
Army assaulted the beaches around Salerno.

The Germans massed against Clark and came close to driving his men from the shore. As the battle raged, two conditions quite apart from the combat infuriated Clark. First, instead of hurrying up the Italian boot to help Clark, Montgomery seemed to dawdle in the toe, making at best a leisurely advance, pausing from time to time to rest and reorganize his troops. Second, a public relations office in Alexander's headquarters, which issued periodic advisories to guide newspaper correspondents and to help them file their stories, called for them to "play up" Montgomery, who was dashing toward Salerno to chase the Germans away from Clark.

A letter from Montgomery several days later hardly improved Clark's disposition. "It looks as if you may be having not too good a time," Montgomery had written, "and I do hope that all will go well with you. We are on the way to lend a hand."

Both men were on the same echelon as army commanders, although Montgomery was a full general and Clark was a lieutenant general. Because of Montgomery's seniority and Clark's comparative youth (he was forty-seven), because Eisenhower insisted on good Anglo-American relations, and because Montgomery was an established figure while Clark was commanding for the first time in combat, Clark put aside his irritation and responded in flattering fashion. "It will be a pleasure to see you again at an early date," Clark wrote. "Please accept my deep appreciation for assistance your Eighth Army has provided Fifth Army by your skillful and rapid advance."

If sarcasm showed through the lines, the prose was at least polite. To disabuse Montgomery, who he thought might claim to have rescued Clark, he added, "Situation here well in hand."

Clark won his battle at Salerno and opened the toe for Montgomery. As the Germans withdrew slowly to the north, Montgomery dispatched an advance party to the Fifth Army headquarters to arrange a meeting with Clark. Clark sent Montgomery a respectful note. "Again," he said, "I want to tell you of our deep appreciation for the skillful and expeditious manner by which you have moved your Eighth Army to the north. We feel it is a great privilege to operate alongside your army."

When Montgomery arrived, he was enormously pleased by Clark's welcome. "The Fifth Army is just a young Army trying hard to get along," Clark told him, "while the Eighth Army is a battle-tried veteran. We would appreciate your teaching us some of your tricks."

Clark's deference fed Montgomery's ego. Taking Clark's statement at face value and understanding it to be a genuine appeal for assistance, Montgomery patronized Clark. He explained his inability to help Clark take his next objective, Naples. For instead of heading north to operate beside Clark's army in the area west of the Apennine Mountains, he was moving across the mountain range and across the Italian peninsula to the east coast, where his immediate task was to seize Foggia. After Foggia, if Clark had failed to get Naples by then, Montgomery offered to strike westward and aid Clark into the city. He then added, "I propose to repeat the same tactics in respect to Rome. But we can discuss that later."

Montgomery's arrogance dismayed Clark. Although he could, of course, hardly show his displeasure, he resolved to take Naples by his own efforts and to capture Rome himself. He needed no help from Montgomery.

A censorship guidance cable from Alexander's headquarters arrived routinely in the next few days and aggravated Clark's feelings. The public relations people encouraged the news correspondents to concentrate on the Eighth Army activities; "Americans may be mentioned."

Clark was positively incensed. Were Clark and the Americans merely junior partners in the enterprise? Were they always to receive lesser mention in the press? He determined to correct the injustice. American troops were playing a major role in the campaign. They merited recognition. To this end, Clark would do his utmost to publicize the Fifth Army achievements. If the Americans, as well as Clark himself, benefited, so much the better.

As Montgomery took Foggia on October 1, Clark entered Naples on the same date. That removed any necessity for Montgomery to come across the peninsula and assist Clark.

The next development in the Anglo-American rivalry took place at Tehran at the end of November and beginning of December, when Roosevelt, Churchill, and the Combined Chiefs of Staff met with Joseph Stalin and his advisers. The conference showed as nothing quite before how the Anglo-American balance in the partnership had changed. Churchill argued for extending the Mediterranean war and delaying Overlord for a few months. He had earlier persuaded Roosevelt to invade French Northwest Africa and to enter the Italian mainland. Now, hoping for Russian support, he could perhaps again modify the Anglo-American agreements. To his surprise and consternation, the Soviets, instead of subscribing to his view—they had long clamored for a second front in Europe—favored Overlord as well as complementary landings in southern France, landings that would be code-named Anvil.

As the sessions continued, Russo-American solidarity seemed to coalesce while British influence waned. A symptom of the growing strength of the United States and the Soviet Union, as well as of the diminishing power of Britain, the decisions installed Overlord, plus Anvil, as the Anglo-American main effort.

In the privacy of his rooms, Churchill, feeling virtually excluded and almost isolated from the alliance, blew up for just a moment before he regained self-control. "A bloody lot has gone wrong," he expostulated. Writing in his diary, Brooke said, "I cannot stand much more of this."

The intramural Anglo-American contest seemed to be over. Although the Americans appeared clearly to have won and to have got everything they wanted, the British refused to accept the reality.

Returning from Tehran to London, Churchill stopped briefly in North Africa. Down but far from out, Churchill, bulldog that he was, resolved to restore British prestige. He found the Italian campaign propitious for his endeavor.

Early expectations in Italy included an Italian surrender, which had indeed occurred, and clear sailing up the boot at least to the Po Valley, which would open vistas in the Balkans. According to Allied intelligence, Hitler had no intention of defending southern Italy. Consequently, with Clark in Naples on the west coast and Montgomery in Foggia on the east coast, there was every reason to anticipate an effortless march by the Fifth U.S. and British Eighth Armies side by side. Separated by the spine of the Apennine Mountains, they would advance easily to Rome and Rimini and beyond. In line with this cheerful prospect, Eisenhower decided to hold off moving his headquarters from Algiers to Naples and to wait until he could, he said, "make the jump straight into Rome."

Hitler punctured the bubble. Instead of withdrawing his troops from positions south of Rome to the northern Apennines, he now directed them to make a stand. In the mountainous and highly defensible country below Rome, they were to block the Allies and keep them from the capital city.

The German decision committed the Allies to slow and painful fighting north of Naples and Foggia. In order to speed progress and get at least to Rome, the Allies studied a variety of amphibious operations, how to go by water around the German defenses and get in place for a quick strike to Rome. Of all the possibilities, a landing at Anzio emerged as the best. Unfortunately, technical reasons connected with distance, shipping, supplies, and the like, made the venture impractical. It was simply too risky. The Allies reluctantly abandoned the idea and resigned themselves to the agony of battling up the peninsula.

That was when Churchill appeared in North Africa. Coming down with pneumonia, Churchill convalesced in Marrakech, Morocco, during the last days of 1943. As he recuperated, he reflected on how to stem the slipping British status. The best way to do so was by generating a striking victory of British arms. But how? and where?

Italy was the only place, and the capture of Rome the best method. Yet whatever Churchill was able to initiate, he would have to act rapidly. Only a few months remained before Overlord and Anvil deprived Italy of substantial assets. Without them, the Italian campaign was bound to stagnate.

Although Britain and the United States were to contribute equal forces in the initial phase of the decisive Overlord invasion, the Americans would eventually far outnumber the British. Anvil was to be carried out mainly by the Americans and the French, with merely token British representation, and these formations were to join Eisenhower's forces in western Europe. How could activities in Italy, where the British were to be the dominant partner, compete for public attention?

The only way was to restore vitality to the sagging operations in Italy, which already resembled a stalemate. Only the capture of Rome could revive public interest. To gain Rome swiftly, Churchill would have to have the Anzio landing. He might thus create sufficient momentum to necessitate abandoning Anvil and retaining the resources in Italy. Telegraphing his Chiefs of Staff in London, Churchill said, "In no case can we sacrifice Rome for the Riviera."

Eisenhower, named to lead the Normandy invasion, was about to leave, and Field Marshal Sir Henry Maitland Wilson, transferred from the British Middle East command in Cairo, was to replace him in the Mediterranean. A British military officer at the top made the area British, with the British Chiefs of Staff serving as the executive agents of the Combined Chiefs. In this state of affairs, Churchill had freedom to maneuver. As John Eisenhower wrote, "Churchill could now pretty much order any operation he desired in that region—so long as the Americans would supply him."

Summoning the principal Allied military men in the theater to Marrakech, he eloquently persuaded them to his wish. They were in accord, the British because Churchill was the prime minister and their ultimate boss, the Americans because they were ambitious and wished to expand the boundaries of their exertions. Churchill cabled Roosevelt, promised that Anzio would in no way delay Overlord, and received permission to hold for a while longer the landing craft designated for transfer to England and needed for Anzio. Brushing aside the technical objections to the landing, he succeeded in putting on the amphibious operation. Risky though it was, Anzio was to gain Rome quickly.

Churchill's "brain child," as it was sometimes called, at first went well. The troops headed inland from the coast, "pegging out claims," in Churchill's words, "rather than digging in beachheads." Then progress halted. When Churchill learned of the eighteen thousand trucks transported to Anzio, he remarked sarcastically, "We must have a great superiority of chauffeurs." Finally, he was doomed to disappointment. Instead of "hurling a wildcat onto the shore," he admitted, the Allies delivered "a stranded whale."

Penned into a plain under German eyes and artillery, the Anzio forces fought for survival. In static warfare reminiscent of the horrors of the Western Front in World War I, the men in the beachhead suffered and endured for four seemingly endless months.

As soon as it was apparent that Anzio would fail to win Rome at once, Churchill called for scrubbing Anvil, the landings in the Riviera, in order to concentrate on Rome. The Americans preferred to abandon Rome in favor of Anvil. Although Churchill claimed that a vigorous Italian campaign would draw Germans from France and thereby facilitate Overlord, Marshall saw the transfer of divisions from Italy to southern France as the best guarantee against British-inspired adventures in the Balkans. The Americans finally agreed to hold off Anvil until Rome was in Allied hands.

Rome fell on June 4, two days before the Normandy invasion. Instead of a great feat of British arms, as Churchill had wished, Mark Clark's Fifth U.S. Army entered the city.

Churchill continued to press for abolishing Anvil in order to use the resources in Italy. The Americans refused. Churchill finally bowed to the inevitable on July 1, and the Allies scheduled Anvil for August 15. Although Churchill harassed Eisenhower until the last minute arguing for canceling the operation, Allied forces invaded southern France. They made virtually unopposed landings. The Germans were in disarray, mainly because of what was happening in Normandy, specifically around Falaise.

CHAPTER 5

The Invasion Plan

CHURCHILL THOUGHT OF A cross-Channel attack as a coup de grace to be launched when Germany was at the point of collapse. Despite Allied progress toward victory, despite Allied inroads damaging German Continental hegemony, Nazism hardly appeared ready to disintegrate. Although Churchill labored mightily for Overlord's well-being—for example, facilitating the building of artificial harbors to be towed to the Continent and anchored off the beaches of Normandy—he visualized all too vividly the difficulties and dangers of what might turn out to be a premature operation.

In the back of his mind was the ever-present memory of Gallipoli in 1916, the failed amphibious venture which he had sponsored and for which he was held chiefly responsible. He recalled all too well the disastrous Dieppe landing in August 1942, when 6,100 troops, mainly Canadians, had departed England and only 2,500 had returned, the rest having been killed or captured. Conditioned by these events, he expected a full-fledged descent on the Continent in 1944 to be what he termed a "slaughter," and he envisioned the offshore waters turning red with the blood of the assaulting Allied soldiers.

The success or failure of Overlord was bound to determine in large part the outcome of the war. Because Churchill dared not lose, he preferred a safer course to a gamble of such magnitude. As late as

February 1944, he again proposed meeting with the Combined Chiefs of Staff to discuss Overlord versus the Mediterranean.

The Americans refused to reopen the issue. A powerful cross-Channel invasion to them was the quickest and surest way to shatter Germany's military power.

As William McNeill has remarked, a "fevered and impassioned note . . . began to appear in Churchill's relations with the Americans in the first months of 1944." Time was running out, and the "Americans were riding roughshod over his artifices and objections, following their chosen path and risking, in Churchill's view, irreparable disaster. But the Americans brusquely dismissed Churchill's arguments as political in inspiration and therefore militarily disreputable."

Not until two months before the invasion, at a formal conference on April 7, when the commanders went over the plans, did Churchill admit in public his satisfaction with the project. "Gentlemen," he said, "I am now hardening to this enterprise." Whether he intended his statement to encourage the high-ranking participants who were gathered or whether he had undergone a sincere change of heart is, of course, open to question.

In either case, obtaining a foothold in France was the *sine qua non* on which all the subsequent endeavors depended. Thus, the Overlord planners devoted much effort to the first step, getting ashore, securing a beachhead. But since the troops entering the Continent could hardly be left to die or to flounder in hesitation at the water's edge, the planners gave much thought to the second step: how to develop the beachhead inland.

The advantages at the outset accrued to the Germans. They were already there in Normandy, and they were preparing—presumably they would be ready when the invading forces arrived—to turn them back and prevent them from landing.

The Allies would be far weaker at the beginning. Some few would come by air, parachuting to earth or descending by glider, but most would travel in ships, then transfer to smaller boats for the assault on the beaches. While they fought for a foothold on the Continent, they had also to build up their strength so that eventually they reached a certain degree of equality and ultimately, they hoped, of superiority when compared to the Germans. Thus, they needed, in addition, space to accommodate their increased numbers and equipment and room to deploy them for the final confrontation.

In the total form of war initiated by Napoleon Bonaparte, the aim of an army in combat is to destroy the opposing army. It is necessary neither to kill nor to maim all the members of the force. Rather, the task is to reduce the efficiency and then the effectiveness of the adversary, making him finally unable to function.

This was what the Allies hoped to accomplish. But before they could engage in the climactic battle for domination, the planners thought, they had to be firmly established on the ground, and they had to have sufficient resources in manpower and matériel to meet the Germans squarely. Presumably, this would occur when the Allies gained certain objectives enabling them to call the invasion a success; or, conversely, when the Allied achievements persuaded the Germans to admit the success of the invasion.

The Allied planning was thus concerned with two preliminaries, getting troops on the Continent and winning a firm footing in sufficient area and strength in order to be reasonably sure of overwhelming the Germans later. Counting from D day, the initial landings, the Overlord plan ran for ninety days. In those three months the Allies were to complete the invasion and fulfill the conditions—enough acreage and troops—to make possible the subsequent all-out battle on the approaches to Germany. The ultimate objective was the "heart of Germany," deemed to be not Berlin, which was too distant for the Western Allies, but rather the Ruhr, the industrial heartland.

Late in April 1943, Sir Frederick Morgan and his small staff began to work on Overlord. By August they had laid out a basic plan. In accordance with the resources tentatively allocated, Morgan's group stipulated not only airborne and special operations but also the basis of the effort, a three-division amphibious assault on three beaches fronting the bay of the Seine in Normandy and centered roughly on the city of Caen. Although Morgan recommended both a heavier initial landing, which required more sea transport, and an extended front to include part of the Cotentin shore, which would facilitate the capture of Cherbourg, the Combined Chiefs of Staff, then meeting at Quebec, accepted the more limited blueprint.

The document passed among a small group of individuals, most of whom found fault. Some preferred a descent on the Pas-de-Calais, across the Channel from Dover, the closest distance from England. Others wondered whether the invasion area was too far from the main German forces. Eisenhower, who read the plan in Algiers toward the end of October, questioned the amount of strength for the initial assault. There was, he thought, "not enough wallop." Together with his chief of staff, Walter Bedell Smith, he favored at least five or six divisions instead of merely three.

Brooke was very much concerned with the bocage country behind the landing beaches, particularly in the Cotentin, for he had spent summers there as a boy and had withdrawn the last Anglo-French forces across the terrain in July 1940 for evacuation to England. He knew well how the hedgerows would impede the Allies as they tried to move their units and expand the Overlord beachhead inland. At the same time, he rationalized, the natural defenses of the region would help the Allies prevent the Germans from dislodging them from their initial foothold.

Despite a variety of reservations, the Overlord concept stood as a foundation on which the forces designated to execute the scheme were to build the structure of the invasion. The British and Americans had thus to name certain headquarters to draw the detailed specifications and to prepare the subordinate units for the crossing.

Bradley had been in England since September organizing the major American headquarters. In November the British designated the 21 Army Group as the senior British headquarters for Overlord. To command it, only Alexander or Montgomery, the most experienced officers, was suitable. Although the Americans had no say in the matter, they privately preferred Alexander, who was amiable, a model gentleman, and easy to work with. But the British chiefs doubted Alexander's intellect and his ability to exert ruthless drive. At Brooke's urging, they chose Montgomery, who, as Lord Gort remarked, was "not quite a gentleman," but who had a relentless clarity of purpose, as well as recognized status as a complete professional. Having agonized over whether he or Alexander would get the prized assignment, Montgomery learned on December 23 of his appointment to head the 21 Army Group and thereby to direct the British and Canadian forces in the invasion.

Aware of American reservations with respect to Montgomery, Churchill, when he informed Roosevelt of the decision, put the blame for the selection on the War Cabinet. He added, somewhat vaguely for him, without his customary forcefulness in language, "I feel the Cabinet are right, as he [Montgomery] is a public hero and will give confidence among our people not unshared by yours."

Eventually, the United States was to put sixty divisions into battle on the Continent; the British and Canadians were never to have more than twenty. The preponderance of American resources in the campaign of northwest Europe dictated an American to be in overall charge. Roosevelt chose Eisenhower. The President informed him on December 7 of his selection to be the Supreme Allied Commander. The appointment became official with a public announcement on the day before Christmas.

Brooke and others still scorned Eisenhower as little more than a coordinator, a good mixer, and a champion of Allied cooperation and unity; he was hardly a real commander as they understood the term. They were indifferent to or unaware of Eisenhower's extraordinary growth in self-assurance since 1942. As Max Hastings has suggested, Eisenhower's authority, to the British, was like that of a constitutional monarch, whose power was less important than his visible possession of the prerogatives, which denied them to others who might be more capable. What they downgraded was Eisenhower's unequaled ability to make the Anglo-American coalition work despite the ever-present frictions.

Eisenhower in particular had hoped to have Alexander, who had served under him in Tunisia, Sicily, and southern Italy, as his ground forces commander in western Europe. Montgomery, he recognized, would be a difficult and abrasive subordinate. But Eisenhower's sensitivity to the idea of alliance led him to accept Montgomery with grace.

Nor did Eisenhower object to continuing the committee-type command marking his earlier experiences. Air Chief Marshal Sir Arthur Tedder was to be the Deputy Supreme Allied Commander, Admiral Sir Bertram Ramsay was to head the Overlord sea forces, Air Chief Marshal Sir Trafford Leigh-Mallory was to direct the Allied air forces in support of the invasion. Thus, British officers delegated to fulfill important aspects of the enterprise were again to surround Eisenhower.

As though wishing to close the circle, to enhance further the British contribution to Overlord, to continue the relationship he had previously enjoyed with Alexander, he asked Montgomery to act temporarily, that is to say, during the initial stage of the invasion for an unspecified length of time, as the Allied ground forces commander. He made the request in Algiers on December 27, when Montgomery came to see him. Because Montgomery was to go to London in a few days while Eisenhower would travel first to Washington for a stay of about two weeks, Eisenhower wished Montgomery to be his personal representative in London during his absence.

To Eisenhower's suggestion, Montgomery was perfectly amenable, and more. He would make substantial contributions to Overlord. His activities with respect to the landings were undoubtedly beneficial. His ideas on the postassault operations, as well as his conduct of them, became highly controversial.

Unlike Churchill, for he lacked the prime minister's political responsibilities and his broad-gauged outlook, Montgomery had never favored extending the war in the Mediterranean. To him the vital place to fight was western Europe. To some, perhaps a large, extent, he was thinking of erasing the shame of the defeat in 1940 and the humiliation of expulsion from the Continent. Despite his involvement in the Sicilian and southern Italy campaigns, he believed in the necessity of a military showdown on the Western approaches to Germany. Early in 1943, he expressed his hope, as he said somewhat flippantly, "to nip across the Channel." Now at the end of the year, he would soon have the opportunity to do so. His leadership and performance in what was to be the decisive theater of the war were to be a fitting climax, he was certain, not only to his abilities but also to his ambitions.

In a letter he wrote to Brooke on the day following his conversation with Eisenhower in Algiers, Montgomery confirmed Eisenhower's request. Eisenhower, he said, wanted him "to be his head soldier and to take complete charge of the land battle." As Eisenhower's ground forces deputy, Montgomery was to carry on in London until Eisenhower returned from the United States.

Having always questioned Eisenhower's military capacity, Montgomery saw Eisenhower's solicitation as confirmation of what was in Montgomery's own mind. Eisenhower's conferral of authority on Montgomery seemed to be an implicit admission of Eisenhower's feeling of incompetence to direct the vital operation of the war. Only Montgomery, no one else, could fulfill this supremely important task. Thus elevated in his own mind, he set out to accomplish the requirements with an assurance verging on arrogance. During the first five months of 1944, while the Allies prepared the invasion, Montgomery demonstrated a boundless ego, together with a lack of generosity toward Frederick Morgan and a cavalier neglect of Eisenhower. So far as Montgomery was concerned, he alone commanded Overlord. When he visited American troops training in the United Kingdom for the crossing, he announced to them, "General Eisenhower is captain of the team, and I am proud to serve under him." The statement was but lip service, a bow, to the Allied concept: Montgomery never repeated the remark elsewhere.

After returning from Algiers briefly to Italy to say good-bye to his Eighth Army, Montgomery traveled to Marrakech, Morocco, on December 31 to see Churchill, who was recuperating from pneumonia. The prime minister gave Montgomery his copy of Morgan's Overlord document to read and asked Montgomery for his comments. After seeing the paper for the first time, Montgomery, on the following day, labeled the scheme "impracticable," not strong enough. Furthermore, the initial beachhead area, he thought, was too small. Forces funneled in after the assault would congest the restricted space. The Germans would be able to block the Allied foothold too easily and prevent expansion inland. The landings, he was sure, should be made on the widest possible front.

Eisenhower, on his way to Washington, stopped in Marrakech on January 1, 1944, and called on Churchill. He discussed the plan with Montgomery. The reactions of both military men were very much alike.

Montgomery arrived in London on January 2, as did Walter Bedell Smith. Both received a briefing on Overlord on the following day. Montgomery immediately criticized the narrow front of the assault. After three days of discussion, the planners modified the blueprint and agreed on the major points. There was to be, in addition to airborne operations to protect the flanks, a five-division amphibious or seaborne assault on five beaches, including one on the eastern coast of the Cotentin closer to Cherbourg, thus extending the beachhead front to about fifty miles. Montgomery had so impressed his colleagues that they informally called the result the "Montgomery plan."

Shortly after Eisenhower reached London on January 14, he was surprised by what Montgomery had accomplished. Not only had he resolved the principal problems but he had also pulled together the threads of an extremely complicated enterprise. He had further stamped his personality on the planning to such an extent that Eisenhower's approval of the arrangements seemed hardly to be necessary.

Eisenhower called a meeting of the principal Overlord participants at the Norfolk House on January 21 to bring everyone up to date and to identify the issues still needing resolution. On the appointed day, when his driver Kay Summersby pulled up to the parking spaces assigned according to rank, she was furious to find the Number One spot occupied by Montgomery's Rolls Royce limousine. Eisenhower grinned and said it didn't matter, forget it; but after he descended and went inside, Lt. Summersby straightened out the misunderstanding with Montgomery's chauffeur. Eisenhower was Number One.

As Merle Miller has said, if Eisenhower presided at the Norfolk House, Montgomery "prevailed." He explained the deficiencies of Morgan's plan and his measures to rectify them. Increasing the assault from three to five divisions required more landing ships and craft. In order to obtain these additional vessels, the Allies had to postpone Overlord for a month. Instead of going on May 1, they pushed the invasion back to June 5.

At the Norfolk House meeting, Montgomery also laid out how he intended to expand the beachhead. His method was at some variance with Morgan's projections.

In the Morgan plan, the Allies were, in three months, to gain what Overlord called a lodgment area. The planners defined the region as that part of western France bounded on the east by the Seine River and the

Paris-Orléans gap, on the south by the Loire River. It thus included that portion of Normandy west of the Seine and all of Brittany. Within that territory the Allies would have sufficient (1) ports to nourish their forces on the Continent—each ally was to have its own supply line and thus its own harbors along a coastline five hundred miles long, (2) airfields to accommodate planes furnishing close support to the combat troops, (3) room to hold the multitude of organizations servicing the armies, and (4) space in which to maneuver. With the lodgment area in firm possession, with adequate ports, airfields, and territory in hand, with a flow of soldiers and supplies building up their strength on the Continent, the Allies would have completed the invasion. They would then mount the post-Overlord operations designed to destroy the German army. In the process they would liberate the remainder of France and western Europe and drive to the frontier of Germany and beyond, probably to the Ruhr.

The British and Canadians in the invasion were to land on the left, the Americans beside them on the right. These positions made sense logistically, for eventually the British and Canadians, as they expanded their foothold, would remain closer to their base of supply in England. The Americans, who were also originally dependent on their supply complex in the United Kingdom, were ultimately to receive their nourishment from the United States, and their proximity to the British Isles was less important. Unfortunately, as Raymond Callahan has said, the forces on the left, those "poised on the edge of the most direct route to Paris— the army therefore likely to be involved in the heaviest fighting from the beginning—was also the army least able to absorb heavy losses: the British." The only way around this unpleasant fact was to shift the burden. As Alun Chalfont has said, "The Americans, with their greater reserves of manpower, would have to take the most casualties." Montgomery would find a way.

How to overrun the lodgment area? The immediate task after the touchdown on the Continent was to secure ports. The British and Canadians, entering Normandy on the Allied left, were to take the minor port of Caen on D day, then go up the Channel coast to Honfleur and Le Havre, which were close to England. The greater part of the replacement troops, equipment, and supplies for the British and Canadians was eventually to funnel through Le Havre. The Americans were to capture Cherbourg as soon as feasible, then head south to Brittany and ultimately drive westward to Brest. In World War I, most of the nourishment for the American Expeditionary Force had come through Brest, and the planners expected the same to happen in 1944. Because the Germans were likely to destroy the port cities, along with their docks and unloading cranes, before the Allies could seize them, initial supply loads were to come across the invasion shore, then through two artificial harbors, one for the British and the Canadians, the other for the Americans, both towed across the Channel and anchored off the invasion beaches as temporary reception facilities.

Providing airfields for the planes to be ferried to the Continent as soon as possible seemed to pose little problem. The best place to build air installations was the ground south of Caen, a vast plain rising imperceptibly for about twenty miles to a place called Falaise. This was in the projected British zone of operations, and the terrain was excellent also for offensive efforts by the Allied mechanized forces, particularly tanks.

For these reasons, the acquisition of both airfields and maneuver space, the Morgan plan chose the Caen-Falaise area for the Allied main effort to expand the beachhead. Furthermore, a quick advance south and east of Caen promised to get the Allies to Paris and the Seine River, sensitive and important objectives.

Montgomery rejected the last idea. The Germans too, he knew, would recognize the Caen-Falaise plain as the best place to fight. They would react strongly to any Allied threat to Paris and the Seine. They were thus likely to mass their forces on the ground south and southeast of Caen against the British and Canadians. Whether he underestimated the skill of the British and Canadian soldiers or whether he realistically understood their shortcomings—weariness in the case of the former, inexperience in the case of the latter—he expected them to have great difficulty holding off the Germans. It would be enough, Montgomery figured, if the British and Canadians prevented the Germans from overwhelming the invasion. The British and Canadians would have to stress defense after landing.

Where then were the Allies to make progress beyond the beaches? While the British and Canadians dealt with the major German forces approaching from the east and southeast, the Americans were to carry the main thrust of the offensive. Unfortunately for the Americans, their zone of operations was in countryside virtually impossible for offense. In waterlogged and hedgerowed terrain so compartmented, so close, so restricted that every tiny field was a potential fortress, in a region where few routes of advance existed, movement was bound to be slow and painful. Through this terrain, in which Brooke despaired of generating forward motion, the Americans were to gain ground once the beachhead was established.

In effect, Overlord, in Montgomery's eyes, was to consist of two phases. During the first, the Allies were to make good their assault, that is, the British and Canadians were to gain Caen and some airfields, the Americans to capture Cherbourg. During the second, while the British and Canadians erected a barrier against the Germans, the Americans were to enlarge the ground held by the Allies; they were to head south to Brittany and the Loire River to seize additional room and ports.

Although the dictates of the terrain would no doubt lead the Germans to concentrate against the British and Canadians no matter what the Allies might do, Montgomery at first talked sensibly of the Anglo-Canadian shield or buffer. When he eventually turned the barrier into a magnet and spoke of drawing or attracting the bulk of the German forces to the best fighting ground opposite the Canadians and British in order to facilitate the American advance, Montgomery was exaggerating, to say the least.

Because the invasion forces could hardly be infected with a defensive attitude, Montgomery endeavored to promote an offensive orientation, particularly among the British and Canadians. They were to thrust quickly, to penetrate deeply, to keep the enemy off balance. They were not to remain quiescent and await the German onslaught but were instead, as he said, "to peg out claims inland."

As a matter of fact, the Caen-Falaise plain attracted Montgomery too. That was the place to strike out, to gain a resounding victory. Had he been a gambler, he might have seized the opportunity. But too much, he decided, was at stake. For he was by tendency a counterpuncher. His strength lay in responding to the initiatives of his adversary. Even his betting book, where he recorded wagers on diverse subjects—the date when the war would end, what kind of government the voters in England would elect afterwards, and the like—symbolically reflected his habit: He never proposed a bet himself but rather chose to accept some that others offered.

Montgomery was far from brilliant in taking the initiative or in pressing an advantage. He lacked the temperament to launch the sudden, swift, ruthless stroke to finish off an opponent, the temperament that athletes, especially boxers and tennis players, term the killer instinct. His pursuit of Rommel across Libya, as Alun Chalfont has noted, was sluggish. Montgomery was unable to destroy Rommel's Italo-German Army during its more than 1,500-mile withdrawal even though the Allied Ultra Secret intelligence intercepts apprised Montgomery almost daily of Rommel's intentions, plans, and strength. Montgomery hesitated to employ the prime European weapon of World War II, the lesson of blitzkrieg, sending tanks forward in rapid movement.

His forte was organizing, training for, planning, and directing an

orderly sequence of events. Balance rather than boldness was his preference. Unlike Patton, who rejoiced in the opportunities of a fluid situation
in which he had to deal with the unexpected on the spur of the moment,
Montgomery was uncomfortable with the unanticipated. He was more
attuned to the well-thought-out course of action.

Rarely in warfare does reality on the battlefield match the plans
laid out beforehand. All too often the unexpected exigency dictates
alterations in preconceptions. Amending original ideas and improvising
would be the case too in Normandy.

Although Montgomery would grapple successfully with the changing
situations of the Normandy scene and show a high sense of poise, he
chose later to claim omniscience. Nothing had surprised him, he insisted
afterwards, because everything had proceeded according to his plans.
The statement was more in keeping with his portrait of himself and with
his propensity for tidiness. The pattern established before the invasion
therefore exerted a heavy burden on the operations he actually carried
out. His preconceptions tended to restrict his choices. For him, altering
the set course to take advantage of opportunities not anticipated in
advance was always a difficult decision.

Montgomery's claim to infallibility also furthered the image of
selfless British-Canadian behavior. Whatever casualties the Anglo-Cana-
dians suffered by holding off the Germans, they would fail to register
much of an advance. To the public following war maps in the newspapers
and noting progress as measured by the forward movement of the front,
gains by the British and Canadians, when compared with those of the
Americans, would be virtually nil. The British and Canadians would
appear to be standing still while the Americans rushed ahead. Montgomery's strategy sacrificed British-Canadian mobility in order, he said, to
benefit the Americans, whose expansion of liberated territory would
confer the glory on them.

A certain ambivalence, nevertheless, crept into Montgomery's view.
The Caen-Falaise plain challenged him. He formally renounced the
gamble, but the attractive ground for offensive combat continued to
hypnotize him. For one brief moment during the campaign, he would be
unable to resist the temptation. He would attempt to blow out the Germans. And he would be unsuccessful.

Fundamentally, the Montgomery strategy promised also to conserve
British manpower. Nigel Hamilton has suggested Montgomery's ignorance, unlike Brooke's, of the hedgerows and the difficulties of fighting
among them. If so, he expected rapid American progress. In retrospect,
as Alun Chalfont has recognized, by compelling the Americans to grind

through the forbidding hedgerowed lowland of the Cotentin, Montgomery made it inevitable for the Americans to bear the brunt of the Allied casualties.

How did the Americans react to this prospect? Omar Bradley, the senior commander of the American ground forces in Overlord, made no protest, nor even a comment. Probably he too was unaware of the problem awaiting in the hedgerows. He accepted the assigned task without question. He envisaged no other way than the plan enunciated by Montgomery. Overshadowed by others more accustomed to basking in the limelight, Bradley remained quiet, obedient, and in the background, as was his habit. No wonder his superiors esteemed him.

Still an unknown personality to the American and British people, Bradley found it difficult to believe in the reality of his eminent position. Hardly at home with the trappings and prerogatives of high rank, he was continually surprised by his elevation to such authority. He showed what was perhaps an exaggerated respect for Montgomery, who had by the time of the invasion, Bradley said, "become the symbol of victory in the eyes of the Allied world." But secretly he chafed under the idea and often wished that he could be a star performer too. During the campaign he would enjoy a flush of success beyond his wildest dreams. That moment would induce in him a self-exhilaration close to dizziness. Unlike Montgomery, who would feel tied to the preinvasion plan, Bradley, to a certain extent, would lose sight of the established objectives and pursue unrealistic goals.

The refinement of the Overlord planning had proceeded far enough by April 7 for a full-scale review. With the principals, both planners and commanders, gathered at the St. Paul's School in London, Montgomery's headquarters, he showed how the campaign was to go. "The object of Overlord," he specified, "is to secure a lodgment on the Continent from which further offensive operations can be developed." The Second British Army and the First U.S. Army were to assault the coast of France side by side, the British on the left. Once they were ashore, the maneuver projected was quite optimistic, indeed, overly so.

Putting aside his earlier cautious estimate of what the British and Canadians could accomplish, Montgomery stressed offensive action. Their immediate objective of Caen, twelve miles inland, was to be taken on D day. Protecting the eastern flank of the Allied beachhead, they were also to move south and southeast of Caen to gain airfield sites. Soon afterwards, they were to seize Falaise, twenty miles south of Caen. Anchoring their left on Falaise, the British and Canadians were to pivot on their right, swing eastward, and sweep the ground between Falaise and Argentan, fifteen miles to the south, and also between Argentan and Alençon, and twenty-five miles farther south. That would put them in position for a drive to the Seine River. At the conclusion of the movement, the Allies would possess a large chunk of the lodgment area.

The First U.S Army had an even larger role. After capturing Cherbourg, the Americans were to advance to St-Lô, about thirty miles to the south, then to Avranches, about thirty miles farther south. They were to move into Brittany, take Rennes, about forty-five miles south of Avranches, strike more than fifty miles south to the Loire River, and wheel to the east to the Seine River and Paris.

Following these formations into Normandy and becoming operational or active sometime afterwards during the campaign, the First Canadian Army, under Henry Crerar, was to cover the British left flank, then drive for Le Havre; the Third U.S. Army, under Patton, was to clear Brittany, seize St-Nazaire and Nantes on the Loire River, and cover the First U.S. Army right flank on the march to Paris.

Montgomery talked about the need for aggressive action on the Continent. He wanted the armies to thrust armored spearheads deep into the enemy defenses. The objectives he set reflected his belief in the power of the Allied forces. But by his ambitious goals, as Nigel Hamilton and Max Hastings have suggested, he meant to inspire his listeners and particularly to assure Churchill, who was in the audience, of his offensive intent. Montgomery thereby exaggerated what he proposed to do, and the result, inevitably, was to prompt disappointment.

The army commanders had by then arrived in England and taken their places at the head of their organizations. Although the magnitude of their tasks and responsibilities compelled outward harmony, they were a mixed lot, hardly well matched and congenial.

Bradley resented Patton, and, as Nigel Hamilton has remarked, "relations between the two American commanders were far from the intimate, friendly ones assumed . . . later." Bradley's aide, who maintained a diary for his boss, recorded, "General Patton . . . is extremely unpopular in the [First Army] headquarters." The antipathy flowed from the top, from Bradley himself, who set the tone.

Also, according to Bradley, "Patton didn't particularly like Monty." Bradley thought Patton considered Montgomery "too cocky." To Bradley, "Possibly too much like Patton himself."

Montgomery believed the American commanders to be less than brilliant. He characterized Patton as a saber rattler, "ignorant of battle" but "a thruster." He found Bradley "conscientious, dependable and loyal," but also "dull." Whether the last referred to his conversation and company or to his tactical ideas, Montgomery did not say.

His attitude toward his two other army commanders was less than enthusiastic. In his letter to Brooke after meeting with Eisenhower at the end of December, Montgomery had suggested whom he wanted to command the British and Canadian armies. His first choice to head the Second British Army in Overlord was the officer who was the logical person to succeed him in command of the Eighth Army, Sir Oliver Leese, who was then under Montgomery as a corps commander in Italy—"easily the best I have," Montgomery said. Leese, who had served in a similar capacity in North Africa and Sicily, was experienced in combat and knew Montgomery's methods well.

To lead the First Canadian Army in Overlord, Montgomery proposed a British officer. Earlier that year, the Canadians had discussed but had reached no decision on putting a British officer in command of their troops in England. In line with their talk, Montgomery suggested another of his corps commanders in Italy, Sir Miles Dempsey. Dempsey had been a student of Montgomery's at Camberley, the staff college, and he had commanded an infantry brigade at Dunkirk. After Dempsey headed one division, then another, he moved up in December 1942, during the North African campaign, to command a corps. Dempsey's service in Tunisia, Sicily, and Italy made him well acquainted with Montgomery's system. Furthermore, he had served with Canadian troops after the Dunkirk evacuation and was well known and well liked by them.

What led Montgomery to suggest a British leader for the Canadians was Montgomery's judgment of the Canadian officer being talked about for the position of army commander. This officer, Montgomery felt, was hardly up to the demands of the job. "The more I think of Harry Crerar," Montgomery wrote to Brooke, "the more I am convinced that he is quite unfit to command an army in the field at present. He has much to learn." The Canadians, Montgomery was quite sure, would prefer to be well handled by a competent British general like Dempsey rather than being "mishandled by an inexperienced general of their own."

There was, in Montgomery's estimation, a fine Canadian division commander in Italy, Guy Simonds. A good friend of Dempsey, Simonds was, Montgomery wrote, "quite first class." Unfortunately, he was rather young to command an army.

When Montgomery left Italy for England at the turn of the year, Leese, in a well-deserved promotion, took his place at the head of the

Eighth Army. Dempsey, who no doubt was aware of Montgomery's having listed him next after Leese, took the Second Army in England. Somewhat lacking in ruthlessness and drive, Dempsey was colorless and tended to be introverted, but he was intelligent and imperturbable, and he satisfied Montgomery's expectations. Patton thought Dempsey to be, as Patton recorded in his diary, "a yes-man."

Against Montgomery's advice, the authorities recalled Crerar from Italy, where he commanded a corps, and gave him the First Canadian Army. Montgomery, who had known Crerar since 1942, doubted his ability on the battlefield. To Patton, Crerar was better than Dempsey, "but not impressive."

Of the four Allied ground commanders designated to execute Overlord under Montgomery, three—Bradley, Dempsey, and Crerar—were quiet and even-tempered. Montgomery easily dominated them. Patton, who strove mightily to curb his exuberance and flamboyance, was an exception and outside the pattern.

The final presentation of the Overlord planning occurred at St. Paul's School on May 15. All the dignitaries were present, King George VI, Churchill, the British Chiefs of Staff, as well as the principal commanders and planners. As the battle projections were exposed, as the drama of what the Allies proposed to accomplish unfolded, Montgomery, as before, was, according to those present, the "driving force" behind Overlord. If Eisenhower remained in the background as the executive, Montgomery stepped forward as the foreman, marshaling his subordinates to explain how they intended to go about their business and what they proposed to do.

Montgomery had, since the last plenary session, scaled down his expectations. According to his tracings on the map, the boundary separating the 21 Army Group (the British and Canadian forces) from the 12th Army Group (the American units) indicated clearly how he expected the campaign to develop. The line he drew ran southeastward from about the middle of the invasion beaches for more than fifty miles to a point below Argentan. There the line turned east and barely northeastward to Mantes-la-Jolie, or Mantes-Gassicourt as it was then called, on the Seine River. According to this concept, at D plus 90 (three months after the invasion), the First Canadian Army, operating along the Channel coast, and the Second British Army, engaged inland, would be up against the Seine River as far upstream as Mantes-Gassicourt. The First U.S. Army, after capturing Chartres and Orléans, would be pressed against the

Seine River and also covering the Paris-Orléans gap. Except for western Brittany, which the Third U.S. Army would be in the process of seizing, the lodgment area would be in Allied hands.

The emphasis was on gaining ground. Both Allies were to overrun the vital part of Normandy, that is, from the Cotentin to the Seine, in equal manner. They were to capture similar shares of the territory liberated. Despite Montgomery's reservations on whether the British and Canadians could really move so fast and so far, such was the concept.

A week before the invasion, Patton invited his major subordinates to dinner—his four corps commanders and their chiefs of staff, his own chief and deputy chief of staff, and the general officer responsible for providing air support to Patton's forces. His purpose was to promote team spirit, but this already existed. The officers were a homogeneous group. They were all good friends, and they worked together in harmony. There were neither jealousies nor reservations on Patton's combat methods. They were completely loyal to him. All, Patton noted with great satisfaction, came originally from Southern states.

Three days later, on June 1, in order to promote Allied cohesion, Montgomery had his principal subordinates to dinner and an overnight at his invasion headquarters near Portsmouth—his four army commanders, Dempsey, Crerar, Bradley, and Patton, as well as his chief of staff, Francis de Guingand. Bradley and Patton were eager to be friendly with Montgomery, particularly on the eve of the invasion, and the evening was pleasant enough. When the port was passed, Montgomery toasted the army commanders. Patton expected Bradley, the senior American, to respond, and after a brief silence, Patton stood and said, "As the oldest Army commander present, I would like to propose a toast to the health of General Montgomery and express our satisfaction in serving under him." Recording this in his diary, Patton added, "The lightning did not strike me" for telling a lie.

When he departed on the following morning, Patton possessed "a better impression of Monty than I had" before. Montgomery told him, "I had a good time and now we understand each other." They were no doubt sincere, perhaps thinking of their cooperation in Sicily. To some extent, both understood, the sentiment was, on both sides, a wistful hope.

As D day, June 5, approached, the weather in England and over the Channel deteriorated. Low clouds, increasing winds, and high seas jeopardized the invasion. The crossing required good visibility and relatively calm waters, and instead, a storm gathered intensity. On June 3, the forecasts for the scheduled time of the landings two days later were pessimistic, announcing overcast skies and high winds. Eisenhower and a few ranking commanders met with meteorologists at four A.M. on June 4 to consider whether to delay or to cancel Overlord. Gale warnings prompted Eisenhower to postpone the operation for twenty-four hours. When the small group came together again at nine-thirty P.M. that night, although a heavy rain was falling and strong winds blew, the news was better. Weather stations in the western Atlantic, in Greenland and elsewhere, promised improving conditions, decreased cloud cover and wind speeds, for the new date. Shortly after four A.M. on June 5, Eisenhower confirmed his decision for touchdown on the morning of June 6.

In the early hours of that day, as transport planes full of paratroopers took off from England, as gliders and other airborne troops prepared to follow, as an armada of ships loaded with soldiers steamed toward the Normandy coast, the Allies banked on the two advantages they enjoyed: the time and the place of the landings were unknown to the Germans.

A vast cover plan code-named Fortitude included dummy camps, fake tanks and trucks constructed of rubber, a flow of false communications, the use of Patton as the fictitious commander of nonexistent invasion forces, and the manipulation of nearly one hundred captured German agents in England. By these means the Allies sought to fix German eyes on the Pas-de-Calais in northern France rather than on the Bay of the Seine as the site of the assault. From the Ultra Secret intercepts of German messages read by the Allies, the effort seemed to be working.

The less than perfect weather added another dimension to the deception. The choppy sea and gusty wind conspired to raise scarcely tolerable conditions for small boats and air transports. To the Germans, an invasion in such circumstances seemed unlikely, even impossible.

The twin Allied needs, first of getting ashore, then of gaining the lodgment area, appeared to have a good chance of attainment. The immediate concern was planting a foothold, but seizing the lodgment area, synonymous with Overlord's success, the essential preliminary for ultimate victory, was in the back of the high commanders' minds.

No one was thinking especially of Falaise, although Montgomery, on the day before, had expressed his confidence in reaching Falaise twenty-four hours after taking the D day objective of Caen. The main purpose was to come into possession of ground.

For, the point was, the Overlord plan was fundamentally a logistical document. It was a blueprint for an invasion designed to gain, during the first three months of action, the Allies the lodgment area. This region contained the bases for continuing support and buildup—the ports to accommodate a constant stream of men and matériel coming from Britain and the United States to Normandy, enough space in which to place the increasing numbers of troops and installations arriving on the Continent, as well as sufficient airfields and maneuver-room to help protect the land already overrun and to help obtain additional terrain. At the end of ninety days, the Allies occupying the lodgment area were to be at least the equal of their adversaries in strength and in capability.

Only then, not before, were the Allies to embark on post-Overlord operations geared to overwhelm the enemy. During the preliminary phase of the invasion, during the Overlord stage, during the initial three months of activity, the planners expected no decisive battle to take place. This was the outlook they imposed on the top battlefield leaders—and it was quite wrong.

PART II

THE
PRECIPITATING
ACTION

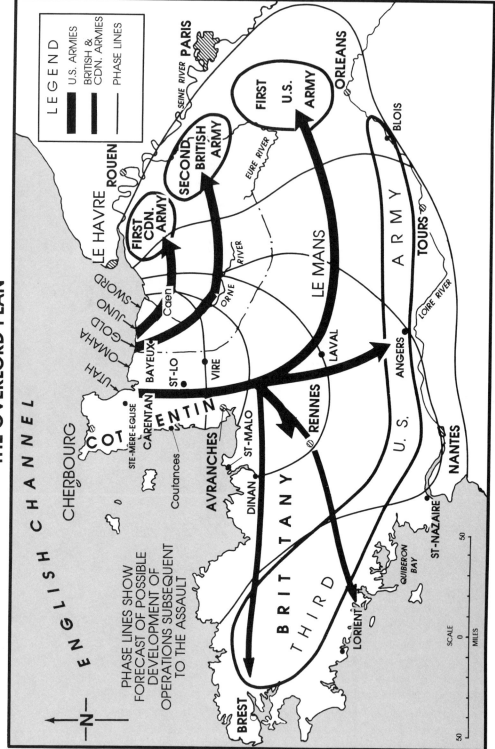

THE OVERLORD PLAN

CHAPTER 6

The Germans

ADOLF HITLER WAS THE beneficiary of luck and intuition. The first brought him to power in 1933 when President Paul von Hindenburg died. The second led him to expect, correctly as it turned out, the failure of French and British nerve in 1934, when, contrary to the Treaty of Versailles, he moved military units into the Rhineland, against merely verbal opposition. Expanding Germany's power bloodlessly, he annexed Austria and took over Czechoslovakia. His pact with the Soviet Union facilitated his invasion of Poland in September 1939.

This was also when he began to lose his touch. His armed aggression, to his mild surprise, prompted Britain and France to declare war against him.

Yet all seemed to go well as Hitler overran Poland and divided the country with Joseph Stalin. He forced Denmark and Norway into the German orbit. And when he unleashed his offensive against the West in May 1940, he gained his greatest success. Rolling over Luxembourg, Belgium, the Netherlands, and much of France, he forced these nations out of the war, occupied them, and expelled the British forces from the Continent.

Had his judgment been better, he would have let his panzers crush the Anglo-French forces at Dunkirk. Instead of finishing them off for good, he allowed substantial numbers of British and French troops to escape.

Master of Europe in mid-1940, with an empire stretching from the North Sea and the English Channel to the Soviet border, Hitler had won the war. His military machine stood omnipotent. He had effectively no Continental enemies. No one challenged his power. Stalin admired his conquests. Francisco Franco in Spain was friendly. Benito Mussolini, who had entered the war on Hitler's side by invading France at the last moment, was both friend and ally.

Only the offshore British were hostile. They were unwilling to conclude a military truce or a political treaty with Germany.

To bring them to their knees, Hitler decided to cross the water and invade England. Gathering shipping and troops in Channel ports, he fought the battle of Britain in the air as a prelude. His luck abandoned him. His outlook was faulty too. His confidence in Hermann Göring and the Luftwaffe was misplaced. His estimate of British obstinacy was wrong. The assault against Britain became a dead end, not even undertaken.

The British were already retaliating. Their early measures were little more than pinpricks, hardly threatening. Yet they were annoying. Small parties of naval raiders descended on the Continent, staying long enough to damage or destroy submarine and radar sites as well as other vulnerable coastal installations. Planes flew over Germany and dropped bombs ostensibly to knock out industrial plants but really to wipe out population centers. Resistance movements in the occupied countries, many initially sponsored and supported by British funds and agents, harassed the Germans by sabotage and a growing violence that spread uncertainty and fear among them. The actions served notice of the intention ultimately to bring down Hitler's Germany.

Propelled by mad ambition and perhaps insatiable greed, Hitler decided to turn to the east. Before he could do so, Mussolini upset his plans. Without advance notice, Mussolini created a mess in North Africa and in Greece, then called upon Hitler for help. Hitler responded. To North Africa he sent Erwin Rommel, who quickly restored the situation. Greece and southeastern Europe were more complicated. Hitler needed a secure southern flank to cover his projected invasion of the Soviet Union, and by the time German troops stabilized the Balkans, it was rather late in the year for a thrust into Russia.

Hitler struck nevertheless. His luck held during the early months of the campaign, then broke down in the face of winter weather and stiffening Soviet resolve. Despite a massive concentration of German forces, Hitler was unable to take Moscow or Leningrad.

At the close of 1941, Hitler's situation deteriorated. As Pearl Harbor aligned the United States alongside Britain, he had to reckon with an eventual Anglo-American attack in the west. He gave some thought and attention to building coastal defenses and erecting an Atlantic Wall. The start of reconnaissance for sites was soon followed by the beginning of construction.

The first real action to prepare for an Allied invasion occurred in March 1942, when Hitler selected Field Marshal Gerd von Rundstedt to be the commander in chief in the west. An austere figure, sixty-seven years old, Rundstedt had with distinction commanded an army group in the campaigns of Poland, France, and Russia. Ill, he retired. When he recovered his health, the Führer gave him responsibility for the defense of the Netherlands, Belgium, and the occupied northern half of France.

Quite by coincidence, several days later, on March 28, the British shocked Hitler. They executed a relatively large-scale raid on the naval base of St-Nazaire. British ships boldly sailed up the mouth of the Loire River and landed troops who caused extensive damage to the installation.

Hitler regarded this operation as a serious threat. Expecting further Allied landings during the summer, he intensified the construction of coastal defenses.

In August, the repulse of the Allied landings at Dieppe seemed to confirm the value of defensive works. Hitler began to talk of a concrete coastal wall put up with what he called "fanatic energy." A month later he spoke of 300,000 troops defending fifteen thousand strongpoints along the western shore.

The Allied detour into North Africa in November, decreasing the danger of a large-scale invasion in the west, allowed Hitler to drain Rundstedt's resources for use in Russia and the Mediterranean. Between April and December 1943, he transferred twenty-seven first-rate divisions to other fronts. Replacing them were units in training; they had fewer and less effective weapons and means of transport, as well as older reservists and troops generally of poorer quality.

In October 1943, looking ahead to the probability of Allied landings during the following year, Rundstedt submitted to Hitler a comprehensive survey of the state of his defenses. His report was pessimistic. The Atlantic Wall was far from ready. As a matter of fact, little had been accomplished.

Hitler responded at once by allocating more labor battalions and increased stocks of building materials to the western defenses. He was particularly interested in strengthening the Pas-de-Calais, opposite Dover. The proximity of this ground to England made it the best place not only for an invasion but also for positioning new and deadly instruments, the long-range rockets and pilotless aircraft called *Vergeltungswaffen*, or reprisal weapons—the V-1 and V-2 rockets—turned toward England. Massive defenses in that area would fulfill two objects: drive back invaders and protect the "miracle" arms on which Hitler counted to win the war.

In addition, in November, Hitler transferred Rommel and his Army Group B headquarters from northern Italy to the west. Rommel was, after Hitler, probably the best-known and most widely admired individual in Germany. His well-publicized exploits had made him a hero. As the commander of the 7th Panzer Division in 1940, he had been in the forefront of the lightning victory, his troops traveling from the German border through Luxembourg, Belgium, and France to the Spanish frontier with blazing speed and amazing effectiveness, capturing thousands of prisoners, taking Cherbourg and Rennes, and losing relatively few troops in the process. In North Africa he kept the British off balance, came close to expelling them from Egypt, and defeated the Americans at Kasserine Pass before succumbing to illness. After his recovery, Hitler was about to give him the supreme command in Italy but western Europe seemed better suited for Rommel's talents. With an independent status under Hitler, Rommel was to study and strengthen the coastal defenses in the west.

Embarking at once on his task, Rommel brought a sense of urgency to all who labored and who defended along the beaches. His presence inspired and invigorated them. With his customary energy, he speeded improvements. His seemingly untiring efforts produced strongpoints, blockhouses, forts, and coastal batteries as if by magic. The number of obstacles he planted multiplied, thousands upon thousands of mines and booby traps of one form or another sowed along the water's edge. The Atlantic Wall took shape and appeared imposing.

Allied landings were the greatest danger to Germany, for western Europe lacked the vast distances of the Soviet Union. If the Allies succeeded in getting ashore, they would be practically on the approaches to the Nazi homeland.

On the other hand, an Allied invasion gave Hitler a most favorable opportunity. If he prevented the Allied forces from coming ashore, he would, for all intents and purposes, win the struggle. The Allies would be so broken that they might be willing to conclude a peace. If not, they would require years of preparation before trying again to penetrate the German defensive crust.

Hitler thus set about to further improve his readiness. He was not only the nominal commander in chief of the German Armed Forces but also the actual supreme commander. He had by 1944 delegated many of his governmental functions to others in order to have time to exercise direct control over military operations. He determined strategy on all fronts, and he supervised closely the formulation and execution of plans. Increasingly he was interested in tactical operations, although he refrained for the moment from issuing the detailed instructions down to battalion level, as he later did when his distrust of his officer corps was almost maniacal.

His first act was to streamline his command structure in the west. Germany had occupied all of France in November 1942, and since then Rundstedt, in addition to his responsibilities elsewhere, looked after the enormous coastline of the Channel, the Atlantic, and the Mediterranean shores. In order to simplify Rundstedt's burdens, Hitler placed two army groups under his control.

In the last days of December 1943, Hitler integrated Rommel and his Army Group B headquarters into the command structure. Under Rundstedt, Rommel became responsible for Holland, Belgium, and northern France as far south as the Loire River. He controlled Armed Forces Netherlands and two armies, the Fifteenth, in Belgium and northern France and covering the Pas de-Calais, and the Seventh, guarding France between the Seine and the Loire rivers.

In May 1944, responding to signs of Allied activity seemingly directed against the Riviera, Hitler activated Army Group G for southern France, with one army along the Atlantic coast, another along the Mediterranean shore.

Of the three hundred or so divisions stationed outside of Germany, about 179 faced the Russians on the Eastern Front. In Italy, 22 fought a delaying action. Combating partisan warfare, 26 were in the Balkans. Scandinavia had 16 divisions, Finland 8. Of the 53 in the Netherlands, Belgium, and France, most were guarding the Pas-de-Calais region.

Exactly how to meet and defeat the Allied arrival in the west was a subject of some debate. Rundstedt, believing in the classic notion, established a strong and mobile strategic reserve centrally located and ready for action. After he distinguished among the various feints, diversions, and subsidiary landings designed to fool the Germans, when he identified the main invasion forces, he would launch his strategic reserve in a swift and powerful counterattack to destroy the invaders before they could reinforce their beachhead. Rundstedt thus counted on a mobile defense in depth, striking power, and a battle of annihilation.

Rommel presupposed Allied air and naval supremacy in the invasion area. He saw little possibility of moving a strategic reserve to the coast under the guns and bombs of Allied planes or of regaining the beaches against naval shelling. If the Germans were to turn back the invasion, they had to do so as the Allies were landing, when they were weakest, that is, when they were afloat, had no cover, and were capable of limited firepower. Rommel counted on his coastal batteries and obstacles and on massed troops along the shoreline to smash the Allies in the first twenty-four hours of the landings, that is, before they could establish a firm footing. Rommel thus advocated a static linear defense, concrete fortifications, and holding stubbornly.

Hitler saw the advantages of both courses of action, yet never decided which he preferred. As a consequence, Rundstedt and Rommel went about their preparations according to their own conceptions, and both were dissatisfied; neither received what he considered to be thorough support.

By May, the mastery of Allied air and naval forces over the entire length of the potential invasion zone made it virtually impossible for the Germans to conduct reconnaissance. The Luftwaffe and the naval units were unable to discover what was taking place in British harbors and along the English coast. The bad weather in the early days of June further hampered attempts to penetrate the Allied air and naval screen concealing the invasion preparations. During the first five days of June, the Germans were without any information from reconnaissance sources.

On June 4, although admitting the paucity of data, the German naval headquarters in the west doubted the imminence of the invasion. Its report that day stated, "The enemy has [not] yet assembled his invasion fleet in the required strength" for landings. A day later, as the Allied invasion armada was heading for Normandy, a total of five German aircraft flew into the overcast sky and over the Channel to carry out routine missions. They found nothing. Rommel's Army Group B, on that day, June 5, reiterated the assumption of the Pas-de-Calais as the "focal point of the major landing" expected. On the same day, Rundstedt's headquarters categorically announced, "There is no immediate prospect of the invasion." The storm led to canceling the naval patrols scheduled for the night of June 5.

Lacking meteorological stations in the western Atlantic, the Germans were unaware of the changing conditions, the potential break in the weather front. As gales raged over western Europe, forecasters continued to discount the prospect of landings. No invasion, they believed, was practical for several days.

Rommel departed his headquarters near Rouen on June 5, his wife's birthday, to spend the night with his family at home, then to continue on the following day to confer with Hitler. Like Rommel, many high-ranking officers were absent from their posts. Quite a few were in Rennes, where a command post exercise was scheduled for June 6.

The invasion took the Germans entirely by surprise. The time and the place were completely unexpected.

The Germans first became aware of Allied paratroopers who arrived in the predawn darkness. Coming to earth on each edge of the assault area, Americans in the Cotentin below Cherbourg, British along the lower reaches of the Orne River, their mission to anchor the flanks of the beachhead, they were widely scattered, particularly in the American zone. Their dispersed locations confused the Germans; they seemed to be everywhere.

The soldiers landing amphibiously had little trouble getting ashore, except at Omaha Beach, where a German division was stationed. Allied intelligence officers had noted the German formation several days before-hand, too late to change the timetable or the touchdown site. As a consequence, the defenders reported throughout much of the day turning back the landings there. Actually, unlike the four other beaches—two British, Gold and Juno; one Canadian, Sword; and one American, Utah; all quickly seized and secured with relatively few casualties—Omaha came into American possession with great difficulty during the afternoon of D day, June 6.

Massed Allied aircraft over the invasion area and sustained Allied naval shelling from ships offshore, as well as stepped-up Resistance harassment, hampered the German reaction. Bridges, railroad yards, and other transportation chokepoints destroyed or damaged by sabotage, by naval gunfire, and by what the Germans called "terrible" and "incessant" air attacks, disrupted the movement of units traveling from the interior of France and elsewhere to the front.

From the beginning of the invasion until well into the summer, the dispatch of German reinforcements to the battle area verged on nightmare. Troops on many occasions had to abandon their trains and march on foot considerable distances with increasing weariness; they often arrived at the combat zone exhausted. Formations were strung out over the countryside and reached their destinations in small packets. Many had to travel at night, and blackout conditions slowed progress, fostered accidents, and enhanced Resistance ambush. A journey normally requiring a single day often took ten. In one instance, a unit needed seven days to cover a hundred miles. Cut telephone wires frequently denied German authorities information on where certain organizations were.

Overlord struck in the area controlled by Friedrich Dollmann's

Seventh Army. Dollmann had commanded the army in the campaign of 1940 and continuously since then. His headquarters was in comfortable billets in Le Mans. The occupation duties had been pleasant despite occasional Resistance disturbance, and the good life had somewhat enervated faculties and deadened initiative among staff members. Still, after a seemingly endless series of false alarms and alerts, the arrival of Allied troops dispelled uncertainties. The army responded promptly to the landings.

About seven divisions were in the general area of the invasion, and Dollmann tried to strengthen them by calling on his forces in Brittany. By the end of the month, five divisions had arrived and a sixth was on the way. Rommel furnished an additional division from those stationed in Holland. Army Group G in southern France dispatched six. Hitler made two available from eastern Europe.

The nearby Fifteenth Army shifted several divisions to Dollmann's command, but continuing concern over the Pas-de-Calais resulted in replacing the departed formations with units coming from Norway and Denmark. The Fortitude deception confirmed Hitler's intuition, and the Fifteenth Army remained inactive and on the alert awaiting the principal Allied descent, which the Germans believed would come from "Army Group Patton." A total of eighteen divisions and four corps headquarters contributed nothing as the Fifteenth Army sat while Dollmann's Seventh Army battled the Allies in Normandy with approximately the same resources.

Rommel returned to Normandy at ten P.M., June 6, and endeavored to stiffen the defenses. By June 9, the fourth day of the invasion, he was so discouraged that he privately conceded Allied success.

Rundstedt, hardly certain whether the Allied presence in Normandy constituted the major assault or a diversionary effort, felt obliged to eradicate the growing beachhead before it became altogether established on the Continent. In conformance with his preparations, he instructed Panzer Group West, his strategic reserve force, to strike to Bayeux, the center of the Allied foothold. The troops were to deliver a powerful blow to cripple, then to destroy the Allied operation and buildup. Before Panzer Group West could get under way, Allied bombers struck the headquarters on June 10, ruined a large number of tanks and vehicles, killed seventeen key officers, including the chief of staff, and brought the attempt to a halt.

A corps headquarters was in place to organize and lead the annihilating stroke, and Rundstedt was about to authorize this action when an Allied bomb killed its efficient commander on June 12.

Already Rundstedt and Rommel doubted whether they could launch a sufficiently devastating attack to dislodge the beachhead. Only a defensive campaign seemed possible. They suggested this to Hitler and asked for a free hand to direct the battle, authority to deploy their troops without waiting for approval from Hitler's headquarters.

Making no response to their request, Hitler reacted by summoning on June 12 an SS panzer corps headquarters and two panzer divisions from the Eastern Front. Once arrived in Normandy, these troops were to carry out the stroke to destroy the beachhead. It would take more than a week for these 35,000 men to reach their destination.

Rundstedt and Rommel, who had been apart in their thinking before the invasion, were soon united on a disagreeable conclusion. If a large-scale attack to obliterate the Allied foothold was impossible, and if a defensive orientation was necessary, the war was as good as lost. They would soon have to withdraw from Normandy and start planning to defend the German border.

The developments hardly daunted Hitler. He placed great faith in the V-1 weapons employed in the Pas-de-Calais. Their campaign against England opened on June 13. For eighty days, the pilotless aircraft, or as the British called them, flying bombs, fell on English soil and brought widespread death and damage. The highest intensity of this onslaught occurred during the first week in July, when observers in England counted 820 missiles entering British airspace. Early in September, the V-2 supersonic rockets made their appearance and sowed increased loss of life and property, as well as dread.

Hitler employed these weapons frankly as terror agents against the civilian population. The great majority struck London. They were, Hitler said, a retaliation for the Allied air attacks on German cities.

Had he instead sent the missiles against military targets—for example, the crowded harbors working at full capacity to nourish the invasion—he might well have paralyzed the Allied buildup.

In mid-June, with the V-weapons starting to be operational and promising to turn the tide not only of the invasion but also of the war, Hitler insisted on turning back the landings. Because intimations of discouragement, even defeatism, had begun to reach him from the front, he decided to go to France to see his principal commanders. A personal visit was sure to raise pessimistic spirits and spur flagging energy.

Hitler traveled to Margival, near Soissons, where engineers had constructed a large and elaborate concrete command bunker for him in 1940. From there he was supposed to direct the invasion of England.

The first time he used the underground structure was on June 17, 1944, when he met there with Rundstedt and Rommel.

He stressed the need to confine the Allies to a small beachhead. The defensive battle had to continue. There were to be no backward looks to positions in the rear. There was to be no withdrawal. "Every man," he said, "shall fight and die where he stands." The field commanders were to continue their efforts to pry the Allies from the shore. The best way to dislodge the Allied beachhead was by a master stroke around Bayeux. The attack was to split and separate the Allies on the beaches, then dispose of each partner in turn.

Hitler thus took increasing control of the fighting. He treated his field marshals with courtesy but regarded them as minor subordinates. He discounted their estimates and distrusted their judgments.

As the troops of the SS panzer corps, the headquarters and the two divisions, arrived in Normandy piecemeal, they started on June 20 to enter the line in the Caen-Bayeux area. It took three days for all to be in position. Once assembled and concentrated, the corps was to launch the strike.

A British thrust on June 25 compelled Rundstedt and Rommel to use these troops. Instead of committing the formation in attack, they had to employ the units defensively to hold Caen. In the touch-and-go situation, the field marshals briefly considered withdrawing from Caen, but the front became stable, the retrograde action, at least for the moment, unnecessary.

Increasingly certain of the need to abandon plans for the annihilating German counterattack and instead to go over completely to defense, Rundstedt so informed Hitler on June 26. "No matter how undesirable this may be," he said, there was no feasible alternative.

Hitler demurred. He ordered the preparations for an offensive effort to continue.

Six corps headquarters had by now assumed responsibility for parts of the front, and that was too many for a single army to direct. The Germans divided the front line on June 28. A reconstituted Panzer Group West headquarters directed the four corps on the right, opposite the British and Canadians. The Seventh Army exerted control over the two corps facing the Americans. Dollmann committed suicide, his act induced no doubt by feelings of guilt over his failure to stem the Allied invasion. His chief of staff announced the death as the result of a heart attack.

The SS panzer corps finally managed to push forward in the Bayeux area on June 29. But the operation was by no means the bold and decisive stroke earlier envisaged. After a brief flurry of success, the German action subsided.

On that day, Rundstedt and Rommel were at Berchtesgaden with Hitler. Having summoned them, Hitler had forbade them to travel the six hundred miles from Normandy by plane or train. The field marshals rode separately in automobiles. They were tired when they reached their destination, and Hitler kept them waiting for six hours before he saw them. Rundstedt remarked on the shabby treatment. It should come as no surprise, he told a senior staff officer, if an old and sick man like himself dropped dead of a heart attack like Dollmann.

Hitler finally received them at six P.M., June 29. What he wanted to impress upon them was the need to hold every inch of ground in order to deny the Allies room for mobility. The German frame of reference was to shift unquestionably from an offensive to a defensive orientation. The Germans, he explained, had confined the Allies to a small and vulnerable beachhead area and must continue to hold them there. The ground the Germans occupied was favorable for defense, and the German forces had organized the terrain skillfully. An equal number of soldiers faced the Americans and the British-Canadians, but because the hedgerowed lowlands in the Cotentin offered natural obstacles inhibiting American offensive action, the 50 medium and 25 heavy tanks arrayed in the region were enough. On the Caen-Falaise plain, in contrast, there were 250 mediums and 150 heavies, three times as much artillery, and all three *Nebelwerfer* brigades in Normandy, the latter called by Americans "screaming meemies."

In the region opposing the British and Canadians, where the ground was favorable for offensive operations, the Germans had massed their resources. They held Caen, the gateway to open country and the best tank route to Paris. They were blocking the British, who were, Hitler was certain, carrying the Allied main effort.

At Berchtesgaden, Rundstedt asked for greater freedom to control the operations in the west. Hitler refused. All actions were subject to review by Hitler and his headquarters.

Rommel had the temerity to ask how Hitler intended to win the war. He received only a baleful glare in reply.

There was scarcely any courtesy on Hitler's part at Berchtesgaden, for he was frankly dissatisfied with his field commanders. They had been unable to turn back the landings. They had failed to mount a decisive counterattack to smash the Allied beachhead. The latest bad news was the disappointing defense of Cherbourg, named by Hitler as a fortress to be defended to the last man, the last bullet, the last stone. Cherbourg had just surrendered to the Americans.

After dismissing Rundstedt and Rommel from his presence, Hitler reported his intentions. "We must not," he said, "allow mobile warfare to develop, since the enemy surpasses us by far in mobility due to his air superiority and his superabundance of motor vehicles and fuel. . . . Everything depends on our confining him . . . and then on fighting a war of attrition to wear him down and force him back." The only possible course of action in Normandy was stubborn defense.

His soldiers' morale was excellent despite shortages of replacements, ammunition, and supplies. Discipline remained effective. Leadership at the lower levels was first-rate. The Germans were far from beaten on the ground.

The worst disadvantage was the absence of air support. The Allies had gained mastery of the skies, and few German planes appeared over Normandy. Where were they? The soldiers joked, "In the West they say they're in the East, in the East they say they're in the West, and at home they say they're at the front." The trouble was, the Allied planes, they said, were painted silver while the German planes were painted an invisible color.

When Rundstedt and Rommel returned from Berchtesgaden to Normandy on June 30, they learned of the failure of the panzer corps attack against Bayeux. The Allied buildup more than ever appeared to be proceeding smoothly. Despite Hitler's long-range plans, the field marshals recommended a limited withdrawal in the Caen area, mainly to straighten and reduce the length of the front, which would then require fewer defenders.

Hitler refused to entertain what he believed was an implicit admission of defeat. On the afternoon of July 1, he ordered: "Present positions are to be held."

In complete disagreement, Rundstedt telephoned Hitler's headquarters. He was, Rundstedt told the staff officer at the other end of the wire with deliberate vagueness, not up to the increased demands.

What shall we do? the staff officer asked nervously.

The opening was too tempting to reject. The field marshal snapped the bait. "Make peace, you fools," he said.

On July 2, Hitler sent an emissary to Rundstedt's headquarters at St-Germain-en-Laye, just outside Paris. He presented Rundstedt with a decoration, the Oak Leaf to the Knight's Cross, and a handwritten note from the Führer politely relieving Rundstedt from his post because of age and poor health.

On that day, Hitler reiterated his orders. The Germans were to restrict and compress the Allies until the Germans could mount the ultimate blow, he said, and "throw the Anglo-Saxons out of Normandy." Perhaps his luck would hold.

CHAPTER 7

The Crisis in Command

READINESS BY THE GERMAN commanders in Normandy to concede Allied success after three weeks, by the end of June, hardly coincided with the view on the other side of the front. The Allies had trouble judging how well the invasion was going. Certain accomplishments were solid and promising. Some deficiencies marred performance and prospects. Touching all aspects of the situation was the question of Montgomery's leadership.

Almost 160,000 soldiers crossed the Channel from England to the Continent on D day. More than 130,000 came by ship. Over 23,000 arrived by air. Casualties were less than 5,000, far fewer than anticipated.

The totals were excellent, but the substantial forces ashore were unable to capture their initial objectives. The most conspicuous failure was Caen.

The British and Canadians were late getting off Sword, Gold, and Juno beaches because an unexpectedly high tide almost flooded the space between water and dune and thereby prompted congestion. There was no time to rest after the strain of the crossing and the exertion of the initial assault. And in some places, according to Major Ellis, "there was little evidence of the urgency" needed to get the troops moving. By the end of the day, they were four to six miles from the Channel.

The Americans landing on Utah below Cherbourg secured a firm foothold of similar depth. On Omaha, after a grim struggle lasting all day, the troops held a precarious toehold no more than a mile and a half deep.

Pushing into the interior was less important for the moment than consolidating the beachhead. Each of the five landing sites was isolated from its neighbor, and a good ten miles separated the British and Americans. It was necessary to close the gaps all along the invasion shore by making lateral contact. Uniting the individual holdings into a single whole would present a stronger face to the Germans and provide a safer base for expansion.

While stretching toward the Americans on the following day, the British liberated Bayeux, the first significant town to fall to the Allies. After a week of effort, the Allies had a continuous if somewhat shallow foothold. The most dangerous spot was between Utah and Omaha beaches, where the Americans were barely three miles from the water line. Caen defied capture.

Patton, still in England and avidly following developments, had a remarkably clear view of the events. As early as the third day, June 8, he had the "impression," as he remarked in his diary, "that people [on the Continent] are satisfied to be holding on, rather than advancing [inland]."

His observation occurred as Montgomery was trying to generate movement off the beaches. Instead of focusing on Caen, he told Dempsey to ignore Caen for the moment and to look ahead to Falaise.

On the following day, June 9, Montgomery at ten A.M. discussed with Dempsey the idea of thrusting to Falaise and beyond Falaise to Argentan. The course followed Frederick Morgan's original Overlord blueprint projecting an immediate strong effort on the excellent operational terrain south and southeast of Caen.

An hour later, when Bradley joined them for a conference, he learned merely of talk about outflanking and bypassing Caen. There was no mention of Falaise or Argentan. The oversight or dissemblance was the first sign during the operation of less than complete mutual trust and confidence between the Allies.

Like the disappointing movement into the interior, the buildup of men and matériel, which seemed to be proceeding smoothly, was in fact behind schedule. Slippage occurred as early as D plus 1, June 7, when only four fifths of the anticipated 100,000 men, only one quarter of the planned 14,500 tons of supplies, and only one half of the 14,000 vehicles listed for shipment were actually unloaded across the beaches.

The difference between plan and reality continued to widen. By

June 20, troops and supplies arriving in Normandy were five days behind the projected totals. The disparity was to some extent beneficial, for the Allied foothold was small and getting crowded.

A shocking event occurred around Villers Bocage on June 13, when a well-seasoned British division, of legendary fame in North Africa, stumbled. The men took the town to open the way to Caen. When the Germans counterattacked, the troops withdrew in some panic for several miles before stopping and reorganizing a line of defense.

The reasons for the reversal were several. The soldiers were said to have been inadequately rested and "mentally unprepared for close combat in the hedgerows." They were veterans who had suffered the cumulative stresses and strains of surviving too many battles, and they wondered why they continued to be in the forefront of combat when other units with less experience and less pain were available. Furthermore, Montgomery's defensive posture, cast over the British and Canadians operating on the eastern flank, diluted boldness and bred caution.

The Villers Bocage incident starkly revealed the precarious nature of the Overlord achievement. The Allies had yet to win a solid footing on the shore.

By the end of the first week, the attempts to encircle Caen and to launch a thrust toward Falaise had come to nothing. Despite Montgomery's later contention—"I never once," he said, "had cause or reason to alter my master plan"—he announced another change in his method.

In a letter to Brooke on the evening of June 13, he told of his intention to go over to the defensive in the Caen sector, "but aggressively so." He proposed to "pull the Germans on to the Second British Army and fight them there, so that First US Army can carry out its task the easier." He was referring to the American effort to take Cherbourg. As soon as Bradley's forces drove westward from Utah Beach to the coast and cut the Cotentin, they were to turn north to capture the port city.

Although Montgomery appeared content, his leadership began to stir concern as early as June 14. At a meeting in England, senior airmen expressed disappointment over and impatience with the small gains on the Continent. They were anxious to have at least part of the Caen-Falaise plain, ground extremely favorable for constructing airfields, and they saw no sign of progress, no prospect of establishing air power on the Continent soon. They questioned whether Montgomery was being too prudent. One high-ranking British officer mentioned "the elements of a crisis" already arising in Normandy. Sir Arthur Tedder, Eisenhower's deputy supreme commander, an air marshal who had worked closely with Montgomery in North Africa before falling out with him, changed the wording slightly. Summing up the sentiment in the room, he said, "The present military situation had the makings of a dangerous crisis." The statement was the earliest overt expression of doubt by a responsible individual on the effectiveness of Montgomery's performance.

Taking his deputy Tedder with him, Eisenhower crossed the Channel to the Continent on June 15. In accordance with military courtesy, he stopped first to see Montgomery, the senior Allied figure on the ground. Montgomery was absent. He was with Bradley inspecting the American front. Perhaps he was avoiding Tedder.

The personal slight made Tedder feel snubbed but had no visible effect on Eisenhower. The party traveled to Dempsey's headquarters, where Dempsey received them warmly. After touring the British area, Eisenhower and his group returned to Montgomery's command post. Montgomery was there. Whether he thought the tactical problems to be none of his listeners' business or whether he thought them unable to follow and comprehend the operational scene, Montgomery outlined his administrative and supply difficulties. Eisenhower paid close attention and penciled some notes to take back with him to England. Appearing to be well satisfied with the conditions on the far shore, Eisenhower, the boss, treated Montgomery, his subordinate, with deep courtesy, even deference. Montgomery showed little reciprocity.

On June 18, Montgomery issued his first written directive. In part he rationalized the Allied inability to expand the beachhead. "After the very great intensity of the initial few days," he wrote, "we had to slow down the tempo of the operation" for two reasons: to get sound positions against German counterattack, and to build up strength for a push into the interior. "All this is good," he said, "but we are now ready to pass on to other things and reap the harvest." What was necessary, he continued, was seizing Cherbourg and Caen, "the first step in the full development of our plans." Bradley's army, which had cut the Cotentin and had thereby isolated Cherbourg, was to attack to the north and capture the port city. Dempsey's army was to take Caen, "really," Montgomery said, "the key to Cherbourg."

Whether Dempsey was to attract the bulk of the German forces to make possible American success at Cherbourg or whether he was to seize Caen to dishearten the Germans and make them loosen their hold on Cherbourg, the statement provoked some snide humor in the American camp. With a broad smile, J. Lawton Collins asked Bradley, "Why doesn't he send us the key?"

Joe Collins had led the forces ashore at Utah Beach, then had pushed his units aggressively across the Cotentin. He was now ready to drive to Cherbourg. Forty-eight years old but appearing much younger, he was the youngest American corps commander in active operations. He had earlier distinguished himself at the head of a division on Guadalcanal in the Pacific. The division's code name, Lightning, described perfectly Collins's methods of operation, and he became known as Lightning Joe. Transferred to England in the spring of 1944 and promoted to command the VII Corps, Collins was impressive. He was enormously energetic, buoyantly optimistic, unshakably confident, and immensely likable. His grin, resembling a teenager's, was sometimes lopsided, always infectious. His professionalism, together with his growing record of success, would make him the best American corps commander in Europe and Bradley's fair-haired boy.

Collins would never have joked about the key to Cherbourg unless he was sure of Bradley's ambivalence toward Montgomery. In public Bradley was respectful toward his superior, as the chain of command required—for example, he consistently addressed Montgomery as "Sir." In private he permitted his associates to poke fun at Montgomery, laughing at Monty for, among other things, taking the Monty legend more seriously than anyone else.

Before Dempsey and Bradley could start their offensives to Caen and Cherbourg, a storm broke in the Channel on the morning of June 19. Strong winds reached gale force and created towering waves. Raging for three days, the disturbance shut down the buildup, threw up and stranded eight hundred vessels on the invasion shore, and knocked out both artificial harbors. The American installation was so badly damaged that it was abandoned; only the British facility was repaired. Not until June 23 did unloading begin again, and by then, despite excellent work, reinforcing Normandy was hopelessly behind Overlord schedules.

In a letter to Sir Oliver Leese, who had succeeded him in command of the Eighth Army in Italy, Montgomery revealed his satisfaction on June 23. "Bradley," he wrote, "is first class as an Army Cmd [Commander] and is very willing to learn; the same with Bimbo [Dempsey]. Both are very inexperienced . . . but both are anxious to learn and are doing so." The two other Army commanders, the Canadian Crerar and the American Patton, had yet to be actively involved in operations, but Montgomery was concerned by their eventual participation in the campaign. "I have grave fears," he confessed, "that Harry Crerar will not be too good; however I am keeping him out of the party as long as I can"—meaning, he was deferring the insertion of the First Canadian Army headquarters into the lineup, a logical decision in view of the small and congested foothold. As for Patton, there was little need to be specific. His foibles were well-known. Montgomery contented himself by saying, "Georgie Patton may be a bit of a problem when he comes into it!!" The two exclamation marks apparently made further explanation unnecessary.

Continuing to Leese, Montgomery set forth his course. Dempsey was to "pull more [enemy] stuff to the Caen sector" to facilitate Bradley's advance. Bradley was about to head north to Cherbourg, and Montgomery had instructed him to thrust south toward Coutances at the same time. "But," strangely enough, "Bradley didn't want to take the risk; there was no risk really."

Was Montgomery unaware of Bradley's thoroughgoing caution, his propensity to go with the odds? Or was Montgomery willing to dispense with prudence on the American side because he cared little about American casualties and wished to speed up the action? In either case, Bradley was beginning to manifest some independence.

As Dempsey prepared another thrust to Caen, Montgomery, in a letter to Eisenhower, promised a "blitz attack," a "show down" fight. Eisenhower responded enthusiastically. He hoped for quick success at Cherbourg, he said, "while you have got the enemy by the throat on the east."

Dempsey's attempt to seize Caen momentarily frightened Rundstedt and Rommel, then petered out. The result spread glumness among the high Allied commanders. The official explanation for the dismal end of the attack was bad weather. Rain and low clouds had prevented the air forces from giving strong support. Nonetheless, Montgomery told Brooke with apparent confidence, everything was working out fine, exactly as he wished.

For Bradley's offensive to the north against Cherbourg had moved vigorously. Collins promoted and sustained a model operation. As it turned out, Caen was hardly the key to Cherbourg. The garrison of 21,000 men in the port city surrendered. As expected, they had methodically ruined the harbor and the machinery beforehand. It took the Allies six weeks to clear and repair the extensive damage and to make possible docking and unloading ships.

On June 30, Montgomery met with Dempsey and Bradley, while Crerar, who had recently crossed the Channel, was present as an onlooker. The main business was obtaining Bradley's consent—he agreed at once—to take responsibility for a small part of Dempsey's front. Doing so allowed Dempsey to remove an armored division from the line and to place it in reserve. Dempsey was then better able to cope with emergencies as he sought to draw German troops to the Caen area, all the while watching for an opportunity to take the city.

No one seemed to remark how illogical Montgomery's strategy was, how mutually exclusive Dempsey's goals were. The more Germans he attracted to Caen, the less chance he had to seize the city.

The Allied situation was still equivocal at the end of June. On the positive side, the Allies were solidly established ashore. Although actual receipts were below those planned, a total of 850,000 troops, 150,000 vehicles, and more than half a million tons of supplies had come to Normandy, a substantial accomplishment. Casualties of 60,000, of whom 8,500 men had been killed, were within the range of expectations and on the low side.

Yet the small amount of ground held was disturbing. The region seized varied in depth from five to twenty-five miles, but was about one fifth of the size projected by the Overlord plan for that date. Instead of possessing a considerable area bounded by Lisieux near the Seine, Alençon in the deep interior, Rennes and St-Malo in Brittany, the Allies still lacked Caen and were distant from such intermediate objectives as St-Lô and Falaise.

Cramming and congesting the available space on the Continent were the large forces ashore. All sorts of units, men and their equipment, together with depots and installations, filled virtually every orchard and field.

What the Allies obviously needed, and quickly, was more land. They required room for maneuver, that is, ground on which combat forces could operate easily, and space to accommodate the variety of support groups streaming ashore in the buildup. Although obtaining the Overlord lodgment area loomed as the eventual goal, more pressing was the requirement to expand the holdings rapidly. The worst bottleneck was German-held Caen, which blocked the approaches to ground favoring tank warfare and airfield construction.

To blast forward quickly, the Allies altered the Overlord schedules. They brought more combat troops to Normandy than originally planned, in order to give punch to the drive for ground. They did so at the expense of supply and administrative personnel.

In his directive of June 30, Montgomery formally set out the next goals. He wanted Dempsey to capture Caen "as opportunity offers—and the sooner the better." But Dempsey's important mission was to hold the enemy in place and to tie the Germans down, to keep them occupied and prevent them from moving substantial strength to the American zone. For Bradley was to drive to the south, first to Coutances, then beyond, at least to Avranches, the entrance to Brittany. Montgomery mentioned additional objectives and spoke of the eventual pivot toward the Seine River, but these matters were simply too far away to count at the moment.

The contrast between the long-range mission assigned to Bradley and the rather static role given to Dempsey raised a few eyebrows in the Allied camp. There was already widespread debate over Montgomery's leadership and intentions. His satisfaction, self-assurance, and promises notwithstanding, the campaign seemed to be making little progress.

Was his plan to attract and contain the bulk of the Germans on the British-Canadian front a rationalization for his inability to take Caen and open the plain to Falaise? Was Caen in enemy hands because of Montgomery's hesitation and excessive caution? Was his strategy a brilliant battlefield expedient designed to conserve British manpower?

To some observers, the Allies appeared to have lost their momentum. The Germans seemed to be shutting down the Allies and imposing a stalemate reminiscent of the trench-type warfare of World War I. Caen and Cherbourg led to inevitable comparison. The Americans had taken Cherbourg with dispatch. The British and Canadians still stood in a semicircle around Caen.

What has been called a "crisis of confidence" in Montgomery grew and reached almost intolerable intensity in July. Simply put, the Normandy campaign had failed to develop. Why were the ground forces unable to get rolling? The trouble was, as Eisenhower's naval aide, Commander Harry Butcher, recorded in the diary he kept for his boss, "Monty has been too slow to attack." According to Carlo D'Este, "Suspecting that the US forces were being used as sacrificial lambs while the British dallied round Caen, American critics began to voice their opinion that the campaign was being badly mismanaged by the British commander who ought to be replaced." Tedder, who was Montgomery's "most vocal critic" at Eisenhower's headquarters, wrote in his diary, "The problem is Monty who can be neither removed nor moved to action."

Restless and impatient by temperament, Eisenhower was anxious to maintain momentum and to show gains. He felt subtle pressures emanating from Washington, for President Roosevelt and the Joint Chiefs of Staff expected exciting consequences to flow from the landings in Normandy, and they looked to Eisenhower for action. Not only Tedder, who displayed what Max Hastings has called "chronic disloyalty to Montgomery," but other members of Eisenhower's staff also grumbled about Montgomery and the slow tempo of the campaign. Ultimately responsible for the results, Eisenhower was unable to influence events directly.

A remedy was for Eisenhower himself to take the reins of the land battle at once rather than to wait until later. Unfortunately, he lacked not only a strong desire to exert such control but also a command post in Normandy. Without a facility on the ground, it would be awkward, if not downright impossible, to exercise proper direction. Ferrying his SHAEF—Supreme Headquarters, Allied Expeditionary Forces—across the Channel was impractical because of the restricted size of the foothold and because of the increased flow of combat troops to France. Eisenhower had no alternative but to permit Montgomery to continue to run the ground campaign.

Actually, Eisenhower wished nothing better than to perpetuate the pattern of his earlier command experience when Alexander had directed the land forces under Eisenhower in the Mediterranean. Eisenhower preferred to exercise a loose general control and to let Montgomery handle the Anglo-American ground warfare on the Continent. Unfortunately for Eisenhower's desire, the stagnation of the campaign made it necessary for him to place a stronger hand on the helm. And the conditions made such action impossible.

Traveling to the Continent on July 1, Eisenhower stayed with Bradley for several days. His primary purpose was to observe and to provide moral support for Bradley's imminent attack to the south. But he had also to discuss with Montgomery the overall command arrangements, specifically, when Eisenhower intended to take over from Montgomery as the Allied ground forces commander.

Accompanied by Bradley, Eisenhower visited Montgomery on July 2 and talked. Originally, Eisenhower had thought somewhat vaguely of letting Montgomery direct the ground operations until it was time to employ the two complete army groups. That is, when Crerar's First Canadian Army headquarters became operational, it would join Dempsey's Second British Army under Montgomery's 21 Army Group. Similarly, when Patton's Third U.S. Army entered the battle, it would, together with the First U.S. Army, come under Bradley's 12th U.S. Army Group. When these events occurred, when Montgomery and Bradley stood on the same echelon as army group commanders, equal in status, it would be logical and proper for Eisenhower to step in and for Montgomery to turn over the Allied ground command to him. Unless, of course, Eisenhower decided to retain indefinitely the original arrangements and permit Montgomery to continue as *pro tem* ground commander.

Still and all, an eventual changeover seemed to be in the offing. Although the Normandy foothold was small and crowded, Crerar's and Patton's army headquarters would soon have to enter the arena, for the combat units were growing so numerous as to strain the span of control. That is, Dempsey and Bradley, as army commanders, had too many corps headquarters and divisions under them to be able to direct the operations easily. Crerar's and Patton's army headquarters would lighten the burden by taking some of the corps headquarters and divisions under their direction.

Since Eisenhower was unable to take over in the near future, he asked Montgomery to continue directing the campaign even after Bradley's 12th U.S. Army Group became operational, a date still to be determined. Montgomery was to go on running both army groups, his own and Bradley's, as well as the Allied land battle.

The action reassured Montgomery. Despite the muffled criticism in the Allied camp or perhaps because of it, Eisenhower, Montgomery believed, was expressing confidence in Montgomery's leadership. His morale boosted, Montgomery interpreted the request as an additional admission of Eisenhower's incompetence and Montgomery's indispensability. No one but Montgomery, he was certain, was capable of leading the Allies to victory.

CHAPTER 8

The July Difficulties

WHATEVER HOPE SPROUTED BEFORE Bradley's offensive to the south in the Cotentin, nothing much happened immediately thereafter. Stifling any success were the natural conditions of weather and the terrain. Normandy is always damp, often cold, even in the summer. The chill and the wetness had been bad in June, but in July they were execrable. The countryside was thoroughly sodden. An incessant downpour of rain turned earth into mud, swamps into lakes, ditches into streams. Low clouds, mist and fog prevented not only artillery forward observers from locating the enemy but also aircraft from flying and doing the same. Among the ubiquitous hedgerows, the earthen dikes out of which grow shrubs and trees, the Germans were concealed in a maze of obstacles. The *prairies marécageuses*, the wide expanses of impassable bogs reclaimed from the sea and now flooded by the Germans, channeled American movements to a few obvious avenues easily blocked.

Three roads led south from Bradley's positions across the Cotentin, one to Coutances, another to Périers, and the third to St-Lô. Down these macadam routes barely wide enough for two vehicles abreast, the First Army attacked. The corps on the Cotentin west coast started on July 3, the neighboring corps joined on July 4, and the next corps in line broadened the effort on July 7. Bradley hoped by these successive hammer blows to crack the German defenses.

From the beginning, the going was painful. The American divisions were inexperienced, and they displayed the ineptness usually marking units new to combat. They were confused and disoriented, tentative and troubled, constantly frustrated. They suffered agonizingly high casualties and measured their gains in yards. Coutances, the prime objective, remained distant, more than twenty miles away.

As early as July 5, a disappointed Eisenhower was convinced of Bradley's inability to generate more than a slow pace through the hedge-rowed lowland. The reasons he noted were the fighting quality of the German soldiers, the nature of the countryside, and the weather.

Eisenhower returned to England on July 5, and Patton, who went to see him that afternoon, found him "a little fed up with Monty's lack of drive." Eisenhower seemed to be thinking of taking personal command of the land battle, an act favored by Patton not only to enhance American prestige but also to speed up the slow-motion campaign. But Patton was unaware of Eisenhower's discussion with Montgomery on the subject and believed Eisenhower to be loath as always to reach a decision. He thought Eisenhower was hesitating to "take the plunge."

Patton had been waiting impatiently in England for authority to go to Normandy, and he filled his diary and letters with his anxiety. "If everything moves as planned," he fretted, "there will be nothing left for me to do." Worst of all, "the fighting will be over before I get in."

Word finally came, and with a profound sense of relief, Patton flew across the Channel on July 6. He stayed temporarily, for a couple of days, with Bradley. Whether he subtly egged Bradley on or whether his presence simply got under Bradley's skin, Patton had a peculiar effect on him. Bradley swelled in self-importance and tended to talk big. He openly remarked his desire to get "out from under the 21 Army Group," as Patton recorded the statement in his diary. Patton understood Bradley's wish and was more than sympathetic. "I hope he succeeds," he remarked. The quicker Bradley's 12th U.S. Army Group became active, the sooner would Patton's Third Army headquarters become operational alongside the First U.S. Army.

A day afterwards, on July 7, Bradley, accompanied by Patton, drove to Montgomery's command post. They all had lunch together, then walked to the war tent for a briefing. "Monty went to great lengths," Patton wrote in his diary, "explaining why the British have done nothing."

Always outwardly correct and respectful toward his superiors, Patton somehow made Montgomery aware of his unspoken criticism. Montgomery was annoyed. He preferred Bradley's subservience. He took out his pique on Courtney Hodges, who was understudying Bradley at the

First Army headquarters. Writing to Brooke that evening, apparently referring to Bradley's eventual move to army group, Montgomery said, "I do not think very much of Hodges. But I shall deal with Bradley; we know each other well now, and he is most co-operative."

By this time there was much more general dissatisfaction with the lack of progress in Normandy. The news media, both in England and in the United States, reflected a mounting sense of unease over the contrast between what the battle maps showed and what Montgomery said. His "unremitting smugness" as he repeated his claim of getting the enemy off balance entirely according to his plan seemed hollow and self-serving, even fictitious. The newspapers looked for towns to fall as proof of success. And a nasty suspicion had arisen in some quarters over a supposition about Allied policy. Were the Allies deliberately marking time in Normandy to let the Soviets do the hard fighting?

Even Churchill was upset. He wanted the British to achieve a great victory quickly—for example, to take Paris—before the Americans completely outnumbered the British forces. Becoming impatient beyond control, Churchill emotionally denounced and castigated Montgomery to Brooke on the evening of July 6. That Brooke flared up in defense of Montgomery indicated how frayed his own nerves were.

Max Hastings and other postwar observers have suggested why the forces on Montgomery's eastern flank were so slow. Much of the fault lay in the weariness and consequent ineffectiveness of the British units. These formations were on ground important to both the Allies and the Germans, and they were worn out. Insufficient manpower reserves made it impossible to suffuse these units with new blood, new strength.

Montgomery was to blame too. He kept himself isolated from the political realities and pressures afflicting most of the leaders on the higher echelons of command. Absorbed exclusively in the tactical concerns of the battle, Montgomery believed all else to be unimportant. Supremely self-confident on the outside, regarding himself as the only one competent to direct the campaign, he exacerbated the situation by his unwillingness to be open and candid with the people who might have shielded and protected him. He never unburdened himself to or confided completely in Brooke, Eisenhower, or even his own chief of staff, de Guingand.

Tormented by the small Continental lodgment, Eisenhower wrote Montgomery an "unhappy letter" on July 7. Because Bradley's offensive had been unable to pick up speed and was likely to be "slow and laborious," Eisenhower questioned whether Montgomery, in his ardor to attract enemy forces, was doing enough to expand the British and Canadian side of the front. "We must use all possible energy," Eisenhower reminded him, "in a determined effort to prevent a stalemate." Bogging down was the worst possibility, for it would compel the Allies to fight "a major defensive battle with the slight depth we now have [on the Continent]." To be forced to do so would be extremely dangerous.

Montgomery responded on the following day. "I am, myself," he wrote, "quite happy about the situation. . . . Of one thing you can be quite sure: there will be no stalemate."

For Montgomery was moving to be rid finally of the embarrassment of having Caen still in German hands. He had launched an all-out effort to take the city. On July 4 the Canadians had initiated what was essentially a preliminary attack on the western side of Caen. Despite vicious fighting, the Canadians were unable to seize the airfield of Carpiquet. Dempsey thought the "operation was not well handled." Two division commanders, one British, the other Canadian, exhibited fatigue and nervousness, and one was relieved and removed from his post.

Three days later, just before darkness fell, the main show opened as 460 heavy bombers dropped 2,300 tons of high explosive in forty minutes on the northern outskirts of Caen, about three and a half miles ahead of the front-line troops.

The use of heavy or strategic bombers in direct support of ground soldiers, that is, to assist them gain ground on the battlefield, was an unorthodox technique. Heavy bombers were supposed to operate against what were called "strategic" targets deep in enemy territory—war plants, refineries, railroad systems, and the like, objectives far removed from the tactical concerns of fighting for the control of terrain. According to contemporary theory and doctrine, destroying the enemy's sources of weapons, fuel, transportation, and the other necessities of warfare would deprive him of his ability to continue the struggle. Air enthusiasts believed victory to be possible by using air power alone, that is, strategic bombardment. They resisted efforts to divert the big planes from their primary role to what they sarcastically termed tactical targets of fleeting importance.

Only twice before in the war had the Allies brought heavy bombers to bear on the battlefield in order to help the ground forces gain extremely difficult and significant objectives. Both instances had occurred in Italy earlier that year. The Allies had subjected Monte Cassino and the neighboring town of Cassino to frightful punishment from the air in February and March. Both attempts had been unable to propel the front through the German Gustav Line and across the mountains to make possible overland advance to Anzio and Rome.

Since then, debate over the tactical use of strategic bombers flourished. Points at issue were the distance required between front-line troops and the bomb targets, the interval needed between bombing and ground attack, and how to avoid craters and debris that impeded vehicular movements after bombardment. Firm agreement had yet to be reached.

Now in Normandy, despite strenuous objections from the proponents of strategic bombing, heavy bombers became available for Caen. Eisenhower insisted on using them, for to him the objective was sufficiently important and profitable, his stated criteria, to warrant the temporary diversion of the big aircraft. There was probably political pressure too, a frustrated Churchill no doubt calling for some way, any way, to wrest Caen from German control. And so the air force people provided the airplanes on relatively short notice.

Six hours after the bombardment, at first light on July 8, three divisions moved forward in attack. The fighting lasted throughout the day.

That evening, without securing Hitler's prior approval, Rommel decided to yield to the pressure and evacuate the main part of Caen. During the night, the Germans crossed the Orne-River, which flows through the city. They took up defensive positions on the other side of the stream and occupied the southern suburb.

On the following morning, July 9, Dempsey's men cautiously entered Caen, an expanse of rubble and ruin. By noon they were in possession of the devastated city as far as the Orne River.

Gaining half the town was a sweet if anticlimactic victory. According to all observations, the bombardment had produced the proper result: it had enabled the ground troops to advance despite strong and well-manned defensive positions. Although later analysis indicated quite otherwise—the bombs actually struck few Germans, had little effect on their defenses, and were positive only in providing a psychological boost to British and Canadian soldiers—only the entry into Caen established in Allied minds the linkage between strategic air power and ground success. Heavy bombers in close support were seen to be effective in overcoming difficult obstacles barring important objectives.

As the troops on both sides of the front settled into their new positions on July 10, the artillery continued to fire. German ammunition supplies permitted expending merely 4,500 shells. The British put out 80,000 rounds that day alone.

Field Marshal Hans von Kluge, who had commanded an army group in Russia before replacing Rundstedt in Normandy barely a week earlier, reported the discrepancy to Hitler. "Although our troop morale is good," he said, "we cannot meet the enemy matériel with courage alone."

The German personnel losses in western Europe after little more than a month of combat were high. Since the invasion, casualties totaled about 100,000 men.

Yet the fact was, the Germans were restricting the Allies to a very small area, denying them the space to develop mechanized and mobile warfare, and making them vulnerable to a campaign of attrition to be won ultimately, they hoped, by Hitler's miracle weapons.

Bradley came to see Montgomery on July 10, a day after the battle at Caen. He was discouraged over his lack of progress in the Cotentin. With Dempsey present, Bradley expressed his dismay over American shortcomings, those of his troops who had been unable to produce a significant advance, as well as his own, for he had been unable to generate any kind of momentum. Since the beginning of the offensive on July 3, the units had hardly budged, and during the two previous days there had been no headway whatsoever.

Despite his low spirits, Bradley was thinking of another way to promote forward movement. He mentioned an idea brewing in his mind, a new attack designed to get the First Army to Coutances. He had no details to give, for the notion was still shaping itself. The only concrete requirement he cited for such an offensive was to have his units out of the mud of the lowland and onto higher, drier ground, where he could use tanks. Suitable terrain was available along the east-west highway joining the villages of Lessay and Périers and the town of St-Lô. The trouble was, the rate of advance thus far attained promised no quick spurt to the desired area.

Pleased by the accomplishment at Caen, Montgomery was in a good mood. He was sympathetic. "Never mind," he said. "Take all the time you need, Brad." Putting two fingers together and placing them on a map, he said in avuncular fashion, "If I were you, I think I would concentrate my forces a little more." A single, full-scale drive at a particular spot, quite unlike Bradley's earlier piecemeal strike of one corps after another across the front, was, in Montgomery's opinion, the best way to proceed.

Bradley was cheered. Montgomery had refrained from blaming or criticizing him and his American soldiers. Furthermore, the preliminary air bombardment at Caen was impressive, instructive, and suggestive. Perhaps Bradley could obtain heavy air support for his new effort, that is, once he reached the Lessay–Périers–St-Lô road.

After Bradley departed, Dempsey proposed to Montgomery a significant attack beyond Caen to the south. If the Americans were unable to attain results in the Cotentin, perhaps the British and Canadians could loosen things up in their area. Or better still, perhaps they could penetrate the German defenses, break free of the close and confining bocage country around Caen, find easier and quicker going on the Caen-Falaise plain, and register a real triumph. As everyone understood, "Caen was not the important point—it was always the airfields."

From the first, Montgomery had been attracted to launching a heavy blow south of Caen. "Of course," Secretary of State for War Sir James Grigg said after the war, "Montgomery's original idea was to break out of the bocage country around Caen and into the open in the first few days after landing." Liberation from the bocage pointed to increased and heightened mobility, even to an Allied blitzkrieg. Yet Montgomery had earlier rejected the idea because of his caution.

His immediate reaction to Dempsey's suggestion on July 10 was negative. It was like a reflex action, an involuntary response to a course already considered and rejected. It was as though Montgomery feared to consider the logical implications of such a move. Accepting Dempsey's thought meant changing the plan again, thereby indicating inconsistency on Montgomery's part. Beyond that, if the attack failed, it might weaken the bulwark erected against the Germans on the British-Canadian flank. If if succeeded, it might precipitate a fluid and completely unpredictable situation difficult for Montgomery to deal with. Both possibilities, success as well as failure, filled him with foreboding.

After some reflection, Montgomery changed his mind. Without embracing Dempsey's notion completely, he asked Dempsey to prepare a plan for what he called a "massive stroke" from Caen toward Falaise. According to Montgomery's written directive, issued that day, Dempsey was to continue his pressure against the Germans by driving toward Falaise, but only if he could do so "without undue losses." Presumably, Montgomery would judge and decide whether the attack was warranted.

Three days later Dempsey had a plan, code-named Goodwood. His design was to "deliver a killing blow" and finally to "crush the German hold on Caen," that is, on the remainder of the city. He hoped to do so by mounting an effort consisting of five steps: (1) destroy the German defenses by a saturation or full-scale bombing, (2) tear a hole in the German lineup by sending 750 tanks forward, (3) outflank the Germans in the southern suburb of Caen on both sides, (4) gain the Bourguebus Ridge, long regarded as the backbone of the German positions, and (5) go beyond the ridge and strike toward Falaise.

Ready to execute the attack should Montgomery signal approval, Dempsey grouped three armored divisions, a powerful shock force, under the control of the 8 Corps headquarters on the eastern side of Caen for the main effort. He built up two corps on each side of the 8 Corps. He alerted a Canadian corps to take the rest of Caen. The weight of these formations was to crush and roll over the German defenses. With the German barrier to progress thus eliminated, the tanks were to move forward in a substantial advance.

By this time too, by July 13, Bradley had conceived, revised, and issued a plan of his own. It was named Cobra. The objective was simply to gain Coutances. But before Bradley could unleash the operation, he needed to have his forward forces on the dry ground of the Lessay–Périers–St-Lô highway. This terrain still lay several miles ahead of his units, which continued their grinding and painful efforts to move forward.

Goodwood and Cobra were both conceived out of frustration. They were meant to be heavy, concentrated blows to achieve decisive breakthroughs of the German front. Each had substantial air power to flatten the German defenses. Each employed tanks to roll over the smashed German field fortifications. Because the Allied air resources were insufficient to carry out both operations simultaneously, Montgomery scheduled them three days apart, as a one-two combination punch. Goodwood was to go on July 18, Cobra on July 21.

Until then, Bradley's attack in the Cotentin continued. It finally came to an end on July 18, the day of Goodwood's start, as St-Lô fell to the Americans after a bitter, week-long battle. The troops were then lined up near the Lessay–Périers–St-Lô road, but Lessay and Périers lay several miles ahead of the forward edge of the combat forces. No matter. The positions were close enough to make possible initiating Bradley's Cobra plan.

To reach that place, the First Army had committed twelve divisions, nearly 200,000 men, in attack. They had fought for seventeen days. They gained less than seven miles at a cost of 40,000 casualties, plus another 10,000 to 15,000 suffering from combat fatigue or shell shock. These figures were the highest proportional losses of the entire European campaign. The relief of three division commanders and several regimental commanders who appeared to be less than efficient helped not at all. Coutances, the prime objective, still lay fourteen miles away.

"We won the battle of Normandy," a survivor said. However, "considering the high price in American lives, we lost." The major impediment to success was, quite simply, "too many hedges." The problem was, "Must go forward slowly . . . take one hedgerow at a time and clean it up." The process was extremely wearisome. "You became so dulled by fatigue," a participant explained, "that the names of the killed and wounded . . . who had been your best friends, might have come out of a telephone book." Those who remained alive were "dead on their feet."

The battle of the hedgerows in July ground down and wore out the Americans. It did the same to the enemy. A German corps commander called the struggle that month nothing less than "a monstrous bloodbath."

To some British who smarted over their long journey to Caen, the difficulties in the Cotentin seemed quite normal. The Americans had done no better than they.

Long before the battle of the hedgerows ended, Montgomery had decided to put on Dempsey's Goodwood attack. As early as July 12 he started to secure the preliminary air power demanded. He wrote to Eisenhower and Tedder, asking for all-out support and promising fireworks. If he could have the "whole weight of air power," he said, his "whole eastern flank" would "burst into flames." The result would be "decisive."

Eisenhower replied on the following day, July 13. He was all "pepped up," he said, "concerning the promise of this plan," so much so that "I would not be at all surprised to see you gaining a victory that will make some of the 'old classics' look like a skirmish between patrols."

On the same day, Tedder assured Montgomery of a sympathetic hearing. The air forces would, he wrote, go "full out" to support Goodwood, what Tedder called Montgomery's "far-reaching and decisive plan."

How far-reaching and decisive Goodwood was supposed to be, whether the primary intention was to help the Americans or to achieve a British-Canadian victory, was left unsaid. All concerned were thinking of reaching Falaise. Dempsey himself, in an order dated July 13, categorically stated the objective to be Falaise, but he was being conservative, for he had in mind Argentan, fifteen miles beyond Falaise, as the final objective. Montgomery altered Dempsey's instruction on July 15 and took out the specific objective, preferring ambiguity apparently because vagueness could be rationalized no matter how the reality developed. According to the written orders eventually published by his and Dempsey's headquarters, the aim was nothing more than to attract and hold the attention of the enemy and to expand the size of the Continental foothold.

As Montgomery informed Brooke on July 14, the British Second Army "has in fact reached its peak and can get no stronger. It will in fact get weaker as the manpower situation begins to hit us"—he was referring to battlefield casualties. If this was the reason for Montgomery's caution, if his Goodwood objectives were truly limited, it was, as Max

Hastings has said, "politically suicidal for him to allow Eisenhower, Tedder and even Brooke to be deluded about them." Montgomery needed, "for political and moral" reasons, a great victory.

At daylight of July 18, as naval vessels in the bay of the Seine fired in support, 1,700 heavy bombers and 400 medium and fighter-bombers, many more than previously employed at Caen, dropped 8,000 tons of bombs to trigger the Goodwood attack. The 8 Corps, directing three armored divisions, then advanced more than three miles in an hour, excellent progress in Normandy.

The Germans had erected a zonal defense in depth on the Caen-Falaise plain. There were several lines, all covered with prearranged fire plans. Reserve units nearby were immediately available for commitment to plug holes in the defenses.

Between nine A.M. and noon, the British were on the verge of penetrating the German positions. The battle on the final German line was desperate.

Montgomery was optimistic. Early in the afternoon he wrote to inform Eisenhower of the results. He was, he said, "very well satisfied." The air power had been "decisive." That evening, for a British news broadcast, he repeated what turned out to be a "wildly overoptimistic evaluation," saying that armored cars and tanks ahead of the main British formations were roaming at will in open country and threatening Falaise.

The battle continued on the following day and again on July 20, until a heavy thunderstorm broke over Normandy in the afternoon. Montgomery then called off further effort.

The British 8 Corps had advanced six miles, gained thirty-four square miles of the Caen-Falaise plain—not very much—and taken 2,000 prisoners, while the Canadian corps captured the remainder of Caen. In exchange, the British and Canadian casualties totaled more than 4,000 men and about 500 tanks, more than one third of all the British tanks brought to Normandy.

This was nowhere near the results Montgomery had led everyone to expect. The discontent was widespread. Many senior Allied leaders felt that they had been had, taken by promises Montgomery had had no intention of fulfilling or had been unable to fulfill. Harry Butcher wrote in Eisenhower's diary, "The slowness of the battle . . . [and] inward but generally unspoken criticism of Monty for being so cautious" brought gloom to Eisenhower's features. Gossips were discussing, Butcher said, "who would succeed Monty if [he were] sacked."

Goodwood damaged Montgomery's prestige, and he never fully recovered. Eisenhower was "disappointed and angered" by the difference between Montgomery's promise and his performance. Tedder's animosity toward Montgomery "redoubled" because Montgomery had deceived the air forces.

Eisenhower and Montgomery met briefly on July 20. Montgomery still believed he, "the supreme professional," could, as Max Hastings wrote, sidestep and delude and soft soap Eisenhower, who was incapable of command. Eisenhower fretted over the campaign's stagnation and was "weary to death" of Montgomery.

On July 21, the day after Montgomery called off Goodwood, Eisenhower wrote to Montgomery to question whether they saw "eye to eye on the big problems." He had been "extremely hopeful and optimistic," he wrote, over the results of Goodwood, "assisted by tremendous air attack." Unfortunately, "that did not come about." As a consequence, he was "pinning our immediate hopes on Bradley's [Cobra] attack." Still, he urged Montgomery to keep Dempsey on the offensive. "While we have equality in size," he said, "we must go forward shoulder to shoulder, with honors and sacrifices equally shared."

Montgomery began to understand how precarious his status had become. He was actually in danger of being relieved and removed. Surprised, then stunned, Montgomery was numb with shock. The awareness shook his confidence. Afterwards, he always seemed a trifle hesitant. His decisions lacked the sharp, cutting directness, what someone called the gemlike quality, they had earlier had.

Upon receipt of Eisenhower's letter, Montgomery instructed Dempsey on July 21, that same day, to continue his effort "intensively." Dempsey's objectives were, first, Falaise, then Argentan.

Montgomery informed Eisenhower of his action, and Eisenhower replied, "We are apparently in complete agreement in conviction that vigorous and persistent offensive effort should be sustained by both First [U.S.] and Second [British] Armies."

That restored Montgomery's equanimity.

A problem of Goodwood had been its confusing motives. Montgomery's ambiguity, whether deliberate or unconscious, shielded and obscured his intentions. The desire to get to Falaise clashed with the wish to avoid overextension. Montgomery had taken the precaution of sending his military assistant to London before the attack to explain to Brooke and to others the restricted purpose he had in mind. All he intended, he said, was to shake up the Germans. Prudence was the key word of the venture. But everyone else assumed Montgomery's expectation of larger results. Otherwise, why was such heavy air support necessary? Or had Montgomery exaggerated the importance of Goodwood to obtain overwhelming air power? If so, he had led his colleagues astray; had, in fact, lied.

Much later, Montgomery explained Goodwood as a preliminary operation designed, like all actions occurring on the Allied eastern flank, to tie down the Germans and prevent them from interfering with Bradley's moves. Goodwood, Montgomery said, suggested "wider implications than in fact it had."

To everyone else, there was, as Lord Carver has gently said, "no doubt that Montgomery wished to take Caen the first day [of the invasion], then extend . . . rapidly, at least to Falaise." According to Max Hastings, Montgomery "hoped desperately to reach Falaise." Actually, Montgomery had anticipated going some fifteen miles beyond Falaise to Argentan.

Credit for the German success in stopping Goodwood belonged to a large extent to Rommel. His foresight in laying out the dispositions on the Falaise plain made it possible to turn back the British. The battle was Rommel's final victory. For on July 17, the day before Goodwood opened, Rommel was out of action.

Having inspected the front, Rommel was returning to his headquarters late in the afternoon when two British aircraft strafed his car as it traveled on the road near Livarot. They killed his driver, and the vehicle crashed out of control into a ditch. Rommel, suffering a concussion and a fractured skull, was unconscious.

Hospitalized, Rommel made a remarkable recovery. He was convalescing at home in September when Hitler forced him to commit suicide. His connections to certain conspirators who had sought to assassinate Hitler on July 20, three days after Rommel's automobile accident in Normandy, incriminated Rommel and indicated his disloyalty to the Führer.

Hitler himself announced the attempt on his life on the following day, saying, "A very small clique of ambitious, unscrupulous and stupid officers plotted to kill me and at the same time to seize the German Supreme Command." The bomb placed under the conference table had exploded with destructive force, killing and seriously injuring several persons in the room but sparing Hitler, who was hurt only superficially.

Although the Allied authorities, quite reasonably, thought the end of the war to be close at hand, the putsch intensified Hitler's suspicions of his military men, but had no immediate influence on the Normandy operations.

Taking command of Rommel's army group in addition to retaining command of his theater headquarters, Kluge reported the results of the Goodwood attack to Hitler's headquarters in East Prussia. In the course of his statement, he wondered whether the Führer and his coterie of military assistants, who were far from the scene of combat, appreciated, as he said, "the tremendous consumption of forces on big battle days."

A day later, at a conference of his senior subordinates, Kluge congratulated them for their stubborn and skillful showing. "We will hold," he said, "and if no miracle weapons can be found to improve our basic situation, then we'll just die like men on the battlefield."

His brave words could hardly conceal a deteriorating situation. So quickly were conditions to disintegrate that he would, in a week or so, call his position an *"ungeheures Kladderadatsch"*—an awful mess.

PART III

COBRA

THE BREAKOUT ATTACK

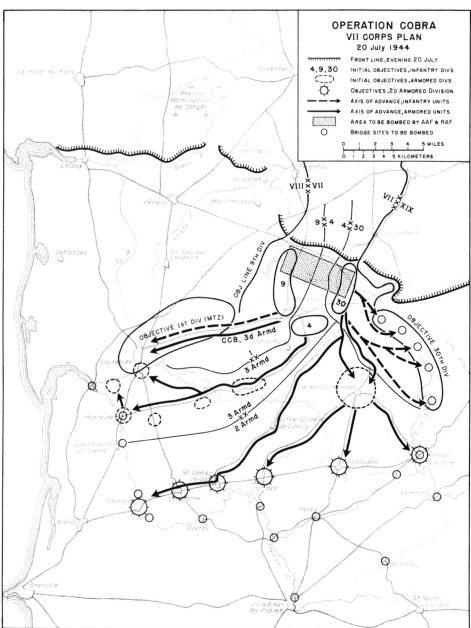

OPERATION COBRA
VII CORPS PLAN
20 July 1944

	FRONT LINE, EVENING 20 JULY
4,9,30	INITIAL OBJECTIVES, INFANTRY DIVS
	INITIAL OBJECTIVES, ARMORED DIVS
	OBJECTIVES, 2D ARMORED DIVISION
	AXIS OF ADVANCE, INFANTRY UNITS
	AXIS OF ADVANCE, ARMORED UNITS
	AREA TO BE BOMBED BY AAF & RAF
	BRIDGE SITES TO BE BOMBED

0 1 2 3 4 5 MILES
0 1 2 3 4 5 KILOMETERS

D. Holmes, Jr.

CHAPTER 9

Bombing

FOLLOWING MONTGOMERY'S ADVICE, BRADLEY drew a blueprint for a concentrated and heavy attack. The plan was relatively simple. There were to be three acts: bombers to blast a three-mile gap in the German defenses; two infantry divisions to enter the gap side by side, then draw apart and press against the sides of the hole to keep the break open; three mobile divisions moving abreast to speed through the opening, swing to Coutances, and go a few more miles to the Cotentin west coast. The conclusion would find Coutances in American hands. If the mobile units reached the coast fast enough, they would have got behind and trapped a substantial group of Germans.

Bagging Germans was hardly Bradley's main purpose. His real intention was to gain ground. As Caen had been a station on the road to Falaise, Coutances was a check point on the way to Avranches. Thirty miles ahead of Coutances, Avranches was the significant place. From the American perspective, Avranches was the bottom of the Cotentin and the entrance into Brittany. Enlarging the Continental foothold was what Bradley and everyone else had in mind.

Bradley made clear on July 12 his hope for a swift advance as he presented the Cobra idea at a conference of his principal staff members and corps commanders at the First Army headquarters. Alluding to the laborious battle of the hedgerows, which was still grinding forward, Bradley called it "tough and costly" combat, "a slugger's match," and "too slow a process" to continue. Cobra, if successful after "three or four thousand tons of bombs" fell on the Germans, was to permit them to shift gears and get rolling.

But Cobra would work only if everyone involved was aggressive and shook up the Germans. "If they [the Germans] get set [again]," Bradley warned, "we go right back to this hedge fighting and you can't make any speed." To pick up the tempo, to blast off to Coutances and beyond, Bradley said, "this thing must be bold."

The boldness devolved in large part and depended on the corps commander charged with directing and managing the main participating formations. As far as Bradley was concerned, only one of his major subordinates could handle numerous elements, mesh their interplay, and instigate an overriding aggressiveness. This was Lightning Joe Collins.

Bradley had been thinking of Collins all along, for he had drawn Cobra to take place in front of Collins's positions. To increase the punch, Bradley narrowed Collins's corps zone to about four miles and gave him five divisions, almost 100,000 men, an unusually large force. In Cobra, Collins was to explode forward.

Before issuing his plan in final and written form, Bradley asked Collins for his comments. Collins had two suggestions.

First, he wanted more troops, specifically another infantry division. If the bombers knocked a hole in the German defenses, Collins wanted to be certain to keep it open. Otherwise, the mobile units would be unable to plunge quickly through the gap to Coutances. The additional infantry division was to help prevent the Germans from closing the passage after the bombing.

Although more troops in the opening might clutter the ground and hold up the mobile divisions, and although giving Collins a total of six divisions in his corps would impose an almost unreasonable span of control, making it difficult for Collins to keep tabs on what all the units were doing, Bradley's confidence in Collins led him to accede to the request.

Collins's second recommendation pertained to the very purpose of the operation. If the mobile elements pushed through Coutances and drove to the Cotentin west coast, they would cut across and be athwart of the routes leading south to Avranches. They would thus block the advance of the neighboring American corps, the VIII. The troops of both VII and VIII Corps were bound to intermingle, and Cobra would come to a pause until Collins and the adjacent corps commander, Troy Middleton, could disentangle their units and reorient them for further movement toward Avranches. Sorting out the formations and getting them started south again would take several days at least, giving the Germans time to recover.

But if Coutances was nothing more than a step toward Avranches, it would be better for Collins to refrain from going beyond Coutances to the west coast. He would thus leave a corridor of advance open for the movement of Middleton's corps. Turning his own units to go south would be a minimal job. Both he and Middleton could press toward Avranches together and side by side.

What Collins proposed in effect was an open end. If the bombardment worked, if the three infantry divisions held open the gap, and if the mobile forces reached Coutances, Bradley would have two options. If a substantial number of Germans were ripe for encirclement on the Cotentin west coast, he could send Collins beyond Coutances to trap them. Or, if the Germans were fleeing or in a state of confusion, he could direct Collins to the south toward Avranches without a perceptible stop. There would be no need to interrupt any momentum created.

Bradley accepted Collins's outlook. He changed Cobra from a plan to penetrate the German defenses and encircle Coutances to a project of broader implication: secure Coutances, disrupt the Germans, and be ready to take instant advantage of their disarray by striking at once to Avranches. "If this thing goes as it should," Bradley said, "we ought to be in Avranches in a week." Collins agreed.

Unlike the ground attack, which lay wholly within Bradley's competence and purview, the bombardment designed to trigger the action was in the hands of others. Although Bradley had watched closely the prior air efforts at Caen, he was no expert in air matters. Yet he knew well what he wished.

He expected to launch Cobra when the First U.S. Army reached and established the front along the ruler-straight Lessay–Périers–St-Lô highway, an old Roman road running across the Cotentin. On the southern edge of the Périers–St-Lô segment, Bradley designated his bomb target, a rectangular area. The long side extended about three miles. The narrow side, or width, was about a mile in distance.

On this ground he wanted an unprecedented number of planes to drop an unprecedented number of bombs in what was called a carpet or saturation bombing. He also wished the bombs released in a minimum period of time: an hour. For he hoped to produce what he called a tremendous "blast effect" from the air to obliterate the defenses in the target area and to stun whatever survivors remained.

He wished the infantry troops to attack at once after the bombardment and advance through the target area. To have them close enough to take immediate advantage of the bombing and also to protect them from accidental or stray bombs, Bradley planned to withdraw them eight hundred yards, about half a mile, just before the planes arrived. If the bombardment demolished the enemy positions, Bradley wanted his troops across the ground before the Germans could restore the defenses. If the bombardment failed to destroy the enemy field fortifications, he wanted his Americans through them before the Germans could raise their heads and realize that the planes had gone away.

In order to enhance further the safety of the American ground troops, Bradley thought of having the bombers make lateral bomb runs. That is, have the planes approach the target from the east or west and use the highway, a prominent landmark, as a guide to keep the aircraft flying south of the road and away from the American soldiers below. A perpendicular arrival over the heads of the American ground troops, although safer for the flyers because there would be no antiaircraft fires rising from the American-held territory, would be dangerous to the ground troops. Flying laterally would expose the aircraft to German antiaircraft guns south of the Périers–St-Lô road, but if the aircraft bombed in the morning, the pilots could fly from east to west and use the sun for concealment; in the afternoon, a reverse course would offer the same advantage.

Bradley was also clear on doing away with the large craters and widespread debris prompted by bombing, for both impeded road traffic. He addressed this tricky question at the conference on July 12. On the one hand, the destructive power of the bombs promised to eliminate enemy defenses and make the subsequent ground advance a walk-through. On the other hand, the bombs gouged craters in the earth and scattered debris over the land, as noted, both of which made it difficult for road traffic to start and keep rolling.

"Do we get heavy or medium bombs, or both?" Collins asked at the meeting.

"Both," Bradley replied.

Some desultory discussion ensued. No one knew exactly how to define heavy, medium, and light bombs, or how to describe their effects. The 260-pound bomb, whatever the type, Bradley thought, did not "make too big a crater." Collins favored "bigger and better bombs," even the 500-pound bomb, and was willing to take his chances on the cratering.

Elwood "Pete" Quesada, who commanded the tactical planes, mainly fighter-bombers, giving the First Army close air support and who had his headquarters, the IX Tactical Air Command, beside Bradley's, came out on Bradley's side. The 260-pound bomb, he said, would be large enough for Collins's purposes and small enough for Bradley's.

Further talk failed to settle the issue. Bradley would have to take up the matter with the men in charge of the planes. He decided to go to England, to see the air force people, to explain Cobra in person, to win the cooperation of the airmen, and to obtain a bombardment conforming specifically to his wishes.

On July 19, Bradley met with his corps commanders and explained how he hoped Cobra would proceed. His battle of the hedgerows had ended on the previous day as St-Lô fell to the First Army. Dempsey's Goodwood had started the day before and was in progress. Cobra was scheduled for July 21, two days hence. The air force, consequently, had one day, the following, to get ready to give Bradley what he wished.

His conference at the First Army headquarters terminated, Bradley, together with his air commander, Pete Quesada, flew from Normandy to England. They landed at Stanmore, on the northern outskirts of London, where the Allied Expeditionary Air Forces headquarters was located. The commander, Sir Trafford Leigh-Mallory, was a tactical air force officer brought up to give close support to the ground troops. As Eisenhower's air chieftain, he loosely coordinated the Ninth U.S. Air Force, the 2nd RAF Tactical Force, and the Air Defense Command of Great Britain, all functioning to assist the ground units. Leigh-Mallory was a consistent advocate of carpet bombings by the tactical air forces, and he favored the occasional use of the strategic air forces in such a role.

In opposition were Carl A. "Tooey" Spaatz, who commanded the U.S. Strategic Air Forces, and Sir Arthur "Bomber" Harris, who commanded the RAF strategic aircraft. They were both strong personalities, not easily intimidated or swayed, and they jealously guarded their functions and their independence to carry out what they conceived to be their own decisive contribution to victory. They were reluctant to relinquish their control to anyone else, to Eisenhower or to Leigh-Mallory. They considered diverting their strategic resources to ground support to be, as John J. Sullivan has said, "tragically wasteful."

According to Sullivan, who put it bluntly and succinctly, "Bitter, protracted arguments at the highest Allied levels" took place before the Normandy invasion over whether, and if so, to what extent, Eisenhower, and by extension Leigh-Mallory, could exercise authority over the strategic air forces. The specific issue was, Could Eisenhower require them to assist the ground forces? "After months of wrangling," no categoric decision could be reached.

As a compromise, Eisenhower received a diluted authority. He exercised direction through his deputy commander, Air Chief Marshal Sir Arthur Tedder. An air force officer, Tedder spoke the flyers' language and understood their problems. Eisenhower through Tedder was to coordinate both functional forces, Leigh-Mallory's tactical formations and Spaatz's and Harris's strategic units. Yet coordination is hardly the same as command, and the arrangement failed to establish clear and undiminished lines of authority and responsibility.

The doctrinal argument over missions created and compounded personality conflicts. Spaatz and Harris quickly lost confidence in Leigh-Mallory's judgment. Tedder sided with Spaatz and Harris until early July, when political pressure compelled them to cooperate with Leigh-Mallory and use the heavy bombers to gain Caen.

Leigh-Mallory's general inability to influence the bomber barons, as they were sometimes called, left him frustrated. His diary entry of July 10 read: "Either I am to be allowed to direct, if necessary, the whole Air Forces available to the full and immediate support of the Army, or I shall resign on that issue. If Tedder does not like it, then he or I will go," meaning, the Combined Chiefs of Staff would have to choose between them and would have to relieve one or the other of his duties.

Knowledge of favorable talk at the highest levels again forced the heavy bombers to participate in the preparation for Goodwood. The failure of Goodwood to produce a breakthrough of the German defenses between Caen and Falaise created the momentum to use them again in Cobra.

For the Cobra bombardment, Tedder was to supervise the planning and execution. Leigh-Mallory was to set the date and the time. Lewis Brereton's Ninth U.S. Air Force, consisting of medium bombers and fighter-bombers, was to plan the bomber attack. Quesada, chief of the IX Tactical Air Command headquartered beside Bradley's command post in Normandy, was to coordinate the air and ground forces. All of the heavy bombers of James H. Doolittle's Eighth U.S. Air Force were to take part. Fighter planes of the Ninth U.S. and the 2nd RAF Tactical air forces were to fly cover, that is, protect the bombers from German aircraft. The RAF Heavy Bomber Command was excluded from the operation because its planes carried only large bombs.

At Stanmore on July 19 to listen to Bradley expound his Cobra wishes were Leigh-Mallory and some of his principal staff officers, together with representatives from the other air force commands involved. They were patient as Bradley presented his desire for a saturation bombing of devastating power on his rectangular target, the bombing to be completed in an hour with only light bombs employed. They approved his target and promised to provide blast effect with comparatively small bombs.

They demurred on his proposal to withdraw his combat troops 800 yards from the bomb target. They preferred pulling back the men at least 3,000 yards. Even this distance, they warned, would hardly remove all the danger of bombing error. Some bombs were bound to fall on American ground soldiers.

To Bradley, 3,000 yards—two miles—was too far. He wanted the combat soldiers to attack immediately after the bombing and to be upon the rectangular target at once. After much talk, the officers in the room reached agreement. The troops would move back 1,250 yards, but heavy bombers would strike no closer than 1,500 yards from them.

The lateral bomber approach to the target area proposed by Bradley, according to an observer, "evoked considerable discussion." Bradley wished to avoid accidental bomb release over the heads of the troops, but the air people deemed the suggestion to be unrealistic and infeasible. The Périers–St-Lô highway, they pointed out, was hardly a prominent landmark to airmen flying at 15,000 feet. Nor could they deliver their bombs in an hour if they flew through the narrow side of the rectangle, the one-mile depth of the target. There would simply be too much congestion in the bomber formations. A north-south or perpendicular approach minimized exposure to antiaircraft artillery and therefore kept flight formations tight and bomb spread constricted. The route also offered better check points for the bombardiers to compute more accurate range sightings while in flight.

Unfortunately, before the parties concerned could clear up the differences in points of view, Leigh-Mallory had to leave for another appointment. Seeing no reason to remain there without his opposite number, Bradley departed too, counting on Quesada to complete the arrangements. Bradley was pleased by what he thought was a "very satisfactory conference." The airmen had been, as Sullivan later wrote, "unusually cooperative." They had refrained from raising their normal doubts over the wisdom of employing strategic bombers in close support of ground troops. They had acceded, Bradley believed, to all of his wishes, including the lateral bomb runs. Quesada too was certain of the air forces' willingness and ability to meet Bradley's requirements without exception.

Contrary to Bradley's and Quesada's belief, the air force officers at the meeting were unable to fulfill Bradley's expectations. Furthermore, they thought that Bradley understood. According to a memo for the record, Bradley "was aware of the possibility of gross errors causing casualties [among the troops on the ground]." Bradley, they had no doubt, "was prepared to accept such casualties no matter which way the planes approached."

The absence of firm understanding and mutual agreement was inexcusable, the failure to button up the arguments indefensible.

Leigh-Mallory's Allied Expeditionary Air Forces headquarters issued an order that day and left "routings and altitudes" to be worked out and coordinated by the participating commands. The directive also warned against bombing short and thus implied a perpendicular approach over the heads of the American ground troops. The Eighth U.S. Air Force was quite specific on this point. Its order cautioned bombardiers against releasing their bombs too soon "because the penetration route [the approach to the target] is directly over friendly [American] troops."

That evening, Leigh-Mallory wrote Bradley a nice note. He told how much he had enjoyed seeing Bradley and how pleasant the conference had been. He apologized for having had to, he said, "rush off" before the end of the deliberations. Yet everything, he seemed to imply, had been settled amicably and satisfactorily.

The thunderstorm bringing Dempsey's Goodwood attack to a close on the afternoon of July 20 opened several days of bad weather. Rain on the 21st and again on the 22nd compelled postponing Cobra. During this period of delay, none of the ground commanders or staff officers involved in Cobra apparently read the air force orders pertaining to the operation. No one evidently noticed the direction of the planes' approach to the target area.

As overcast skies on July 23 once more prevented the heavy planes from engaging in precision bombing, Bradley replied to Leigh-Mallory's note. In a nice and kidding letter, Bradley assumed blame for having, he said, "failed to make arrangements for proper weather." He seemed quite satisfied with the conditions of the impending air attack.

Forecasters on July 23 predicted improving weather conditions on the 24th, thus making it possible to put on Cobra. At Leigh-Mallory's headquarters, his deputy commander, an American named Major General Hoyt Vandenberg, who was to become the U.S. Air Force chief of staff after the war, reviewed the planning documents and the published directives for the air strike. Remarking the perpendicular bombing approach, Vandenberg recalled Bradley's desire for a lateral flight. According to Vandenberg's memory, what made it impossible to fly to the target area along the narrow or lateral side was Bradley's requirement to complete the bombing in an hour. To check his understanding, Vandenberg telephoned from the Allied Expeditionary Air Forces headquarters in Stanmore to the Eighth U.S. Air Force, the heavy bomber command.

Reaching Doolittle's operations officer at the Eighth U.S. Air Force headquarters, Vandenberg asked whether his recollection was correct. Was Bradley's wish for a bombing of no more than an hour responsible for the direction of the heavy bomber approach to the target?

The operations officer was unable to confirm and to verify Vandenberg's memory. Sensing the potential importance of Vandenberg's question, the operations officer promised to call Vandenberg back. Seeking higher authority, he asked Spaatz's deputy commander at Strategic Air Forces headquarters, an American named Major General Fred Anderson, to phone Vandenberg and refresh his remembrance of the problem.

Anderson did so. He corroborated Vandenberg's statement. He too, Anderson said, "was worried about the repercussions that might arise" from the approach route. As Vandenberg noted in his diary, Anderson "wanted it clarified"—that is, recorded beyond question—"that the time factor which was set by AEAF [Leigh-Mallory] was the controlling one for their direction of attack."

Vandenberg offered to check out their understanding and to explain the problem to Leigh-Mallory, and Anderson apparently acquiesced. For Vandenberg "called him [Leigh-Mallory] and suggested that perhaps Bradley might prefer to extend the time [for the bombardment] . . . and thus allow parallel bombing. . . . [He, Leigh-Mallory] assured me that he had just spoken to Bradley and that the additional time to deliver the bombing attack [by means of a lateral approach] was too great for Bradley to accept and that, therefore, he [Bradley] had decided to accept the additional risk of perpendicular to the [Périers–St-Lô] road bombing."

This seemed to settle the matter from the air force point of view.

Despite the reservations of forecasters at the Eighth U.S. Air Force headquarters who recommended further delay, Leigh-Mallory set the Cobra bombardment for noon of July 24. Reports of heavy clouds over Normandy that morning led him to fly to France to check the scene personally. He arrived at Bradley's First U.S. Army headquarters at 11:20 P.M., forty minutes before the initial aircraft were scheduled to appear over the target area. To his dismay, the overcast skies prevented precision bombing. Leigh-Mallory therefore canceled the air attack. Unfortunately, his order reached the Eighth U.S. Air Force too late. Most of the big bombers were already airborne and en route to the Périers–St-Lô road.

The majority of the bombardiers found the cloud cover too thick to attack and refrained from dropping their bombs. But about 350 heavy bombers released their loads, about 550 tons of high explosive and 135 tons of fragmentation bombs in all. Some fell short of the Périers–St-Lô road and on American ground troops, killing 25 and wounding 131. The soldiers had been particularly vulnerable because, after withdrawing from their positions overlooking the highway, only a few had dug foxholes for protection.

Quesada was astonished and shocked. He sent a telegram of indignant protest to Brereton at the Ninth U.S. Air Force. Why, he asked, had they used "another plan"? Why, he reiterated, had they switched the plans without informing him?

Bradley was upset and angry over the casualties among his soldiers, but when he learned how the aircraft had approached—over their heads—he became livid with rage. Seeking out Leigh-Mallory still at the First Army headquarters, he demanded to know why the bombers had flown a perpendicular course to the target.

According to a memorandum dictated by Bradley on the following day, Leigh-Mallory pleaded ignorance. Was he simply unable to stand up to Bradley's blazing anger? Leigh-Mallory promised to check with Doolittle's Eighth U.S. Air Force and to report his findings to Bradley.

If Bradley's account was accurate and true, Leigh-Mallory not only admitted his lack of knowledge of a basic fact in an operation he was supposed to coordinate but also contradicted Vandenberg's diary entries. If Vandenberg's notations were correct, Leigh-Mallory understood the issues of the Cobra bombardment perfectly. The only other explanation is distasteful to contemplate. Were Bradley on the one hand and the air forces on the other building a case to absolve themselves of responsibility for the short bombs?

In any event, Collins ordered his three infantry divisions to attack and regain the ground they had given up by withdrawing just before the bombing. The troops recovered the terrain after sharp fighting. They thereby misled the Germans, who were certain of having repulsed a major American ground attack after a heavy and serious air strike.

Meanwhile, Bradley awaited word from Leigh-Mallory. From Stanmore, he finally phoned at 11:40 P.M. The bombing, he informed Bradley, could go again on the following day, on July 25, but only under the same conditions. Nothing had changed. Given the time restriction of releasing the bombs in an hour, only a perpendicular approach was feasible. What did Bradley want to do, cancel or repeat?

The choice was brutal. Bradley had no option. He accepted the repetition.

Leigh-Mallory rescheduled Cobra for the following morning. Both air and ground forces hastily added some precautions—additional artillery-smoke markings—to reduce the chances of bombing errors.

At eight A.M., a weather plane flew over Normandy and reported good visibility over the target area, cloud cover along the route. The latter condition compelled pilots already in the air to descend from planned altitudes; bombardiers had to recalculate data and to reset bombsights. The result loosened plane formations and consequently spread bomb patterns.

About half an hour late, fighter-bombers flying a parallel approach to the target area dropped their loads along the Périers–St-Lô road and opened the air attack. The explosions created great clouds of dust and smoke rising from the ground. As the armada of heavy bombers came in from the north, pilots searched for the highway and other landmarks. Artillery flashes and the bomb bursts, together with the drifting smoke and dust, obscured the terrain below. A breeze blowing from the south wafted the cloud toward the American ground troops. Although the Eighth U.S. Air Force later judged the bombing of 1,500 heavy bombers dropping more than 2,000 tons of high explosive and almost 2,500 tons of fragmentation, together with some white phosphorus and napalm, to be good and on target, the bombardment killed 111 Americans on the ground, wounded 490, and sent almost 200 more to the hospital with combat exhaustion and shock.

Despite the unexpected casualties, Collins's infantry divisions attacked upon the conclusion of the bombing. They met surprisingly solid resistance from German soldiers who, unlike the Americans, had been sheltered in tunnels, trenches, foxholes, and dug-in armored vehicles. Heavy fighting throughout the afternoon failed to crack the German defenses. The Americans could barely get across the line of departure, the Périers–St-Lô highway. According to the immediate verdict, the bombing had had "negligible" effect. The "breakthrough for which we had all hoped," a notation in that evening's First U.S. Army diary read, had failed to materialize.

In the gloom arising out of the First Army's estimate of the Cobra bombardment's failure to open a hole across the Périers–St-Lô highway, Bradley dictated a memorandum that evening. He leveled charges against the air force in general and the Eighth U.S. Air Force, the heavy bombers, in particular, for the perpendicular approach, "calling it a primary cause of the bombing casualties" among American troops. The airmen, he insisted, had promised to make the bomb run parallel to the Périers–St-Lô road. "It was duplicity," Bradley wrote in his two books of memoirs after the war, "a serious breach of good faith in planning," and again, "a shocking breach of good faith."

According to Sullivan, who is categorical, "This claim is false." Many airmen had told Bradley of the impossibility of the parallel approach, "given the size of the target area, the number of bombers, and the time permitted for bombing." Bradley had apparently accepted that fact.

Anger over the air force spread from the First Army to Eisenhower's headquarters in England, and Bedell Smith, Eisenhower's chief of staff, charged the bomb mishaps to the airmen's lack of enthusiasm for close ground support. Informed of his remark, Spaatz at once told Eisenhower, on July 26, of the warnings Bradley had received. Casualties were sure to occur among American troops because, Spaatz said, "We were attempting to place too heavy a concentration [of bombs] in too small an area." Even a lateral approach would hardly have been foolproof. Some bombs would inevitably have spilled over beyond the designated target and struck the ground troops.

If the state of the art of bombing at the time excused all those involved, if no one could have averted the accidental short bombs and the American ground casualties, why did such misunderstanding and resentment arise?

Some of the problem lay in the Army–Air Force relationship. Although the flyers had by 1944 gained virtual autonomy and would soon after the war win independence, they were still at this time part of the Army. After thirty years of uneasy cohabitation, as well as bitter interservice argument over the role of air power, ground and air officers were deeply suspicious of each other. Ground officers had traditionally outranked and dominated the flyers, and Bradley had perhaps acted under the influence of this attitude in postulating his Cobra requirements. In his mind, he had but to state his needs, and the Air Forces, he expected, would acquiesce and obey.

The rise in prominence of the Air Force grated on many ground officers who, as Sullivan wrote, believed airmen to be "overpaid, over promoted, overdecorated, and incorrigible publicity-seekers who invariably claimed for themselves a far greater importance in the nation's military establishment than their battlefield record warranted." Bradley shared this outlook because, according to Sullivan, forty years after the war, Bradley still refused in his memoirs "to acknowledge the great benefits that air supremacy gave his forces in France—supremacy that had been won . . . in fierce air battles over Germany."

If Bradley was at fault for expecting too much, Tedder failed to exercise the close supervision with which he was charged. Once the decision had been made to employ strategic and tactical bombers to support Bradley's attack, Tedder disappeared from the scene and played no role. He might well have suggested or insisted on having the heavy bombers strike first, ahead of the fighter-bombers, whose attack had raised the great cloud of dust and smoke obscuring the landmarks.

Sharing in the blame was Leigh-Mallory, who displayed a masterful insouciance throughout the operation. He was wrong to depart the initial conference at Stanmore before Bradley completed his presentation, wrong to set the bombardment for July 24, wrong to arrive in Normandy too late to check the weather that morning and too late to cancel the bombing. Finally, as a colleague, a British officer, described Leigh-Mallory, he was a "man in whom nobody has any confidence, a man who in addition to a widespread reputation for incompetence, has a peculiar knack of rubbing everybody up the wrong way with his pompous arrogant attitude."

Was Eisenhower also at fault for giving Leigh-Mallory "patient, unwavering support . . . in the face of the constant criticism" directed against the airman? Did Eisenhower, in the interest of furthering coalition harmony, err in keeping Leigh-Mallory?

The entire event remains as clouded as the air over the target. Everyone involved was to blame to some extent for failing to button up a firm and common understanding.

Whatever the confusion, the ground side of Cobra had to roll.

CHAPTER 10

Breakthrough

ACCORDING TO THE COBRA plan for the ground action, three infantry divisions were, immediately after the bombing, to attack across the target area. The one in the middle was to plunge straight ahead. The two others were to peel off, the one on the right to the village of Marigny, the one on the left to the village of St-Gilles. These rural places, about three miles apart and the same distance south of the Périers–St-Lô highway, defined what Bradley hoped would be the Marigny–St-Gilles gap. Sweeping the area clear of enemy troops would constitute a breakthrough of the German defenses.

Only then, after seizing Marigny and St-Gilles, did Collins intend to commit his three mobile divisions and to send them speeding to Coutances. On July 12, when Bradley had first presented the Cobra idea, Collins had made plain the difficulty of attaining rapid advance in the hedgerow region with mobile, mechanized units. "The only doubtful part of it [Cobra] to my mind," he had said, "is we shouldn't count too much on fast movement of armored divisions through this country. If we make a breakthrough, it is OK [to use armored divisions] but until then . . . [they] can't move any faster than the infantry."

Now, late in the afternoon of July 25, despite his earlier reservations, although the infantry divisions had hardly so much as started toward Marigny and St-Gilles, Collins changed his mind. Telling the infantry to continue on their missions but to get off the roads, he decided to commit the better part of his mobile forces, two of his three available divisions, on the following morning. Instead of pointing them directly to Coutances, he told one to seize Marigny, the other to capture St-Gilles. With these villages in hand and the way to further advance open, he would, presumably, send the third to Coutances, the final objective.

Collins's decision was the vital action for Cobra's subsequent development. The key piece in the operation, it was very much of a gamble. For the Germans seemed strong and effective. There was no sign of an impending breakthrough. The risk of committing large armored forces in constricted space lay in the distinct possibility of cluttering the roads, congesting traffic, and utterly paralyzing movement.

Unknown to the Americans, the bombing had inflicted considerable damage on the Germans south of the Périers–St-Lô highway. In addition to creating a frightening lunar landscape, the bombs had buried men and equipment, overturned tanks and trucks, and, most tellingly, severed telephone wires and broken radio antennas. The disruption of communications isolated combat groups, cutting them off from knowledge of what was happening elsewhere and from orders of what they were supposed to do.

They stopped the Americans immediately after the bombardment because of reflex actions on both sides. The Germans who survived the bombing put up a spirited defense as a matter of habit. The Americans, conditioned by their previous experience in the slow-moving and close-range battle of the hedgerows, were cautious and tentative in their advance. Having expected the bombers to annihilate their opponents and to allow them to walk through the target area unopposed, they were disconcerted when they encountered resistance.

Kluge received fragmentary reports from his subordinate commanders at army, corps, and division levels who were out of touch with their units. Ignorant of what was happening to their soldiers, they assumed the worst. The bombardment, they believed, had eliminated their troops and destroyed their defensive positions. A yawning hole, they were sure, lay open ahead of the Americans. This was what they told Kluge. On this basis, Kluge informed Hitler's headquarters that evening, "As of this moment, the front has . . . burst."

To restore a firmly fixed front required swift action by a responsible commander on the scene, someone who could take the necessary measures without looking over his shoulder and awaiting approval from Hitler's distant headquarters in East Prussia. Kluge was that person, and he asked for what he believed would be denied him. Would Hitler give him a free hand in Normandy? Miraculously, the answer was yes.

Kluge set about to plug the gap, then clean up the damage. He ordered reserve troops up to reestablish defenses along the Périers–St-Lô highway. As the units traveled toward their destination, the situation spun out of German control. The Americans moved too swiftly to be contained.

Except for German resistance around Marigny, opposition in the target area on July 26 melted away. Moving off the roads and across the fields, American infantrymen began to go forward quite easily. In the evening, riflemen were five miles below the Périers–St-Lô road. The armored division rolling across the highway at noon drove through St-Gilles in midafternoon, then kept heading south. By the end of the day, it was nearly ten miles into what had been German territory.

Collins's accomplishment was quite clear. He had broken cleanly through the enemy defenses. This was no time to stop or to relax. He ordered all units to continue their exertions during the night.

Progress on July 27 everywhere in the Cotentin confirmed the achievement. "This thing has busted wide open," exclaimed an astonished and exultant Leland Hobbs, commander of the 30th Division.

With communications almost nonexistent and details therefore scarce, Kluge remained in the dark. What seemed absolutely evident, he told Hitler's headquarters that afternoon, was that the Americans were "running wild."

To Bradley, the decisive development was the retirement of the Germans along the Cotentin west coast. They had at first pulled back to establish a new line to protect Coutances. With Americans constantly threatening to outflank and encircle them, the Germans accelerated their retrograde movements on the afternoon of July 27. In response, Bradley issued new orders that evening. He thereby brought the Cobra operation to an end after three days, although some units continued to pursue the objectives assigned to them in the Cobra plan.

As far as Bradley was concerned, Coutances, still in German hands, was no longer important. Avranches had come into view and within reach. He instructed his subordinates to exert what he called "unrelenting pressure" on the Germans, to destroy those who still resisted and to pursue those who were in flight. Cobra had created a fluid situation, a war of movement favorable to the Allied forces, and Bradley wished, above all, to sustain and extend the German disarray.

Expecting soon to come into possession of Avranches and with it the entrance into Brittany, Bradley, in accordance with Overlord plans, began to prepare to change the command structure. With Brittany, the province where Patton's Third U.S. Army was to operate, looming beyond

Avranches, Bradley alerted Patton to his impending insertion into the campaign. Late in the afternoon of July 27, Bradley asked Patton to look after Middleton's VIII Corps on the First U.S. Army right. Advancing along the Cotentin west coast, Middleton was to pass to Third Army control when he turned the corner at Avranches into Brittany. Patton was then officially to enter combat. Until that moment, Bradley requested Patton to manage informally the VIII Corps progress.

The activation of Patton's Third Army headquarters would require bringing the 12th U.S. Army Group into existence. Eisenhower had given Bradley permission on July 25, two days earlier, to do so whenever he wished, and Bradley decided to open the new headquarters when the Third Army came to life. Because Bradley himself was to step up and assume the army group command after turning the First Army over to Courtney Hodges, Bradley asked Hodges, also on July 27, to "keep close track of," he said, the three corps on the First Army left, Collins's VII, the XIX, and the V, positioned across the front in that order.

Thus, when the new arrangements went into effect at a date still to be determined, the three U.S. commanders, with Bradley at army group directing Hodges and Patton at the armies, would already be in place. The transition promised to be smooth.

Montgomery had similarly altered the command structure on the British side. With the First Canadian Army headquarters under Henry Crerar becoming active on July 23 and taking responsibility for a small part of the front, Montgomery at 21 Army Group headquarters now directed both Dempsey and Crerar. In addition, he continued to act as temporary Allied ground forces commander, thus as Bradley's immediate superior.

The Montgomery-Bradley relationship, at first quite categoric and direct as a boss-subordinate connection, began to show signs of dislocation. Montgomery had always exercised command over the Americans through Bradley with considerable restraint and circumspection, as well as finesse, allowing Bradley great latitude and thereby conforming with coalition courtesy. For example, he conferred more freedom on Bradley than on Dempsey.

As the Americans gradually built up their forces and occupied increasingly more territory on the Continent than did their partners, Bradley started to show some signs of independence. The snide remarks about Montgomery and the British broke down Montgomery's omnipotent stature. Besides, Bradley's self-esteem was rising. He had directed his army in combat for almost two months in Normandy, and he had overcome the difficulties of the invasion, the capture of Cherbourg, and the battle of the hedgerows. He was also the object of flattery from his fellow Americans, who rarely ceased to remind him of his preeminent place in the campaign. He was, after all, the senior American troop commander on the Continent. He had won his spurs by his victories, he was about to step up to army group, where he would be Montgomery's organizational equal, and he was entitled to certain additional, if somewhat vague, prerogatives. The success of Cobra extended and deepened these tendencies.

With Cobra, strictly speaking, for the most part over, with Coutances as good as captured, and with American energies directed on attaining Avranches, the First U.S. Army advance to the south continued unabated on July 28. Below the Lessay–Périers–St-Lô highway, Collins's infantry troops mopped up small, bypassed German groups. Ten miles and more beyond the original line of departure, his mobile armored forces were chewing up the countryside and moving quite at will. So rapidly were they going that they found themselves behind the bulk of the withdrawing German units in the Cotentin. Their presence in the German rear threatened to block further retrograde action, to encircle substantial numbers of men, and to upset German plans completely.

On the Cotentin west coast, where Patton had informally taken over and was supervising Middleton's VIII Corps, a Patton trademark appeared. Two armored divisions wriggled forward through the infantry troops and emerged at the head of the procession. Leading the way side by side, they hustled toward Avranches. As Eisenhower had already remarked, Patton was able not only to exert "an extraordinary and ruthless driving power . . . at critical moments" but also to get "the utmost out of soldiers in offensive operations." His actions were soon to produce a whirlwind.

On the German side, all seemed to be confusion. The left flank had collapsed. And Kluge was powerless to impose order. The Americans were simply moving too fast, refusing to pause and give the Germans a chance to reorganize their defenses.

From his vantage point in London, Brooke watched the Americans gather momentum with awe and some discomfort. In comparison, the British looked passive and static. To avoid criticism, Brooke urged Montgomery to attack on Dempsey's front. According to Major Ellis, Montgomery passed the word to Dempsey. "Step on the gas," he ordered.

Dempsey organized an effort on July 30 near Caumont with the objective of Vire, an important road center. According to Alun Chalfont, the attack was "a disaster." The British enjoyed a superiority of three to one on the ground and an absolute domination in the air, but they went nowhere. German counterattacks drove them back to their line of departure. The performance of the corps and division commanders was well below par, and Dempsey dismissed both from their posts.

In contrast, the Americans were flushed with victory. On July 29, there was little German resistance. Many Germans holed up during the day and at night moved along back roads in long columns of vehicles, many horse-drawn, making their way to the south.

The weather, cold and rainy with lots of fog in June and throughout most of July, turned clear and summery, with brilliant sunshine, and the tactical air forces came out in great strength. Fighter-bomber pilots discovered near the village of Roncey a pocket of German troops, traffic stationary, bumper to bumper, and, as one reported, "triple banked." For the better part of six hours, the flyers attacked, bombing and strafing an estimated five hundred vehicles of all sorts.

Abandoning their transports, the Germans fled on foot. Many blundered into American outposts strung seemingly everywhere across the Cotentin, and they were quickly swept up and herded into makeshift prisoner-of-war cages.

Nothing changed on July 30 as American infantrymen and tankers raced to the south through terrain marred by a profusion of destroyed and wrecked equipment, hundreds of dead horses, and the spilled and scattered miscellaneous debris of defeat. Just before dark, a German signal crew manning a telephone relay station in the northern outskirts of Avranches reported the approach of American troops.

As dusk was falling, these men crossed the Sée River and rode up the long incline into the town of Avranches, which sits on a bluff two hundred feet high and overlooks the bay of Mont-St-Michel. Across the water eight miles away was the famous rock of chapels and churches, but the troops paid little attention to the magnificent sight rising from the sea. They moved quickly through the streets, scooping up an occasional surprised German, and taking control of the strategic prize.

The ease with which they seized Avranches proved illusory, for the peaceful night soon exploded into gunfire. Behind them up the hill into the town came a column of German tanks, artillery pieces, trucks, and ambulances, all carrying soldiers as passengers, all seeking escape, all ignorant of the prior arrival of Americans. The confrontation quickly developed into a battle, and both sides fought desperately until morning. At first light, the Americans, although reduced in effective numbers, still occupied Avranches; the surviving Germans had been deflected to the east, and they headed toward the town of Mortain, twenty miles away.

The American triumph in Cobra came to completion on July 31. One high-ranking commander instructed his troops, "We face a defeated enemy, an enemy terribly low in morale, terribly confused. I want you in the next advance to throw caution to the winds . . . destroying, capturing, or bypassing the enemy, and pressing—" he paused a moment as he searched for the proper word "—pressing *recklessly* on to the objective." Another commander directing his men said, "We *must* keep going to maintain contact and not give the Boche a chance to dig in."

The Americans complied with vigor and skill. Those in Avranches might have thought they had accomplished their mission, but during the course of the morning, they received word to take another objective. A few miles south of the town at the hamlet of Pontaubault, a bridge crossed the Sélune River. Reconnaissance pilots to their great astonishment had found the bridge miraculously still standing, still intact. The Germans, through ineptness or simple oversight, had failed to demolish the single structure giving Americans easy access to what in effect was the rest of France.

Discovering the existing crossing site about the same time, the German commander in Brittany dispatched a force of about a thousand men to Pontaubault. After destroying the bridge, they were to dig in and set up defensive positions along the riverbank and deny the Americans the best place to cross the stream. They were to confine the Americans to the Cotentin and prevent them from emerging into open country.

Neither side had knowledge of the other's activity, and both forces arrived in Pontaubault about the same time, the Germans shortly after the Americans had crossed and outposted the bridge. A shootout took place and, with the help of tactical aircraft, the Americans dispersed the *Kampfgruppe*.

With Pontaubault in hand, routes beckoned the Americans in three distinct directions—to the east toward the lodgment area boundary of the Seine River and the Paris-Orléans gap, to the south toward the Loire River, another designated edge of the lodgment area, and to the west into the expanse of Brittany.

Pontaubault marked the southernmost point of the Allied advance on July 31, but what happened ten miles east of Avranches at the town of Brécey showed further the extent of the German disintegration. Late in the afternoon, a tank-infantry task force in Collins's corps had gained its objective, cutting a major highway in the Cotentin, and was about to halt for the night when a message arrived from Collins. Because of the late hour, he requested rather than ordered the task force to drive twelve miles farther if possible. The troops responded. Barreling down the main road, they made what was referred to as a Hollywood-type entry into Brécey early in the evening. As they sped through the streets toward the Sée River, they took potshots at German soldiers in dress uniforms spending a night on the town.

The bridge across the stream had been blown, but the task force members carried rocks to the river to build a ford, then waded across in the face of some small-arms fire. Three miles ahead, they reached a small wooded hill, and there they halted for the night. The leading element of Collins's movement, the task force was more than thirty miles south of the Périers–St-Lô highway.

Shortly before Cobra, on July 24, Eisenhower had written to Bradley to wish him well and to offer some mild advice. "My high hopes and best wishes," Eisenhower said, "ride with you in your attack. . . . Pursue every advantage with an ardor verging on recklessness and with all your troops without fear of major counteroffensive from the forces the enemy now has on his front. . . . [If you will do so], the results will be incalculable."

What had been "incalculable" to Eisenhower before the event was surpassingly clear afterwards. While the First U.S. Army had captured 8,000 prisoners of war during the first twenty-five days of July, it had, in advancing more than thirty miles during the last six days of the month, taken 20,000. The Americans had also gained possession of the last natural defensive line barring their egress from the Cotentin and their entrance into Brittany.

They had, in addition, saved Montgomery's neck. In much the same way that the successful conclusion of the North African campaign in 1943 had rescued Eisenhower from relief, possible disgrace, and certain oblivion, Cobra dissipated all the talk of sacking Montgomery. It would have been next to impossible to dismiss Montgomery anyhow, for his reputation as the victor of El Alamein and his status as a hero had made him a mighty figure not easily cast aside. Removing him from command in Europe would have been a blow to British national confidence. Yet who knows, Merle Miller has asked, what would have happened to Montgomery had not Cobra blown the Continental stalemate to smithereens and opened the prospect of quick victory?

Although Collins was responsible for a good part of Cobra's success, the triumph was indubitably Bradley's. He had created and formed the operation, and he had blasted out of the hedgerows, out of the Cotentin. He had transformed the entire campaign, for the projected Cobra breakthrough had become a breakout.

Ernie Pyle, the American journalist who was in Normandy during the Cobra bombardment, later evaluated the development correctly. "I have a hunch," he wrote, "that July 25 of the year 1944 will be one of the great historic pinnacles of this war. It was the day we began a mighty surge out of our confined Normandy spaces, the day we stopped calling our area the beachhead and knew we were fighting a war across the whole expanse of France."

A distinct phase of the invasion had ended. On the first day of August, as Bradley stepped up to army group and Patton's army appeared officially on the scene, a new stage of development opened.

As for Kluge, he was dumbfounded. "It's a madhouse here," he exclaimed on the morning of July 31. Talking on the phone from Le Mans to his chief of staff in St-Germain-en-Laye, a Paris suburb, he described the scene as a *"Riesensauerei"*—one hell of a mess. "You can't imagine what it's like," he said. "Commanders are completely out of contact [with their troops]." The left flank in the Cotentin was shattered, smashed, and, he added, "cannot hold." As for defenses in the rear to which the Germans could withdraw, he said, "All you can do is laugh out loud." Hitler and his advisers? "Don't they read our dispatches? Haven't they been oriented? They must be living on the moon." The terrible thing was, there was not much anyone could do. "It's a crazy situation," he concluded.

How the Germans tried to restore sanity led directly to the Falaise pocket.

CHAPTER 11

Breakout

DURING WARTIME, IN EVERY U.S. headquarters above regiment, that is to say, in ascending order, division, corps, army, and army group, the commander presided over a daily meeting, usually held early in the morning, of his staff. Each staff officer, speaking in his area of competence and expertise, briefed the boss. Summarizing the events of the past twenty-four hours, each brought the commander, as well as the other staff members, up to date on the developments. Occasionally the commander questioned his advisers to clarify their remarks.

The G-2, or intelligence officer, and the G-3, or operations officer, prepared a written record of their oral presentations and usually added documents to extend their comments or to illustrate conditions. Mimeographed in a large number of copies and widely distributed, both internally in the headquarters and to other headquarters, these daily reports carried information and guidance.

The G-3 Periodic Report, listing the results of operations, was a straightforward and factual document, although guesswork sometimes appeared. The G-2 paper was somewhat more speculative. Although the intelligence officer tried to be down-to-earth and matter-of-fact, he dealt with his perceptions of the enemy, which were, to some extent, subjective. He offered his view of the enemy's strengths and weaknesses, capabilities and possible intentions. Building on past events, the G-2 sought to identify trends in enemy behavior, then extrapolated in order to predict the more or less immediate future.

The product of the staff section regarded as having the best brains in the headquarters, the G-2 account represented a rigorous logic applied to knowledge obtained from observation of the battlefield, interrogation of enemy prisoners of war, and secret sources of information. The interpretation also mirrored, quite unconsciously, the mind-set, that is to say, the current assumptions or the bias, of the key people in the community, the decision makers and their chief assistants and advisers. The assessment therefore more or less reflected the danger of all intelligence reporting, the tendency to find what one wished or expected to see. Listeners and readers always treated the comments with caution.

The First U.S. Army G-2, an especially brilliant officer who was widely admired for his perspicacity, distributed a particularly heady and optimistic estimate of the enemy situation on August 1. His judgment emerged out of the backdrop of Cobra, the attempted assassination of Hitler twelve days earlier, and the general losses suffered by the Germans during the two months of Continental combat. As a result of these circumstances, he had come to doubt whether, he wrote, "the German forces in Normandy can continue for more than four to eight weeks as a military machine. One more heavy defeat such as the recent breakthrough battle which commenced 25 July will most probably result in the collapse of the forces now . . . [in the Avranches area]. Surrender or a disastrous retreat will be the alternative. . . . The current situation may change with dramatic suddenness into a race to reach a chaotic Germany."

In other words, the Germans could hardly last one or two months more. The war in Europe appeared to be as good as won. The dissolution of German cohesion on the battlefield was bound to end quickly in total defeat. All the Allies had to do, the G-2 intimated, was to finish the Germans off. What the Allies had to do, the G-2 implied, was to continue the pressure. He could go no further than to intimate and imply, for the question of how to accomplish the task involved decisions residing in the G-3 or operational realm.

In retrospect, although the perception was quite ahead of the reality, although the Germans on August 1 were far from ready to throw in the towel or give up the ghost a month or two later, in September or in October, the document was remarkably accurate and on the mark. American expectations were usually exaggerated, and the G-2 projections on all levels of command tended consistently to be in advance of actuality and to anticipate coming events long before they occurred. But the report of August 1 fixed accurately the vulnerability of the German forces in Normandy to defeat, as well and specifically around Avranches, where the First U.S. Army responsibility lay.

Already on July 31, Eisenhower was writing to Montgomery, not only to spur Montgomery on, but also to bolster his ego by placing the American success in Cobra within the larger Allied context. "From all reports," Eisenhower said, "your plan continues to develop beautifully. I learn that you have a column in Avranches. This is great news and Bradley must quickly make our position there impregnable. Bradley has plenty of Infantry units to rush into forward areas to consolidate all gains and permit armor to continue thrusting."

Two days later, Eisenhower again communicated with Montgomery. "If my latest reports are correct," he said, "the enemy resistance seems to have disintegrated very materially in the Avranches region. Our armored and mobile columns will want to operate boldly."

The messages were vintage Eisenhower. Encouraging his subordinates, he advocated energy and audacity. Yet he refrained from suggesting where the columns ought to go, what they ought to do, and what purposes they ought to fulfill.

In the fast-moving situation where the Germans had lost control of the events unfolding in the breakout area, the Allies faced the same hazard. High-ranking commanders could hardly keep up with the locations of the leading elements to know what was happening on the front. Without a firm hand to steer the units to certain ends, the offensive growing out of Cobra might explode in all directions and serve no useful purpose.

To orient and marshal the speeding formations toward a meaningful goal, the Allies needed a plan to capitalize specifically on the real world as it then existed. There was no plan because Cobra and its immediate consequences had happened so rapidly. Eisenhower, Montgomery, and Bradley, individually and as an institutional whole, had been unable to cope with the exigency.

Lacking a pattern tailored exactly to the measurements of the moment, they fell back on the preinvasion Overlord planning. Even though the Overlord planners working long before the Channel crossing had been unable to imagine a scene resembling the near-confusion at the beginning of August, nothing else existed to direct the Allied forces.

An Overlord assumption was the necessity to own Brittany, which was to serve as the principal American supply base, and the Breton harbors, which were to become the chief American ports of entry. Brittany and its assets were part of the Overlord lodgment area for reasons of logistics, and the entire lodgment area, the planners felt, had to be in Allied hands before the Allies could venture beyond its boundaries. Thus, in accordance with the Overlord blueprint, while the other armies set about to capture that part of the lodgment area east of Avranches in the ancient provinces of Normandy, Anjou, and Maine, the major portion of Patton's Third Army was to swing to the west and overrun and seize Brittany.

This determined the immediate movements out of the Cotentin. The 4th Armored Division in Avranches and Pontaubault started south to seize Rennes before rushing off to the southwest to take the port of Lorient on the Breton southern shore. Immediately behind it came the 6th Armored Division heading west directly to Brest. Following was a provisional task force of 3,500 men who were to prevent the Germans from demolishing several high trestle bridges on the railroad linking Brest to the interior of France.

Getting these units through the narrow Avranches-Pontaubault corridor in forty-eight hours was quite an accomplishment. Only two main highways led south, and they were sown with mines and littered with dead horses and wrecked vehicles. In some villages, buildings had collapsed and tumbled into the road, and before vehicles could pass, bulldozers had to clear the streets of rubble. All the while, German planes appeared in strength and bombed and strafed the traffic.

A well-organized effort squeezed the forces through the bottleneck. Some division commanders personally directed the flow of vehicles at vital crossroads. Transports moved in accordance with meticulously drawn schedules and timetables. After the two armored divisions and the task force came an infantry division and, to direct the operations in Brittany, Troy Middleton's VIII Corps headquarters. All were part of Patton's Third Army and under Patton's command.

Middleton was a West Pointer who had been the youngest American regimental commander in France in 1918. Afterward, he resigned from the service and eventually became president of Louisiana State University. World War II brought him back to active duty. He led a division in the invasion and campaign of Sicily, then moved to southern Italy for a few weeks until a bad knee required rehabilitation in the United States. When he returned to Europe, he took the VIII Corps through the grueling battle of the hedgerows and into the exciting aftermath.

Big, balky, and imperturbable, bred in the infantry, Middleton was accustomed to conducting orderly operations developed by units in compact formation and pursuing distinct and successive objectives. The slow systematic battle in June and July had deepened his habits. Even before he entered Brittany, he looked ahead to St-Malo, the nearest port city located on the northern shore, and enunciated its capture as his "immediate task."

Patton, in effect, overrode him. He paid no attention to St-Malo, and his orders were silent on the place. Consequently, the subordinate commanders planned to speed past St-Malo, as one of them said in high spirits, "without even looking at it."

A cavalryman, Patton spurned plodding forward, particularly in the existing fluid situation, which offered the opportunity to exploit enemy weakness, opened marvelously long vistas and little opposition, and promised quick and exciting conquest of distant places. Favoring, as he said, "a good plan violently executed *now*" over "a perfect plan next week," Patton regarded warfare as a simple exercise requiring "self-confidence, speed, and audacity." He strode upon the stage at the very moment when he was exactly needed, when everything, at least on the VIII Corps front, was in flux, when rapid decision was the order of the day. No one was more suited by temperament and experience than he to take charge and to impose his will.

Unfortunately, Patton's authority was limited to his army and subject to the supervision of, in order of ascendance, Bradley, Montgomery, and Eisenhower. Whatever Patton did had to be in accord with their view of the scene. However much Patton found his subordinate position galling, he resolved to make the best of the situation and to enjoy the prerogatives and responsibilities of army command.

Even Eisenhower's relegation of Patton to anonymity failed to curb Patton's exuberance. Because the Germans still expected the fictitious "Army Group Patton" to cross the Strait of Dover and invade the Pas-de-Calais, Eisenhower sought to maintain the deception, tricking the Germans into keeping a good part of the Fifteenth Army in the area and far from the combat in Normandy. He ordered the commitment of Patton's Third Army to be kept secret. There was to be no public mention of Patton's entrance into battle. The imposition of press censorship on his name and organization served merely to infect Patton with increased energy. In the doghouse since he had slapped the soldiers in Sicily about a year earlier, in disgrace once again after apparently talking too much in England several months before, Patton was firmly resolved to reestablish his stature as a military genius. The challenge in August sharpened his faculties.

He sent his units into Brittany with a figurative wave of his hand, dispensing with intermediate objectives, routes of advance, boundaries for units, and other usual appurtenances of offensive warfare. For example, standing at a crossroads near Avranches with one of his armored division commanders, Patton put his arm around the officer's shoulder and, speaking of an objective more than two hundred miles distant, said, quite simply, "Take Brest."

His subordinates below Middleton were tank officers who had a close affinity with Patton and his methods. They knew what he wanted. Untouched by the depressing combat in the hedgerows, triumphantly leading the way into Brittany, they joyously pounced on their distant destinations and quickly disappeared from sight and sound in a cloud of dust.

Middleton soon lost touch with them. After a few days, his contact with them was, he admitted, "practically nil." Communications were virtually nonexistent. "The expensive signal equipment," Middleton explained after the war, ". . . was never designed apparently for a penetration and pursuit of a magnitude of the Brittany operation." And, he might have added, its speed.

Having dispatched Middleton and his VIII Corps into Brittany, Patton turned to the next entity available to him. This was Wade Haislip's XV Corps headquarters, which had arrived on the Continent in mid-July. Haislip was a stocky West Pointer who had fought in France in the Great War. He had a deceptively mild manner. Behind the shy and boyish smile was an iron will.

In accordance with existing plans, Haislip was ready to follow Middleton's corps into Brittany. But congestion on the roads matched a certain confusion in command concepts, and Haislip, as late as the morning of August 1, had no clear idea which divisions he was to control and which direction he was to go. At noontime, he had some news. Instead of traveling southwest from Avranches into Brittany, he was to turn toward the southeast. Specifically, he was to plug a gap of spreading dimensions between Middleton's VIII Corps going west and Collins's VII Corps heading to the east.

Haislip had by this time acquired two divisions, one armored, the other infantry. He was to get another infantry division later, but no one knew which. Slow traffic prevented him from moving his armored division through Avranches, but he sent the infantry to blocking positions a dozen miles east of Pontaubault. Haislip thus broadened the Avranches corridor. This, together with short advances made simultaneously by Collins's VII Corps, established a barrier facing east against possible German interference with the American units streaming into Brittany.

On August 2, a contretemps marred the Bradley-Patton relationship. Patton, happy and cheerful to be in the midst of combat again, pursuing his duties with infectious enthusiasm, sincerely admired Bradley's achievement in Cobra. "Bradley certainly has done a wonderful job," Patton informed Eisenhower on July 28. "My only kick," he added, kidding, "is that he will win the war before I get in." Three days later, in a letter to his wife, Patton wrote, "Brad has realy [sic] pulled a great show and should get credit for it."

Now on August 2, Patton ordered a division to cover the VIII Corps flank. At another location and without knowledge of Patton's action, Bradley directed a different division to fulfill the same mission. Bradley thus committed an unwarranted intrusion into Patton's affairs and prerogatives. On the surface, his interference indicated Bradley's loss of confidence in Patton.

When the two officers met that afternoon, Bradley admitted to Patton what he had done and apologized. Patton was taken aback and upset when he learned of Bradley's meddling, but he swallowed hard and said it was okay.

But Bradley's switch of units compounded the state of confusion in the area. The XV Corps headquarters had "no [telephone] wire to either [of its] division[s]." One division had "no wire to anybody." The other seemed "to have wire [only] to VII Corps." And one division was simultaneously and absurdly attached to two corps going in opposite directions.

This was not seriously disruptive, but Patton's discomfort was potentially so. He was unable to choke down his anger completely, and before he could curb his tongue, an impertinent remark slipped out. Forgetting for an instant their new status, Bradley the boss, Patton the subordinate, reverting to their earlier association in Sicily, where such comment was apropos, Patton told Bradley, as Patton recorded in his diary, he "feared he [Bradley] was getting the British complex of over-caution."

The comment stung Bradley, but he said nothing. He was very much aware of having committed an error, a gaffe, and of needing to make amends. As a result, he tended, in the next few days, to listen more sympathetically to Patton's occasional advice and urging.

Patton judged the extent of the German predicament as requiring the Allies to complete the job begun by Cobra, to widen and deepen the devastating effects of the breakout, to dispense with by-the-book caution, and to speed ahead to victory. He was fitted to play such a role. But his place in the chain of command and his extreme care in dealing with Bradley made him hesitate to grasp the reins, even figuratively or behind the scenes.

Alerted by Bradley on August 2 to indications of change in the air, Patton altered Haislip's mission. Instead of holding defensively in place,

Haislip was to embark on a new venture. He was to advance to the southeast, but for the moment Patton was unable to tell him exactly where and how far to go. Conversations and decisions on higher levels were about to transform the shape of the campaign.

The impetus had come late in July from long-range planners at Montgomery's headquarters, a group of senior British and American officers. They were familiar with the Overlord preinvasion plans denoting Brittany as the place for the Third Army commitment. They were aware also of a caveat in those documents. If the Germans were at the point of collapse or about to withdraw from France, the planning papers said, the Allies might well dispense with Brittany altogether. If the war was about to be won, there was no reason to expend energy and resources in pursuit of Brittany, a long-term logistical investment. It would be far bolder as well as more rewarding to drive eastward and obtain the Seine River ports of Le Havre and Rouen.

As the long-range planners studied the German disintegration in the Cotentin, they noted the conditions mentioned in the preinvasion plans. The Germans indeed seemed to be on the verge of collapse or withdrawal from France. In this case, Brittany had lost its importance. A new course was feasible. A single corps with an armored division and three infantry divisions, they reported, "might take about a month to complete the conquest" of Brittany. During this time, the rest of the Allied forces could "round up" the Germans west of the Seine and destroy them inside the lodgment area. With this accomplished, the Allies could head across the Seine River at Paris, scoot through the Paris-Orléans gap, and speed to Germany.

This became the prevailing view, and Eisenhower informed Marshall of it on August 2. Bradley, he wrote, would "so manhandle" the German left flank that "within the next two or three days" the Allies would be able to go wherever they wished. In these circumstances, Eisenhower "consider [ed] it unnecessary to detach any large forces for the conquest of Brittany."

On the following day, Bradley ordered Patton to clear Brittany with "a minimum of forces." The primary mission now was to expand the lodgment area to the east.

Montgomery told Brooke on August 4, "I have turned only one American corps westward into Brittany as I feel that will be enough."

As a consequence, while the other Allied forces drove eastward to crush the Germans, Middleton and his VIII Corps set about to overrun Brittany.

The language of Eisenhower, Bradley, and Montgomery, in recording the diminished value of Brittany, carried a tinge of regret over the size of the forces already committed there. No large forces, a minimum of forces, and only one corps for Brittany, as they said, indicated a subtle wish for even fewer troops in the province. The two armored divisions, the task force, and the infantry division committed in the region totaled more than 50,000 men. They equaled the number of Germans located there, for the motive behind their dispatch had been offensive in nature. These troops were to take the territory in accordance with the Overlord planning.

After the fundamental change in perception and plan, with the major Allied energy now directed to the east, the Allies could have sent a lesser force into Brittany to fulfill, for example, a blocking mission. Unfortunately, the speed of the movement into Brittany had sucked in more troops than were necessary, and it was too late to redress the flow of units. Those streaming westward into Brittany were lost for the main Allied effort east of Avranches.

The place and the time of the basic decision at the highest Allied levels were never altogether clear. Yet whoever made the decision, Eisenhower or, more probably, Montgomery, and perhaps Bradley as adviser on the American role, on August 1, 2, or 3, had been unable to grasp the reins of leadership firmly and in good time. Important combat elements had slipped into Brittany on a wave of misplaced momentum in search of the Overlord lodgment area.

A single unfettered spirit remarked the flaw and tried to remedy the error. He was John Shirley Wood. An athlete endowed with a brilliant mind, Wood had breezed through college at the University of Arkansas and had had a good time as quarterback of the football team. In order to play a few more years, he attended and graduated from the Military Academy at West Point. He had no trouble with his studies and gained the nickname "P," for Professor, because he helped his classmates with their lessons. Somewhat of an eccentric, he maintained this image when he was a student at the Command and General Staff College at Leavenworth—he ostentatiously read a newspaper in class while his instructors lectured. As a tank officer, he became closely associated with Patton. Some thought him to be Patton's most intelligent disciple. He raised and trained his 4th Armored Division to a high pitch of efficiency, then led it effortlessly and effectively in the Cobra breakout.

His troops having taken Avranches and Pontaubault, they covered the forty miles to Rennes on the afternoon of August 1. At the city that evening, the advance guard bumped into solid opposition. Judging the defenses to be too strong for him to penetrate into the capital of Brittany and take control of the important communications hub, Wood radioed Middleton for help. Besieging and reducing an urban center, in Wood's opinion, was hardly a task for an armored division, which was designed for speed and mobility. He needed, he said, an infantry regiment, about 4,000 men, to crack the defenses and seize the place. Middleton agreed and complied with Wood's request.

While waiting for the regiment to arrive on the morning of August 2, Wood conceived a revolutionary idea. His mission, after capturing Rennes, was to head swiftly to the southwest and take the port of Lorient. But obviously, so far as Wood was concerned, the main lines of the campaign in France were bound to develop in the other direction, toward the east. To proceed to the city of Lorient, lying to the southwest, was simply to go in the wrong direction. At Lorient, Wood was sure to confront the same problem as at Rennes. He would be required to undertake street fighting to seize the metropolitan area, again, hardly a proper mission for an armored division. What was more significant, Wood at Lorient was certain to be at a dead end and facing the wrong way, with his back to the real action.

How could he correct the situation? His solution was a flash of genius and at the same time quite simple. Instead of going through Rennes, then swerving to Lorient, Wood determined to swing around the western edge of Rennes. He would thereby cut the many roads into and out of the city and prevent German reinforcement from or escape to the west. He would then continue through the outskirts and cut the southern exits and entrances. At the conclusion of his circling maneuver, with the infantry regiment having by then surely liberated Rennes, Wood's armored division south of the city would be facing east. There he would be poised to drive to such exciting and worthwhile objectives as Angers, Chartres, or the Paris-Orléans gap. How wonderful to be in on the kill!

Careful not to jeopardize the infantry attack on Rennes, Wood embarked at once on this course. On the following day, August 3, in great elation, Wood sent Middleton a detailed picture of his proposal, which naturally modified the existing orders from the headquarters of Bradley's 12th Army Group, Patton's Third Army, and Middleton's VIII Corps.

With the transformation of the campaign becoming clearer and the region east of Avranches emerging as the major place of battle, Middleton found himself in sympathy with Wood's concept. Wood's solution was all the more striking because it was painless. Saying nothing, Middleton let the situation unfold. But on August 4, Patton's chief of staff, Hugh Gaffey, noted the unauthorized location of Wood's division. He pointed

Falaise, where the pocket was supposed to close

Trun, where the pocket closed temporarily

Chambois, where the pocket finally closed

General George C. Marshall, U.S. Army Chief of Staff. The ranking Army officer and the President's closest military adviser, he placed his protégés in the most important American positions of authority and responsibility.

From left: Field Marshal Sir Alan Brooke, Chief of the Imperial British Staff, General Marshall's counterpart, military adviser to the Prime Minister; General Dwight D. Eisenhower, Supreme Commander, Allied Expeditionary Forces, General Marshall's favorite subordinate, the American officer in Europe who made the Anglo-American coalition work; General Sir Bernard L. Montgomery, pro tem Commander of the Allied Ground Forces in Europe, Commanding General, 21 Army Group, the leading British soldier on the Continent, and Field Marshal Brooke's favorite subordinate

Generals Montgomery (*left*) and Eisenhower smiling for the photographers

From left: Elwood "Pete" Quesada, Commanding General, IX U.S. Tactical Air Command, responsible for giving First U.S. Army close air support; Omar N. Bradley, Commanding General of First U.S. Army, later of the 12th U.S. Army Group; William B. Kean, General Bradley's Chief of Staff

From left: Courtney H. Hodges, Omar N. Bradley, George S. Patton, Jr., America's battlefield commanders

The top American commanders in Europe *(from left)*: Eisenhower, Patton, Bradley, Hodges

General H.D.G. Crerar, Commanding General, First Canadian Army

J. Lawton "Lightning Joe" Collins, Commanding General, VII U.S. Corps, here uncharacteristically grim *INFANTRY JOUR.*

Hoyt Vandenberg, Ninth U.S. Air Force

John Shirley "P"(for Professor) Wood, Commanding General, 4th U.S. Armored Division, who was sure that the High Command was winning the war the wrong way

Troy H. Middleton (*left*), Commanding General, VIII U.S. Corps, who struck west into Brittany; Wade H. Haislip, Commanding General, XV U.S. Corps, who drove east to the Seine River

Walton H. Walker, Commanding General,
XX U.S. Corps, who would go anywhere

Leonard T. Gerow, Commanding General,
V U.S. Corps, who couldn't get started

Jacques Leclerc, Commanding General, 2d French Armored Division, who had
Paris on his mind

Roosevelt and Churchill, the Allied leaders who directed the war

Scenes of ruin such as this (and on next page) are typical of the destruction left in Normandy as the Germans were driven out.

out the discrepancy to Patton. Patton's response was categoric: comply with Bradley's 12th Army Group orders, he said. Gaffey then reminded Middleton of Wood's assignment to take Lorient.

According to Max Hastings, Patton was "desperately anxious not to become entangled in a wrangle with Bradley when his own position"— as a consequence of having slapped the soldiers in Sicily and having apparently talked out of turn in England— "remained that of probationer." However much Patton favored getting Wood and his division out of Brittany and involved in the east, he "had no intention of crossing his [Bradley's] wishes." Not directly, at least.

To get Wood turned around and headed for Lorient, Middleton drove forward to see him. When Middleton arrived at Wood's command post, he received a warm welcome. Just as big and burly as Middleton, Wood threw his arms around the corps commander and gave him a bear hug.

"What's the matter?" Middleton asked with dry humor. "Have you lost your division?"

What he meant of course was, did Wood know where his division was, which way it was facing, and where it was supposed to go? Or had the division escaped from Wood's control?

"No!" Wood cried. He knew well where his division was and what it was doing.

The problem was much more serious. Wood was altogether upset. Referring to the high command, Eisenhower, Montgomery, Bradley, and whoever else were making the decisions, calling the shots, and running the campaign, Wood said, "They are winning the war the wrong way."

However much Middleton agreed with Wood, there was nothing to do but get Wood on the road to Lorient. The city, as Wood expected, was well defended. He ringed the landward side of the port and waited for reinforcement or relief. As he had anticipated, he was at a dead end.

Impatient to get going again, Wood on August 6, on the basis of his friendship with Patton, bypassed Middleton—an unusual, even illegal action—and sent a message directly to Patton. "Trust we can turn around," he wired, "and get headed in right direction soon."

Middleton quickly learned of Wood's appeal and understood Wood's anguish. He replied gently that evening. "Dear John," he wrote, "George [Patton] was here this P.M. and made the following decision . . . remain in that vicinity and await orders." He signed the note "Troy."

On the following day, August 7, reading the events of the campaign correctly, Wood implored Middleton again. "We should be allowed . . ." he said, "to hit again in a more profitable direction, namely to Paris."

Patton and Middleton were both working to free Wood from his trap. He and his division were too precious, too efficacious to waste at Lorient. And additional forces were needed on the main battlefront.

On August 8, Middleton, with Patton's explicit permission and Bradley's official approval, asked Wood to move part of his division to the east to take Nantes. Joyously, Wood complied. Five days later, Wood found release. Detached from Middleton's VIII Corps, he finally had the green light to head eastward.

He was lucky. The 6th Armored Division, entering Brittany behind Wood and speeding to Brest, stood similarly around the harbor city with hands figuratively in pockets until the end of the month. Only then, two weeks after Wood escaped from Brittany, did an infantry division arrive at Brest and allow the 6th Armored Division to scurry off, also to the east and toward the main battle.

Sending Wood's armored division to Lorient and "away from the pursuit of a disorganized enemy [in the east]," Wood said many years later, ". . . was one of the great mistakes of the war."

"Looking at it with hindsight," Middleton said long after the war, "Wood was right, of course."

Middleton went on to equivocate. "But," he continued, "the high command was absolutely right in . . . [wanting] the ports" in Brittany.

The last was anything but an objective judgment. The Allied leadership, and more particularly the American commanders, had to make some effort in Brittany. But they committed two errors. They sent too many troops into the province, a useless waste of resources. And they fought a bitter and protracted campaign to gain ports that were never used, a tragic waste of men.

It took two weeks of siege warfare by a reinforced infantry division of more than 20,000 soldiers to seize St-Malo, which was destroyed in the process. It took more than three infantry divisions suffering almost 10,000 casualties in a month-long operation terminating late in September to reduce and capture Brest, also ruined by the fighting and by German demolitions. The task force succeeded in preserving the trestle bridges, but with Brest a field of rubble, the railroad was unnecessary. Nantes, relatively quickly taken, was also battered and unable to discharge vessels. Lorient and St-Nazaire remained under German control, ringed and contained by American troops until the end of the war.

There was no point to rehabilitating the harbors in hand, for Brittany had become a backwater of the war, too distant from the combat action to serve as a means of supply and support. Logistically, the Brittany campaign was a strategic failure. The territory was unnecessary for victory, and the leadership should have avoided committing forces to gain what turned out to be worthless.

Two positive gains resulted. The first was to liberate the province, except for the two ports of Lorient and St-Nazaire, from German occupation. The second was to give meaningful employment to 20,000 or so armed members of the underground Resistance movement, the French Forces of the Interior, who were awaiting the arrival of American units and who then provided them with close and enthusiastic assistance everywhere.

The peripheral campaign in Brittany deprived the main arena to the east of substantial troop elements. For this unacceptable diversion of forces, the unnamed members of the high command, as Wood and Middleton called them, were responsible and to blame.

While the VIII Corps was becoming embroiled in Brittany, while the situation south and east of Avranches remained extremely fluid, the Germans elsewhere in Normandy maintained the battle line they had firmly fastened down. Allied units hammered against German troops who refused to panic or even to give way. Although the Allies made some gains of a few miles during the early days of August, the German defenses remained solid and virtually in place.

Courtney Hodges, who had acceded to the command of the First U.S. Army, found the situation altogether to his liking. No tricky maneuver was necessary or even possible. All he could do was to smash straight ahead. These exertions were so wearing by early August that many units were extremely tired. The troops began looking forward to some rest and, as one division commander said, "hot showers, hot food, USO shows . . . [and] Red Cross doughnut girls." Unfortunately, shortages of new formations and replacements prevented the relief from combat of worn-out units.

Dealing with the distinctly dissimilar conditions along the front, Eisenhower, Montgomery, and Bradley enunciated orally and in fragmentary fashion on August 3 the major points of the new blueprint designed to shape the campaign beyond Cobra. On the following day, August 4, Montgomery issued a full-scale directive formally setting out the Allied course.

He estimated the enemy front to be "in such a state that it could be made to disintegrate completely." As he read the alternatives open to the Germans, "the only hope" they had of saving their armies, he believed, was to initiate an orderly or, as he called it, a "staged withdrawal to the Seine." How could he disrupt the German retrograde movement? By swinging the Allied right flank "round towards Paris," by jostling the Germans and making them retire more quickly than they wished, Montgomery hoped to force them up against the Seine River, where Allied air attacks and French Resistance demolitions had apparently destroyed all the bridges. Unable to cross the river with sufficient speed to escape, the Germans faced potential destruction west of the stream. Best of all, the Allies would come into possession of the Overlord lodgment area, the prerequisite, according to the Overlord planners, for the climactic drive to Germany and victory.

Montgomery envisioned the first step in the projected German withdrawal to be to a line extending generally south from Caen, through Mayenne, to Laval, possibly as far south as Angers. Leaving Bradley to deal with the southern extremity of the supposedly new German defensive line, Montgomery turned his attention to the British and Canadian precincts. The task he set there was to "cut off the enemy now facing [the British] Second Army." Against the broader wish to pin the Germans against the Seine, an action requiring a longer period of time, Montgomery wanted Dempsey and Crerar to encircle a substantial body of German troops between them in the immediate future. The major instrument in this concept was to be a Canadian attack to Falaise. He ordered Crerar to have his First Canadian Army ready to strike toward Falaise "*as early as possible*," italicizing the words to underscore the urgency, "and in any case not later than 8 August."

The most exciting events were occurring in the south, on the Allied right, in the American zone, in Patton's area, where the German front had crumbled. Acting in compliance with Montgomery's outlook expressed on August 3, Bradley ordered Patton to move the bulk of his forces to the southeast of Avranches. Patton was to secure, then penetrate, the bottom part of the north-south German defensive line anticipated by Montgomery. Specifically, Bradley directed Patton to go up against sixty miles of the Mayenne River and take three towns, Mayenne and Laval along the stream, and Angers near the juncture of the Mayenne and Loire rivers. By this advance, Patton was to protect the Allied right flank and expand the Overlord lodgment area to its southern boundary along the Loire.

Complying, Patton told Haislip to move his XV Corps thirty miles to the river line, to cross the Mayenne River where all the bridges but one were demolished, and to seize the towns of Mayenne and Laval. Road congestion prevented Haislip from starting at once, and Patton went to see him again on August 4. He had talked with Bradley and had halfway persuaded Bradley to start thinking of the Paris-Orléans gap as the proper Third Army long-range objective. He therefore told Haislip to be prepared to continue his advance beyond Mayenne and Laval to

Le Mans, a city of 75,000 inhabitants, forty-five miles to the east. Before Haislip could begin to go to Le Mans, Patton had first to have Bradley's okay. If he obtained Bradley's approval, Patton would give Haislip more explicit instructions. In any case, Patton said, "Don't be surprised." Haislip might suddenly receive orders to go eastward, to the northeast, or perhaps to the north. Unlike Montgomery, who envisaged a small and partial encirclement of the Germans in the north, Patton smelled the opportunity to form a more inclusive and much larger trap.

Haislip sent his forces off early on the morning of August 5. "Nobody knows anything about the enemy," his G-2 reported, "because nothing can be found out about them." Lack of knowledge of the enemy hardly restrained Haislip and his men. They proceeded ruthlessly. Before noon, units swept across the single bridge still standing and seized Mayenne. Early on the following morning, other formations took Laval.

As soon as Mayenne fell, Patton asked Bradley for permission to go on to Le Mans. Bradley hesitated. This was moving a little too fast for his liking. But with Patton's urging and his remark on caution sticking in his craw, Bradley granted approval. Patton passed the word to Haislip.

Haislip spurred his troops forward. Like Patton, he understood the advantages of speed and daring. To his subordinate commanders, Haislip announced, "Push all personnel to the limit of human endurance." If the word "personnel" seemed impersonal and out of place, perhaps it was because Haislip's previous post had been as War Department G-1, the assistant chief of staff for personnel. His division commanders and their troops knew what he wanted, and they responded. Without stopping, against the barest of opposition, the XV Corps barreled down the roads toward Le Mans.

Patton meanwhile was trying to fulfill the remainder of Bradley's instructions. To proceed south to Angers and the Loire River, Patton called upon his next corps component awaiting commitment to battle. This was the XX Corps headquarters, and Patton at first set Angers as the corps objective. But as Patton talked Bradley into letting him send Haislip on to Le Mans, he persuaded Bradley to allow him to order the XX Corps across the Mayenne River near Angers and conduct a parallel drive to the east. To Bradley, the important function of this advance was to protect Haislip's southern flank. To Patton, who was trying to wheedle Bradley into designating the Paris-Orléans gap as the eventual Third Army objective, the ultimate goal was to dispense with Angers and the Loire River and to have the XV and XX Corps both rush eastward side by side at breakneck speed to get behind the German armies and impose complete chaos on them.

Unfortunately for Patton's desires, two things interfered. Bradley insisted on having the towns of Nantes and Angers to augment the safety and security of the Allied flank at the Loire River. And the XX Corps had no troops. No combat unit was available for immediate assignment to the corps.

The best that could be done was to seize upon the 5th Infantry Division at the other end of the American zone. It had been pinched out of action by the convergence of corps boundaries and was in a rest area. An hour before dawn on August 4, word came to move to Avranches. The men quickly packed and departed on a road march lasting three days. Just before noon on August 7, the advance elements of the division entered a designated assembly area forty miles south of Avranches.

The XX Corps mission consequently remained unfilled. Capitalizing on the occasion, Patton eventually talked Bradley into allowing him to bring Wood's armored division out of Brittany from Lorient to Nantes. By this action, Patton accomplished part of Bradley's wishes and also liberated Wood from a static mission and made him available to act in the main arena. At the same time, Patton came closer to persuading Bradley to recognize the Paris-Orléans gap as the Third Army objective.

Montgomery issued another directive on August 6 and emphasized his thinking of two days earlier. The Germans, he said, had dismal choices to make. If they held on the right, in the British-Canadian area, they offered the Allies the opportunity to swing around their left and to cut off their escape. If they weakened their forces on the right to bolster their positions against the Americans, they gave the Allies access to the shortest route to the Seine River. In either case, they faced the prospect of being destroyed west of the Seine.

The Allied objective emerging in Montgomery's view was the Seine River, and to get there he wanted the following action. Crerar's First Canadian Army was to take Falaise, then swing east toward the Seine River. Dempsey's Second British Army was to move southeast, then east through Argentan and head for the Seine. As for Bradley's 12th U.S. Army Group, Montgomery left the details to Bradley. He ordered simply a thrust to the east and northeast to Paris.

Montgomery's gesture of leaving the American steps to Bradley was important for Bradley's self-esteem. He specified Alençon, lying to the east, as the next objective of Courtney Hodges and the First Army. Such an advance would parallel the surge of Haislip's XV Corps, which Patton had sent rushing toward Le Mans.

Some American G-2s had noticed some disconcerting signs among the Germans during the past three days. These indications seemed to portend, but only vaguely, German preparations for a counterattack. No one paid much attention to the mild warnings. Such a course of action appeared to be madness. Besides, everything was going beautifully. The end of the war seemed to have come within reach.

Patton especially was feeling mellow. He was conducting the kind of warfare he preferred. He seemed to be influencing Bradley toward his views. Everything was going as he wished. Less than a week after the entrance of his Third Army into battle, his elements were kicking up a storm in three widely separated places—Middleton's VIII Corps in Brittany to the west, Haislip's XV Corps moving across the Mayenne River toward Le Mans in the east, and the XX Corps, as soon as units became available, about to go to Angers and the Loire in the south.

After dinner on the evening of August 6, no doubt enjoying a cigar and perhaps a snifter of calvados, Patton dictated to his male secretary, a warrant officer, a letter to an old friend, Kenyon Joyce, a cavalry officer who had been Patton's superior before the war and who was then commanding a corps in the Pacific Northwest. Referring to his Third Army, Patton said, "We are having one of the loveliest battles you ever saw. It is a typical cavalry action in which, to quote the words of the old story, 'The soldier went out and charged in all directions at the same time, with a pistol in each hand, and a sabre in the other.' "

Patton chuckled over the picture brought to mind.

That was about when, as G.I.'s used to say, all hell broke loose. Disregarding Montgomery's logic, the Germans, instead of withdrawing from Normandy, turned and sprang at the Americans.

PART IV

THE ENCIRCLEMENT

HAISLIP'S SWERVE TO THE LEFT
(FROM LE MANS)

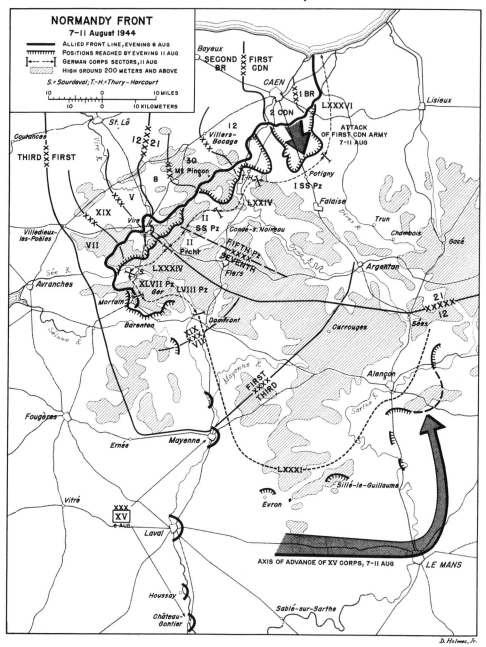

NORMANDY FRONT
7–11 August 1944

ALLIED FRONT LINE, EVENING 6 AUG
POSITIONS REACHED BY EVENING 11 AUG
GERMAN CORPS SECTORS, 11 AUG
HIGH GROUND 200 METERS AND ABOVE

S.= Sourdeval; T.-H.= Thury - Harcourt

10   10 MILES
10   0   10 KILOMETERS

Bayeux

SECOND   FIRST
BR   CDN

CAEN

Lisieux

1 BR

2 CDN

LXXXVI

ATTACK
OF FIRST CDN ARMY
7–11 AUG

St. Lô

12   21

THIRD   FIRST

Coutances

12   21

Villers-
Bocage

30
Mt Pinçon

8

Potigny

I SS Pz

T.-H.

Falaise

LXXIV

Trun

Chambois

Gacé

XIX

V

Vire

Villedieux-
les-Poêles

VII

II
SS Pz

Condé-s. Noireau

FIFTH Pz.

SEVENTH

II
Pzcht

Flers

Argentan

LXXXIV

XLVII Pz
ger. LVIII Pz

Avranches

Mortain

Barenton

Damfront

XIX
VII

Carrouges

Sées

21
12

Alençon

Mayenne R.

FIRST
THIRD

Séé R.

Seiune R.

Fougères

Ernée

Mayenne

LXXXI

Sillé-le-Guillaume

Vitré

XXX
XV
6 AUG

Evron

Sarthe

Laval

AXIS OF ADVANCE OF XV CORPS, 7–11 AUG

LE MANS

Houssay

Château-
Gontier

Sablé-sur-Sarthe

D. Holmes, Jr.

CHAPTER 12

The Mortain Counterattack

THE GERMAN GENERALS WERE no less professional than Montgomery. Their training, experience, and outlook gave them much the same military perceptions. They too favored a withdrawal from Normandy and from France.

Hitler disagreed. He decided otherwise. The solution he imposed was unorthodox, but hardly mad. His concept contained a well-reasoned logic.

Tormented by the disloyalty to his person and leadership in the July 20 putsch and fearful of a widespread circle of plotters, Hitler ever more distrusted his military men, particularly those in France. Increasingly, it appeared to him, he had to direct the war himself.

As he viewed the battlefields ringing Germany toward the end of July, he saw Normandy as the most immediate problem. He could do little in Finland and the Balkans, which he was about to lose. He had started work on a new defensive line from East Prussia to the Carpathians to slow and halt the Soviet advance. His forces in Italy were tying down numerically superior Allied contingents. The most pressing concern was France.

The obvious step, to withdraw, presented considerable disadvantages. Retiring would jeopardize the German armed forces, for their dependence on horse-drawn transport made them less mobile than the Allies and consequently vulnerable to mechanized pursuit. Pulling back from the rocket bases in the Pas-de-Calais must hamper the effect of the so-called miracle weapons. Giving up France was to expose Germany to immediate Allied invasion.

Furthermore, no prepared positions existed in the rear. Where could the troops move back to? The deep bends and twists made the Seine River difficult, even impossible, to defend. In contrast, the Somme-Marne-Saône river and the Albert Canal–Meuse River waterway behind it, both anchored on the Vosges Mountains near Switzerland, were excellent barriers, although unmanned. Best of all, the West Wall, which the Allies called the Siegfried Line, was the obvious place to stop an Allied incursion into Germany. Neglected for four years and partially dismantled of its guns, the belt of fortifications required repair and rearmament. Hitler ordered the West Wall strengthened at once.

Needing from six to ten weeks, according to his calculations, to place defenses behind the front and also to complete new production and training schedules, Hitler chose to stabilize the conditions in Normandy, at least temporarily, and perhaps longer. Because other Allied landings on the Continent now seemed out of the question, he could concentrate his efforts on the existing front. The lack of major ports, in Hitler's view, was the weakest segment of the Allied achievement. He therefore reaffirmed his program of naming major ports as fortress cities—Dunkirk, Calais, Boulogne, and Le Havre along the Channel coast, and those immediately threatened in Brittany, St-Malo, Brest, Lorient, and St-Nazaire—all to be defended, he instructed, "to the last man, to the last cartridge" and destroyed in the process.

He told Kluge on August 1 to forget the Americans entering Brittany. There was no way of stopping them anyway, and besides, the fortress policy would keep them from seizing the ports they were after. To reestablish the conditions of the static warfare in June and July, Hitler charged Kluge with preventing the Allies from moving eastward to the Seine River. While holding firmly in place all along the front he was to prepare a bold offensive thrust. By striking to the west to Avranches, Kluge was to rebuild the German left flank. He was to reattach and reanchor the flank on the Cotentin coast. He was thus to restore a cohesive front firmly tied down at both ends, at Avranches and near Caen.

Kluge had no reserve to carry out his mission, for all the forces in Normandy were already engaged. But six divisions were traveling to the battleground, one just arriving, two crossing the Seine River, two coming from southern France, and one under way from the Pas-de-Calais. These additional units allowed Kluge to gather the necessary power for the blow.

Having informed Kluge informally of what he wished, Hitler issued his official order on August 2. He specified Avranches as the goal, nothing more. During the next few days, Hitler expanded his idea into a somewhat grandiose plan, at least a two-step venture to seize Avranches, then turn north to tear the Americans apart.

To Kluge and his major subordinate commanders, the Germans had a good chance of recapturing Avranches. There could be little hope of holding the town indefinitely, much less of swinging northward and launching an offensive sweep. In any event, a twenty-mile surge to Avranches had its positive aspects. It would divert the Americans from important supply bases, mainly of ammunition and gasoline, around Alençon and Le Mans, both of which were threatened by Haislip's advance to the east. The Germans had to act quickly before their positions disintegrated under Allied pressure. For this reason, except around Avranches, their defenses remained strong and unyielding.

Kluge assembled four panzer divisions. Three were to jump off abreast, roll through the town of Mortain, and proceed as far as they could. When the initial momentum ran out, the fourth, immediately behind as an exploiting force, was to go through the leading elements and plunge ahead the rest of the way.

What the Americans later called the Mortain counterattack and the Germans referred to as the Avranches counterattack started in the early minutes of August 7. In the darkness, German tanks rolled toward Mortain.

A small town then of 1,600 inhabitants, Mortain is located in wooded highland and broken terrain sometimes called "*la suisse normande*," Norman Switzerland, a region of narrow, winding roads and steep inclines. Mortain itself sits at the foot of a rocky eminence rising to the east. From the top of this hill, called 317 after its height in meters, the bay of Mont-St-Michel, twenty miles to the west, is visible on clear days.

A division of Collins's VII Corps had entered Mortain on August 3. When Collins came to see the place soon afterwards, he pointed and said to the division commander, "Ralph, be sure to get Hill 317."

"Joe," he replied, "I already have it."

Three days later, on August 6, Collins moved this division from Mortain to Mayenne, there to attack eastward to Alençon in a parallel movement north of Haislip's effort to Le Mans. Replacing the departing troops in Mortain that day was the 30th Division.

Already a veteran outfit, the 30th Division had fought in the battle of the hedgerows, received most of the short bombs in the two days of the Cobra bombardment, and led the infantry advance through St-Gilles in the Cobra target area. Having suffered heavy casualties, the division was pulled out of the line toward the end of July. The troops had ridden to the rear and entered a rest area, where they took showers, exchanged their clothing for new uniforms, played ball, and relaxed. They had also welcomed 800 replacements. The new men were hardly settled in, adjusted, and acclimated when orders abruptly canceled the rear-area stay. Although two of the nine infantry battalions were absent on other duties, thus making the division understrength, the rest of the soldiers picked up their things and mounted trucks and other vehicles for the ride to Mortain on August 6.

Traffic snarls held up movement, and the troops arrived in town late that afternoon. The long road march had tired them. They had no maps of the new area and no time for reconnaissance, thus little knowledge of where the adjacent American units or the enemy were. The soldiers dropped into shallow foxholes of the departed men. The incoming artillery battalions took the positions already established. The signal units assumed the existing telephone-wire nets and used them, but they were so unfamiliar with the system that they were unable to repair breaks and eventually they had to lay their own wires. At eight P.M., August 6, the division commander, Leland Hobbs, took responsibility for the Mortain area.

Four hours later the Germans struck. The effort was somewhat ragged, hardly well massed and coordinated. Only three of the six designated assault groups jumped off on time. Even so, they attained surprise. Encircling Hill 317 occupied by nearly 700 Americans, about seventy panzers overran several roadblocks on the edge of town, drove through Mortain, and headed west. By noontime they had penetrated the American line for a distance of six miles. The attack then came to a stop. Committing the fourth and exploiting division had no effect.

Despite initial confusion, the Americans at Mortain stood their ground. Fighting out of unfamiliar positions, they stemmed the German advance. Artillery fires, effectively called by forward observers on Hill 317, and air support, particularly from rocket-firing RAF Typhoons and Hurricanes, compelled the Germans to halt and throw camouflage nets over their vehicles and to dig foxholes in the fields.

The 30th Division sustained about 600 casualties that day. Leland Hobbs, who had been an outstanding football lineman at West Point, was touched by and proud of his men's performance. "There were many heroes today," he said, "both living and dead." Hill 317, which he called "the key to the whole area," remained in American hands even though the Germans tried repeatedly to storm the surrounded height. Of the seventy German tanks in the initial penetration, only about thirty were still operating at nightfall.

Kluge had that morning issued a stirring order of the day. "The decision in the battle of France," he announced, "depends on the success of the attack. . . . [We have] a unique opportunity, which will never return, to drive into an extremely exposed enemy area and thereby to change the situation completely."

It was true. Near Mortain was an important American complex of supply installations. If the Germans overran and destroyed this logistical base, they would nullify the effect of Cobra. Furthermore, taking Avranches would cut off the Pontaubault corridor and separate the First and Third U.S. armies.

American G-2s began to appreciate the German thrust, as one report read, as "a major counterattack." Bradley in effect took control of the First Army from Courtney Hodges and attached all nearby divisions, a total of seven, plus an eighth alerted for additional reinforcement if necessary, to Collins's VII Corps and allowed Collins to coordinate the defense.

Hitler was profoundly disappointed. He had expected, he said, "to throw the Americans into the sea." By afternoon, having sought a scapegoat, he fixed the failure on Kluge and castigated Kluge's poor judgment, unnecessary haste, and utter carelessness. There seemed to be no alternative but for Hitler himself to take overt charge.

Categorically, he ordered the effort continued with a larger force pressing forward aggressively. "I command the attack to be prosecuted with daring recklessness to the sea"—to Avranches. Kluge was to take three panzer divisions out of the front facing the British and Canadians "regardless of risk" and send them to Mortain to join the elements already engaged. Kluge was to disrupt the American advance "by a thrust into the deep flank and rear of the enemy." The whole future of the campaign, Hitler said, depended on success. "Greatest daring, determination, imagination," Hitler insisted, "must give wings to all echelons of command. Each and every man must believe in victory. Cleaning up in rear areas and in Brittany can wait until later."

To Kluge, the attack had completely bogged down. There was little point to prosecute the venture further. It was better to withdraw. Holding the four panzer divisions in and around Mortain made him uneasy, for they occupied a salient, a bulge, and were thus exposed to flank attacks and eventual encirclement. The loss to the Americans that day of the town of Vire, twenty miles north of Mortain, heightened his concern. But the most troubling part of Hitler's harangue was his instruction to divert forces from the Falaise area, where the Canadians seemed to be building up their strength.

Dispirited, Kluge admitted his pessimism to one of his subordinate commanders that afternoon. "I foresee that the failure of this attack [to Avranches]," he said, "can lead to collapse of the entire Normandy front, but the order [from Hitler] is so unequivocal that it must be obeyed." He directed three panzer divisions to move out of the British-Canadian area and to head for Mortain during the night.

Kluge's anxiety became acute shortly before midnight, when he learned of an immense aerial bombardment along the road to Falaise. The bombing presaged a full-scale Canadian attack. Kluge therefore needed all the units he had in the area for defense. One of the three divisions he had ordered to depart for Mortain had already left the Falaise sector. Kluge canceled the movement of the other two. Continuing the attack to Avranches, as Hitler wished, would have to wait. The Germans could hardly afford to lose Falaise.

CHAPTER 13

The Canadian Attack

THE ATTACK TOWARD FALAISE on the night of August 7 was a major Canadian operation. Given the felicitous though accidental timing of the effort, twenty-four hours after the Mortain counterattack, the blow promised to be one of the most significant actions of the Normandy campaign. Unfortunately, the Canadian military experience during the interwar years and immediately thereafter conditioned the event and blemished the results.

In World War I, Canada had placed four elite divisions in France and grouped them into a Canadian corps commanded by a Canadian officer. The troops distinguished themselves at Ypres, Vimy Ridge, Passchendaele, along the Somme, and elsewhere, and gained the enviable reputation of being first-rate soldiers.

The operational skill and expertise amassed on the Western Front largely vanished afterwards. According to R. H. Roy, neglect of the military was a Canadian tradition, and the armed forces "barely managed to exist" during the two decades following the Great War. The emphasis was on the militia, "the amateur soldier who trains in his spare time." As John A. English was written, "The long legacy of Canadian institutional neglect of the essential elements of the profession of the arms could not be easily or quickly overcome" in World War II.

When the country followed Britain and entered the conflict early in September 1939, Canada was totally unprepared to wage combat. The

Army consisted of sizable reserve forces but less than 5,000 full-time regulars. The necessity of expanding the Army at once was nowhere debated, although the purpose of enlargement, whether for home defense or for overseas commitment, was bitterly argued. Proponents of the former were called isolationists and obstructionists, while advocates of the latter were charged with being warmongers. Prime Minister Mackenzie King seemed to equivocate on what Canada's role in the struggle ought to be and offered less than all-out guidance and support to the military. Nonetheless, a division composed of volunteers sailed for the United Kingdom in November. In command was Andrew G. L. McNaughton, Canada's most respected and best-known military man.

McNaughton had seen action in World War I as a gunner and was twice wounded and twice mentioned in dispatches. Chief of the General Staff from 1929 to 1935, he was headstrong, crusty, and uncompromising. According to Stephen Harris, he "cultivated and manipulated friendship with senior bureaucrats and politicians" and wielded extraordinary power. His main interests were technological and educational, and under his aegis, knowledge of battlefield techniques declined.

Training his men in England, McNaughton was alerted for action in Norway in the spring of 1940, then warned of commitment in France to oppose German blitzkrieg in the West. He finally received word to ship some Canadian units to Brittany and lower Normandy. The troops hastily crossed the Channel, but before they could assemble and deploy against the Germans, the campaign was over. The Germans had won. The Canadians retired from the Continent without engaging the enemy.

With the Germans threatening to invade the British Isles, McNaughton commanded a corps of several Commonwealth divisions in defense. He was difficult to work with and overly sensitive to imagined slights against Canada. Montgomery came to detest him, and many British officials disliked him. As more Canadian troops arrived in England, the authorities transferred McNaughton to a strictly Canadian position, and he moved up to corps, then army, level, although Brooke thought him "quite incompetent to command an army."

The soldiers were, by this time, as Colonel Charles P. Stacey has written, "tired of inaction," upset by their "static employment," and envious of other Commonwealth forces, Australians, New Zealanders, and South Africans, who had fought against the enemy. The long inactivity of the Canadians in England undermined their morale. McNaughton, "after nearly three years of disappointment and frustration," was quick to endorse the Dieppe operation in August 1942. The tragic end of this venture gave McNaughton the reputation of having poor tactical judgment.

Despite a widespread wish to get Canadians into action as soon as possible—in order to give them combat experience, to rebuild their self-respect and confidence, and to provide a claim to some influence in the postwar world—McNaughton, much like Pershing in World War I, argued vehemently for committing all the Canadian contingents together as a single national entity, presumably in the invasion and campaign of northwest Europe. Over what Brooke, according to Carlo D'Este, called McNaughton's "fanatic antagonism," the Canadian government decided to have formations participate in the Sicilian operations.

A Canadian division fighting there under Montgomery was good. The troops made an excellent impression. "The Canadians," Montgomery wrote to Brooke, ". . . are very willing to learn and they learn fast." Guy Simonds, the division commander, functioned extremely well. McNaughton wished to visit the Canadian troops during the campaign, but Montgomery refused him permission to land until the combat had ended.

Despite talk of bringing the Canadians back from Sicily to the United Kingdom and once again uniting all the forces, additional units went to Italy and fought in Montgomery's Eighth Army. In December 1943, in exasperation and protest, along with some governmental pressure, McNaughton resigned.

It took three months to choose McNaughton's successor. In March 1944, rather late to prepare the troops for Continental operations, Henry Crerar took his place. According to a variety of Canadian observers, Crerar was neither sound nor expert. He had served as an artillery battery commander in World War I. Chief of the General Staff in 1940, he resigned the office in order to command the I Canadian Corps headquarters in England. Sent to Italy in 1943, he was there for five months without participating in combat, his corps headquarters held in reserve. Montgomery suggested his taking command of the Canadian division to gain some battle experience, but Crerar refused to step down from his corps.

Jealous and envious of Simonds's success and high standing with senior British officers, Crerar, as several contemporaries and historians have noted, schemed to remove Simonds from command. When Crerar had assumed command to the First Canadian Army, he decided to keep Simonds, for Simonds was too young to threaten Crerar's primacy and was, besides, an abler practitioner, better versed than he, in the business of war. An uneasy relationship developed. Simonds often accompanied

Crerar to conferences at Montgomery's headquarters, not only to be sure of understanding what was required but also to suggest improvements in ideas and plans.

Simonds, who was forty-one years old in 1944, was, according to J. S. McMahon, Canada's "most competent field general." English by birth, Canadian by upbringing, he graduated from the Royal Military College of Canada in Kingston, Ontario. With his beret, heavy eyebrows, piercing eyes, small clipped mustache, firm cleft chin, Oxford accent, and polite manners, he was dashing. He had the bearing and the look of what the military approvingly call command presence. A "military innovator, a perfectionist, and a ruthless authoritarian," he was also hot tempered, cold, silent, grumpy, intolerant of others' faults, and less than a generous man. He was, Dominick Graham has said, "by no means popular in the Canadian Army, although admired." A lieutenant general, he commanded the II Canadian Corps headquarters.

"Montgomery much preferred Simonds [over Crerar]," Dominick Graham has written, "but as the British had, quite rightly, got rid of McNaughton, they obviously could not do the same to Crerar, and so he survived although Montgomery found him tiresome."

Canadian units had been in combat from the beginning of Overlord. The 3rd Canadian Division landed on Juno Beach on D day. After hard fighting on the approaches to Caen, Canadian soldiers, together with British troops, entered and liberated part of the city a month later.

Immediately thereafter, on July 11, Simonds's II Canadian Corps headquarters became operational in Normandy under Dempsey's Second British Army. Simonds took responsibility for the area astride the Caen–Falaise road. His troops captured the rest of Caen south of the Orne River during Goodwood.

On July 25, the day that Cobra started in earnest, Simonds's corps attacked down the Caen–Falaise road. The battle lasted throughout the day, but the Canadians made no progress. "By any measurement," John A. English has written, the operation "was an unmitigated tactical debacle and Simonds was obviously deeply upset about it." The Canadian soldiers were brave, but they were in large measure badly led on the battalion and regimental levels.

Crerar also made his entrance into combat on the same day. His first Canadian Army headquarters had become operational two days earlier, on July 23. Seeking to break Crerar in gradually, Montgomery put him in charge of a small front held by a single British corps on the extreme left of the Allied dispositions. Montgomery hoped to have Crerar learn much from his subordinate corps commander, J. T. Crocker, who was sound and solid, one of the best. For his initial assignment Crerar was to perform a minor task. He was to make a limited advance, a small push forward, to cover Caen's port of Ouistreham and permit its safe use.

The attempt fizzled as Crerar floundered and bore out Montgomery's unflattering appraisal of his capabilities. Instead of working carefully with Crocker, Crerar became embroiled with him in immediate misunderstanding. As John A. English had detailed, Crerar was inflexible and overbearing. He accused Crocker of insubordination. According to Crerar, Crocker, whether for personal reasons or "because of the fact I am a Canadian . . . resented being placed under my command and receiving any directions from me" and consequently displayed neither "tact nor desire to understand my views."

Montgomery had to intervene to straighten out and smooth over the uncomfortable matter. He wrote to Brooke on July 25, "Harry Crerar has started off his career . . . by thoroughly upsetting everyone; he had a row with Crocker the first day, and asked me to remove Crocker." Hoping to let Crerar settle in and improve gradually, Montgomery gave him a vague assignment—"to keep the Boche worried" by forays, incursions, and raids.

"Looking at Canadian . . . performance in Normandy up to the end of July 1944," John A. English has concluded, "it would seem fair to say that the lives of many soldiers were unnecessarily cast away. . . . The responsibility must rest with the high command."

Montgomery extended Crerar's front on July 31 to include Simonds's II Corps. On these two officers, who showed "a marked disparity in their operational abilities" and who harbored "residual tensions between" them, Canadian military fortunes depended.

On August 4, Montgomery ordered Crerar to "break through the German positions astride the road Caen–Falaise," drive eighteen miles to Falaise, cut off enemy forces facing Dempsey's Second British Army, and unhinge and hasten the German withdrawal from Normandy expected by Montgomery. The task was difficult because of the terrain and the German defenses in depth. The highway to Falaise is straight for the first fifteen miles, rising gradually across acres of wheat fields broken by an occasional village, a clump of woods, an unexpected orchard. The open country, useful for tank operations, also offered excellent fields of fire for defensive weapons.

Crerar sought a way to get infantry through the formidable enemy defenses on the Falaise plain and found a gunner's solution, the close integration of fire and movement, that is, an infantry advance closely coordinated with artillery shelling.

Simonds was more imaginative. Concerned about how to get tanks as well as foot soldiers through the massive German gun screen, he devised a clever and somewhat complicated maneuver. He decided to attack at night in order to rob the enemy artillery of accuracy; he would dispense with an artillery preparation in order to gain surprise; and he would move infantrymen in armored carriers in order to protect them against enemy fires as they accompanied the tanks forward. Participating in the endeavor were three infantry and two armored divisions, plus two armored brigades. As in the Caen, Goodwood, and Cobra operations, heavy bombers were to deliver a massive effort to start the attack.

At 11:00 P.M., August 7, a total of 1,020 heavy bombers dropped almost 3,500 tons of bombs on the flanks of the projected ground assault. Fighter-bombers then delivered high-explosive and fragmentation bombs on the Germans. Altogether, 720 artillery barrels shelled the enemy and lighted the battlefield with flares. Bobors machine guns fired streams of tracer bullets to mark the direction of advance. Searchlights sent beams into the clouds, which deflected the rays to the ground and thus provided what was called "artificial moonlight."

On the heels of the major bombardment, at 11:30, the ground attack started as two armored brigades moved forward across the line of departure three miles south of Caen. In the lead were tanks with flailing mechanisms, huge turning wheels swinging chains to detonate mines laid in the ground. Then came eight columns of tanks, each consisting of four tanks abreast, a total of thirty-two tanks side by side across the front, to roll over and flatten whatever obstacles existed to bar their progress. Behind them, infantrymen rode as passengers in armored personnel carriers, closed wagons protected by light armor, their job to detruck when necessary to mop up Germans surviving the bombardment and the tank advance.

The bombs and the shells, together with the tank movements, created great clouds of dense smoke and dust, which combined with a heavy ground mist to obscure landmarks. Despite the tracer bullets and the artificial moonlight, the tankers had to drive in low gear, searching their way. Many became bewildered and wandered off course. Collisions occurred.

Yet the weight of the destructive forces from the air and from the ground, as well as the impetus of the tank-infantry pressure, gained the Canadians three miles during the hours of darkness. At dawn of August 8, the troops were through the main line of German defense. Shortly thereafter, although the road to Falaise lay open, the exertion came to a halt.

To get the endeavor started again, Simonds ordered his two armored divisions, one Canadian, the other Polish, both inexperienced in combat, to come forward. They were to pass through the leading formations on narrow fronts at 2:00 P.M. and press on to Falaise, fifteen miles away. To provide an initial push, Simonds asked for a bombardment at 12:30 P.M.

The Poles, equipped and trained by the British, had arrived in England by a variety of routes. Many had escaped from Poland individually and in small groups after the debacle in 1939, some through Norway, others by way of Hungary, still others elsewhere. Quite a few had crossed the Channel after the French surrender in 1940. Several volunteer units formed in the Middle East had traveled by ship to the United Kingdom. On February 21, 1941, the 1st Polish Armored Division came into existence in London, with 16,000 effectives, 4,500 vehicles of all sorts, and 380 tanks.

Motivated by a fierce pride and an intense patriotism, the Polish soldiers wished ardently to prove their efficiency and their effectiveness in battling the Germans, not only to avenge their defeat in Poland in 1939 but also to bring their country back into existence. They had role models in Italy, where a Polish corps under Wladyslaw Anders serving in the Eighth British Army had thrilled the Allied world in May 1944 by driving the Germans from the virtually impregnable height of Monte Cassino. Hoping to emulate the exploits of their compatriots in Italy, the Polish armored division under Stanislaw Maczek crossed the Channel and debarked at Arromanches and Courselles on August 2. The Polish insurrection in Warsaw was just beginning.

Both armored divisions, Canadian and Polish, entering combat on August 8, committed the mistakes normal to inexperienced and unblooded units. In the morning, as they moved forward to the front, the hesitations and confusions of troops who had yet to learn and to become accustomed to the sights and sounds of warfare produced immense traffic congestion. General George Kitching, commander of the 4th Canadian Armoured Division, cited the slowness of both divisions to get to the start line and to set up their artillery. Some units got lost and wound up on the wrong terrain features.

As they struggled to pass through the leading elements, then to push on to Falaise, 492 Allied bombers dropped loads along the road to Falaise and tried to facilitate the ground progress. Some bombers released prematurely and struck both divisions, killing 65 soldiers, wounding 250, and disorganizing the attack. The units on both sides of the highway to Falaise could hardly get started in the afternoon, and the Germans restructured their defenses, once more barring the way to

Falaise. Crerar blamed the Poles for the breakdown of the effort. By nightfall, he said, the Poles had advanced "not more than a few hundred yards."

Simonds ordered both divisions to continue through the night. The ensuing struggle during the hours of darkness, as well as throughout August 9, carried the corps forward a few miles. On August 10, the attack "sputtered out."

According to Chester Wilmot, an Australian war correspondent sympathetic to Commonwealth forces, "The evidence suggests that the thrust from the north was not pressed with sufficient speed and strength." As for Kitching, he blamed the Poles. They hardly moved, he said, and were of no help. Because negative sentiments among Allies were hardly a monopoly of the British and Americans, Kitching added, "I formed a poor opinion of the Poles."

The offensive was deemed "a failure." Despite superiority in air and artillery, the five divisions and the two armored brigades numbering a total of 600 tanks were unable to handle two depleted German divisions equipped with a total of 60 tanks and tank destroyers. Falaise lay more than a dozen miles to the south.

The disappointment on the Canadian side notwithstanding, the Germans were pessimistic and somber. Kluge spoke on the telephone at nine P.M. on August 9 with the commander of the Falaise sector. "We didn't expect this to come so soon," Kluge said, "but I can imagine that it was no surprise to you."

"No," came the mournful reply. "I have always awaited it and looked toward the morrow with a heavy heart."

Kluge could think of nothing to say to raise his spirits.

CHAPTER 14

The Short Hook

WHILE THE CANADIANS SLUGGED down the road toward Falaise on August 8, the Americans continued to battle the Germans at Mortain, trying to keep them from breaking through to Avranches. Leland Hobbs, alternately elated and depressed, was cheerful in the afternoon. "We are holding and getting in better shape all the time," he informed Joe Collins. "It was precarious for a while." He continued earnestly, "We are doing everything in God's power to hold."

The danger persisted. Those in the midst of the fighting called combat a matter of "infiltration and counter infiltration" and "a seesawing activity" with "minor penetrations by both sides." A 30th Division staff officer asked a regimental commander on the telephone, "What does the situation look like down there?" The reply he received was, "Looks like hell. We are just mingled in one big mess, our CP [Command Post] is getting all kinds of fire, [German] tanks within 500 yards of us."

From the American point of view, the situation was improving, though to what extent was unclear. Could the Germans create more damage? Or had they been stopped? From most indications, the counterattack had "apparently been contained." Even though Bradley seemed to be confident of Collins's ability to smother the Germans at Mortain, he was glad to have insurance from Eisenhower, who was visiting Bradley that day. If the Germans advanced and drove a wedge between Patton's and Hodges's forces, thereby cutting their supply lines, Eisenhower promised to nourish both armies by air shipments.

On the other hand, if the Americans had halted the Germans, what appeared positively exhilarating was the opportunity to surround the German forces in Normandy. By pushing westward toward Avranches, the Germans had, as a periodic report stated, "incurred the risk of encirclement from the South and North."

Before the Mortain attack, Patton had expected the Allies to outrun the Germans and to outmaneuver them so as to expose them to partial or full-scale encirclement. Haislip's drive to the east—his corps was approaching Le Mans—had moved the Americans eighty-five air miles southeast of Avranches, around the German left flank, in the incredibly short duration of a week. About to capture Le Mans, Haislip would then be seventy-five miles short of the Paris-Orleans gap farther to the east. Few Germans barred the way. To Patton, sprinting to Orleans would present a marvelous prospect. Turning north from Orleans to Paris would quickly liberate the capital, the most important city in France. Even more vital, crossing the Seine River and heading down the right bank to the sea would get Americans behind the Germans and surround all who were west of the river. Trapping them was the prelude to destroying them. All the roads to Germany would then be open to the Allies. In this vision and in this context, the Mortain counterattack simply facilitated the American task and gave more time to complete it.

Bradley had no such outlook. Pragmatically concerned by what was happening at Mortain, uncertain whether the situation had stabilized, he searched for a direct way to relieve the German pressure. The recent sequence of events—Haislip's movement to Le Mans, the Mortain counterattack, and the Canadian thrust toward Falaise—suggested the immediate feasibility of fashioning a hook to threaten the Germans at Mortain. Bradley's motivation was less the prospect of bagging German prisoners than of dissipating the menace. What he sought, above all, was safety.

For that reason, the Loire River hypnotized him too. Troops at Nantes and Angers would provide flank protection for his army group. Furthermore, the river was the southern boundary of the Overlord lodgment area, and, as such, one of his final Overlord objectives. While the opportunity to surround the Germans in Normandy begged for single-minded precedence, the Loire claimed some of Bradley's attention.

Patton had little interest in the Loire River, because few Germans were there. If the Allies eliminated the Germans in Normandy, there was no point to securing the Overlord lodgment area. With the Germans destroyed, the allies could head triumphantly to Germany any way they chose. In Patton's mind, the immediate, as well as the overriding and ultimate, task was encircling and defeating the Germans.

Yet Patton was unable to disregard Bradley's desire, and he used Bradley's wish as an excuse to move Wood's armored division eventually out of Brittany. This was the positive aspect. On the negative side, Patton told Walton Walker, the XX Corps commander, to look after Nantes and Angers with the 5th Infantry Division, which had traveled for three days from the First Army left flank to an assembly area forty miles south of Avranches. Although Patton would have preferred to move the division eastward to bolster Haislip's corps or to get Walker involved in the drive to the east, he had to accede to Bradley's views.

Walker was a short, stocky West Pointer who wanted continuous activity and immediate results. He appeared to be constantly dissatisfied and irritated. He was a superb leader whose attitude was, "Do something, goddammit, anything." He had fought in France in 1918 as an infantry-man, later transferred to the tanks, and was a great admirer of Patton. Receiving control of the 5th Division on August 7, the day of the Mortain counterattack, Walker told the division commander, Le Roy Irwin, to take both Nantes and Angers.

A hero of the battle of Kasserine Pass in Tunisia in 1943, Irwin thought it impossible to seize both cities at the same time because they were fifty-five miles apart. He chose Angers, an urban center of 95,000 inhabitants, and by evening had units on the outskirts. Angers appeared too large for Irwin to capture easily and alone, and he began to invest his objective.

At noon, August 8, an impatient Walker telephoned Irwin and shrilly told him to take both Nantes and Angers at once. Irwin was used to operating with the more methodical First Army, and he plodded on. Late in the day, Walker let Irwin know his displeasure. He was, Walker said, "much exercised" because nothing was happening at Nantes and Angers. Suddenly understanding, Irwin hurriedly sent out a call for trucks to transport soldiers to Nantes.

Despite Walker's incessant calls for action, it took several days, until August 11, for Irwin and Wood to seize Nantes and Angers and provide the security Bradley was after. In the meantime, Walker and Irwin had been unavailable for the operations developing in the east.

On August 8, with Eisenhower at Bradley's headquarters in the morning, Bradley discussed with him the opportunity offered by the Mortain counterattack. Bradley preferred and suggested the simplest act, turning Haislip north from Le Mans. Instead of heading to the Seine to start a grand envelopment, Bradley proposed, as Russell Weigley has said, "a shallower and surer movement" aimed at the Germans around Mortain. The drive would complement the Canadian thrust to the south. If the Canadians reached Falaise and continued on to Argentan, and if Haislip got to Alençon and went beyond to Argentan, their meeting would trap an estimated twenty-one German divisions west of the town.

Later that day, as Bradley grasped the full and staggering import of the potential event, he revealed the enormity to Secretary of the Treasury Henry Morgenthau, who was visiting the European theater and who was then at Bradley's headquarters. They faced an occasion, Bradley said, arising "once in a century." According to Russell Weigley, Bradley continued, "We're about to destroy an entire hostile army." With success, the Germans would have "nothing left with which to oppose us."

To so alter the course of events required Montgomery's assent. In Eisenhower's presence, Bradley telephoned Montgomery. He mentioned Eisenhower's being in the room, indicated Eisenhower's approval of the idea, and talked only of the American part of the new concept, that is, of Haislip's role.

Montgomery quickly concurred. According to Nigel Hamilton, Montgomery said something about sending no more troops to Brittany than were necessary. Echoing "P" Wood's thinking of a week earlier, Montgomery said, "The main business lies to the east."

He and Bradley agreed on a general line of action. They would encircle the Germans who were west of the north-south line running from Falaise to Argentan and Alençon. The Canadians in the north were to push south through Falaise to Argentan. At the other end of the front, Haislip was to turn to the north at Le Mans and head toward Alençon. Once through Alençon, Haislip was to go as far north as Carrouges and Sées, small towns on the army group boundary drawn by Montgomery three days before, a line eight miles south of Argentan. The interior armies, Dempsey's and Hodges's, were to continue their blows to dislocate German cohesion and to herd them into the trap being set by the Canadians and by Haislip's corps of Patton's army.

This settled, Bradley at once passed his instructions to Patton, who was disappointed. He tried half-heartedly to talk Bradley out of the notion, which, to Patton, appeared to be a local solution. He attempted to convince Bradley of the soundness of a deeper envelopment, either north from Orléans to Paris or at least northeast from Le Mans through Dreux or Chartres on the way to the Seine River. But, he said later, "Bradley won't let me." The decision had been made. Montgomery and Eisenhower, along with Bradley, favored a short hook.

According to Michel Dufresne, Patton told Everett Hughes, a friend who was Eisenhower's logistical troubleshooter, why he disliked the shallow movement. "We oblige the tanks," he said, "to deploy in the manner of infantry"—meaning, the maneuver was cramped instead of wide-ranging, restrained instead of audacious. Privately he wrote to his wife that evening to say, "I am the only one to realize how feeble the enemy is. He is finished. We can end the affair [the war] in ten days." What was required was unhampered boldness. But since his superiors were after something quite different, Patton set about to make their operation work.

He knew exactly what Bradley wanted by eleven A.M., August 8. Bradley had passed on a list of instructions, and to make a record of Bradley's wishes, Patton wrote or dictated a memo for his chief of staff, Hugh Gaffey. First, Bradley was releasing three divisions to the Third Army—as it turned out, only two were able to travel to join Haislip's XV Corps, for the third remained near Mortain caught up in the defense. Secondly, the Third Army, Bradley repeated, was to secure Angers and the 12th Army Group right flank with one division—Patton had already given Walker the 5th Division for this task. Next, Patton was to hold a division at Le Mans for general security—Patton had in mind an inexperienced outfit in Haislip's corps as best suited for that role. Finally, using all the other troops available in the area, Patton was to attack from Le Mans to Alençon, then to Carrouges and Sées—he would have the XV Corps headquarters carry out this effort with four divisions advancing, while the fifth and inexperienced division stood at Le Mans.

"To recapitulate," Patton concluded his memo for Gaffey, the Third Army was to cover the army group right flank along the Loire River and guard against what he called "a doubtful attack." More importantly, the Third Army was to change direction at Le Mans and go north. "The purpose of the operation," he stated clearly, "is to surround and destroy the German army west of the Seine."

The last statement indicated Patton's focus on the principal task, destroying the Germans. Fiddling around at the Loire River and thereby losing the services of the XX Corps headquarters and the power of the 5th Division for the main job bothered him.

Patton sent Haislip a letter of instructions, talked with him on the telephone, and went to see him. "You initially take Sées and Carrouges," he told Haislip, "and prepare for further advance." What Patton hoped to do, he informed Haislip, was "to eventually operate with two corps abreast" going north, the XV and the XX. On which side of the XV Corps he would place the XX Corps, he could not yet tell. The XX Corps could go on Haislip's left to cover an unprotected opening of some fifty miles between the First and Third Armies, more specifically between Collins and Haislip, bound to develop so long as Hodges's army remained on the defensive around Mortain. But if Patton could get Bradley to move Hodges into the open ground, Patton would commit the XX Corps on Haislip's right flank. Two corps pushing north would broaden and strengthen the envelopment from the south.

Haislip was hardly surprised. Patton had warned him earlier of a possible change in direction. Now he was to meet the Canadians, as Patton said, "to surround and destroy the German army west of the Seine." Haislip was to move thirty miles to Alençon, a major crossroads, then go eleven miles beyond to the east-west road between Carrouges and Sées, small towns on the American side of Montgomery's army group boundary. Patton instructed him to lead with his armor, that is, his two armored divisions, in order to speed ahead.

Progress of the XV Corps, in whatever direction, north or east, was bound to be risky because of two conditions. Haislip was creating an ever-increasing salient, a bulge, and both of his flanks were uncovered and exposed. Although Patton was quite prepared to accept the risk, he could hardly overlook it completely. He thereby alerted Walker's XX Corps headquarters, which was looking after Nantes and Angers, to be ready to come up beside Haislip's XV Corps in order to protect one flank or the other.

Entering Le Mans at five P.M. on August 8, Haislip's XV Corps was in control of the city by midnight. It would take one day for him to gather his forces and prepare his attack to the north.

The Canadians, together with the Poles, continued to struggle along the Falaise road, and their threat to take the town distressed Hitler early on the morning of August 9. He had firmly taken the direction of operations into his own hands, and he ordered tanks, as well as antitank and assault guns, to move out of the Fifteenth Army in the Pas-de-Calais in order to defend Falaise. There would be, he had said before, no additional Allied invasion of the Continent and therefore no need to keep useful weapons far from the battlefield.

Having thus apparently disposed of the problem at Falaise, Hitler turned to Avranches. He wanted another attack to jump off that evening. Six panzer divisions abreast, he specified, were to advance, and two additional exploiting divisions were to bolster them. In a gratuitous slap at Kluge, Hitler told him to avoid the mistakes of his original enterprise, which Kluge, according to the Führer, had launched "too early, too weak, and in unfavorable weather," meaning weather permitting Allied aircraft to fly.

German commanders in Normandy called Hitler's order "pure utopia" and "the apex of conduct by a command ignorant of front line conditions, taking upon itself the right to judge the situation from [Hitler's command post in] East Prussia." Having vented their frustration, they tried to follow orders.

They were unable to do so. Increasing Allied pressure at Falaise, at Mortain, and at Le Mans forced Kluge to delay the effort that afternoon. The earliest date he could put on the new advance to Avranches, Kluge decided, was August 11. Yet even that day was less than propitious. With only about 120 tanks available, and with a night movement necessary to avoid Allied air attacks, the tankers required the light of a waning moon. The next favorable phase of the moon was August 20, and Kluge set that date for the thrust to Avranches. It seemed inconceivable for the Germans to maintain for so long the conditions permitting a resumption of the endeavor to secure Avranches, but there was no alternative.

The battle around Mortain continued to rage on August 9. Leland Hobbs talked on the phone with Joe Collins and characterized his activity as "trying to plug up these rat holes." In a later conversation, Hobbs wondered aloud whether his positions were "practically untenable." Weary of the up and down reports, Collins flared in exasperation and anger: "Stop talking about untenable."

In Le Mans on August 9, as Haislip prepared to attack to the north on the following day, he received two additional divisions sent by Patton, an American infantry division and a French armored division, both inexperienced in combat. Haislip placed the Americans in Le Mans to occupy the city and to be in position to react against a German threat to either of his open flanks or to his unprotected rear. In compliance with Patton's wish to lead with his armor, Haislip put the 2nd French Armored Division up forward to operate side by side with the 5th U.S. Armored Division, whose commander, Lunsford Oliver, had performed in outstanding fashion in North Africa and was doing the same in Normandy.

The French troops had arrived in Normandy on August 1, over Utah Beach, commanded by Jacques Leclerc, wartime pseudonym of Philippe François Marie de Hautecloque. He had served as a captain in the campaign of 1940, then made his way to England and joined de Gaulle's Free French Forces, the first Regular Army officer to do so. Tempered in fire, possessed of a formidable will, barely concealing an interior fury, headstrong and impatient, Leclerc burned to erase the shame of the French defeat. He generated immense charisma.

Leclerc was short, thin, and intense, with a small mustache. He generally carried a cane, a necessity springing from a bad fall from a horse, and although it seemed too large for him, it became his personal trademark. Sent by de Gaulle to Chad, Leclerc raised and trained a mobile column, traveled with it through the interior of Africa to Libya, attacked and defeated Italian troops at Koufra, attached himself to Montgomery's British Eighth Army and fought on his desert flank. In the process, he gained a legendary reputation. Having advanced rapidly in grade and having functioned more or less independently, Leclerc was little suited to the discipline of the chain of command.

He formed the 2nd French Armored Division in North Africa toward the end of 1943 from a variety of sources. "Never, at least never in more than a century," wrote General de Langlade, one of Leclerc's major subordinates, "has there been reunited such a mosaic of peoples, races, religions, and political convictions." Free French from the United Kingdom and Syria came together with men from French North Africa and Equatorial Africa. Catholics, Protestants, Jews, Moslems, and animists mingled in amity, as did communists, reactionaries, socialists, radicals, free thinkers, militant Christians, and Quakers. What bound them together was hatred of the Boche, love of France, and the spirit of Leclerc. The latter imparted a sense of adventure to a body of men who sometimes exhibited the exuberance of freebooters.

After training in Algeria and moving to England, the division was placed on the Overlord troop list, the planners said, "primarily so that there may be an important French formation present at the re-occupation of Paris." It was only just and fair, the Allies recognized, for Frenchmen to have the responsibility and the honor of liberating the capital.

Leclerc and his men had a glowing precedent to emulate. French units reequipped by the Americans in North Africa had fought in Italy in Mark Clark's Fifth U.S. Army. The French Expeditionary Corps under Alphonse Juin, numbering eventually four divisions, had fashioned a brilliant record. Juin and his troops had broken the Gustav Line in May 1944 and thereby opened the road to Rome. Withdrawn from Italy soon afterwards, the French soldiers, ultimately to form a French army under Jean de Lattre de Tassigny, were preparing to follow Americans ashore in the invasion of southern France scheduled for August 15.

Like Leclerc, the members of his division were eager to avenge the defeat, to display their courage and skill, and to erect a standard of glorious achievement. Although quite a few had participated in combat in western Europe, North Africa, the Middle East, and elsewhere, they would enter battle as a single formation in Haislip's XV Corps. Their appearance in metropolitan France was the beginning of a climax which could reach culmination as they freed Paris from German occupation, and their anticipation of this ecstasy made them difficult to control.

Patton called in Leclerc for a talk shortly after the division arrived on the Continent. He offered to let Leclerc join the battle at once, that is, without resting after the division's movement from England. If Leclerc accepted, Patton said, he would have the opportunity to fight before the inevitable German collapse. For "one had the right, at that date," Patton said in his imperfect but fluent French, "to wonder whether the [German] capitulation was to come in a matter of several days."

The Third Army commander was, of course, stimulating Leclerc, heightening his anticipation. Patton wanted the French to skip the normal period of rest before engaging the enemy, for Patton was short of divisions and needed Leclerc's organization. As Patton guessed, Leclerc snapped the bait. He jumped at the chance to go against the Germans immediately.

Patton then told him what he was to do. He was to go north from Le Mans and through Argentan to Falaise in order to meet the Canadians descending from Caen. Leclerc was thereby to close the pocket being formed around the Germans. And Paris? asked Leclerc. Patton waved the query aside. Later, later, when Paris came into reach.

As Leclerc revealed afterward to Langlade, he was willing to take Argentan. But instead of continuing to Falaise, he preferred to join the British and head east toward the Seine. That would put him closer to Paris, his ultimate objective. In addition, he would be more comfortable, he was sure, working with the British again, for he had become familiar with them and their methods in North Africa.

Patton and Haislip—the latter had been a student at the École de Guerre in Paris—both spoke French easily. They were, besides, patricians, like Leclerc. They tried to make Leclerc feel at home, but he was skeptical of the Americans. He had ingested some anti-American British attitudes, and, like the British, tended to think of the Americans as newcomers to the war. As a consequence, he downgraded them. He could see battlefield problems and solutions in an instant's glance and could come to a quick decision, whereas the Americans, he believed, required time and paperwork to understand in great detail the ramifications of a situation.

To his subordinates, Leclerc stressed the need to obey only him. If the Americans committed stupidities, there was no reason for the French to follow and do the same. As Langlade understood this and paraphrased it: "If an American is an ass, there is no reason for a Frenchman to be one too."

A good part of the outlook came from resentment. France was the *patrie* of the French, but the Americans were running the show in which Leclerc was involved. The French were the proprietors, the Americans merely transients. On the road to Alençon and Argentan, Leclerc and his division would try Haislip's and Patton's patience.

On August 9, after dinner, Patton wrote to his wife. "If I were on my own," he said, meaning, if he had an independent command, if he had no need to cope with Bradley, Montgomery, and Eisenhower above him, or if he were in Bradley's or Montgomery's or Eisenhower's shoes, "I would take bigger chances than I am now permitted to take. Three times I have suggested risks and been turned down and each time the risk was warranted."

Patton never specified his recommendations, but what was on his mind and what he wanted to do seem clear. He wished to get to Orléans, advance to the Seine River, have the gap on Haislip's left closed, and insert the XX Corps on Haislip's right. These actions encompassed a broad perspective of shrewdly calculated risk. They showed an audacity daring to grapple with the unknown. They demonstrated a deep confidence in his ability to meet and surmount potential crisis, to dominate the battlefield, and to win clear-cut victory.

Instead, Patton was engaged in carrying out the doings of others. Their outlook seemed small potatoes, overly cautious, and hardly to his liking.

About the same time that Patton was communicating with his wife, Montgomery was writing to Brooke. "We hold Le Mans," he said, "and strong forces [are to] advance toward first Alençon, then Argentan. . . . The Canadian Army has worked well today. . . . Falaise is close to our artillery," meaning, within range of the guns. "The actual situation offers grand possibilities. . . . If we can arrive at Alençon [the American objective], Argentan and Falaise [the Canadian objectives] rapidly enough, we have a good chance to encircle a large part of the German forces."

Yet at bottom, Montgomery doubted his ability or the Allied capacity to stop the full-scale withdrawal he still expected the Germans to make. His lack of confidence showed in his conclusion: "If the Germans escape us here," he said, "I will rapidly apply the plan [designated] in my directive [of two days earlier]," that is, push the Germans up against the Seine River.

To this more or less official report, Montgomery added a personal note, saying, "I think the Americans will have no difficulty reaching Alençon, for nothing opposes their advance. If we can arrive at Falaise and also hold Alençon, we should then be able to close the breach between the two." Exactly how to close the breach, meaning, how to close the pocket, he had still to decide. But he had plenty of time, he thought, before he had to make up his mind. He had forgotten how fast the Americans could move.

In a gossipy vein, Montgomery continued to Brooke, "So far, the Poles have not displayed the dash we expected, and have been sticky." Changing the subject, he talked about Crerar, who was "fighting his first battle and it is the first appearance in history of a Canadian [Army] H.Q. [Headquarters]. He is desperately anxious that it should succeed. He is so anxious that he worries himself all day! I go and see him a lot and calm him down. He will be better when he realises that battles seldom go completely as planned . . . and that if you worry you will eventually go mad!" He mentioned Crerar's row with Crocker and Crerar's wish to sack Crocker. A problem was Crerar's belief in the artillery. A good initial fire plan, Crerar thought, would make the Germans run away. "I fear he thinks he is a great soldier."

Although Montgomery, like Patton, was giving his prime attention to the encirclement in progress, Bradley in contrast was concerned on August 9 also with Brittany. Heavy fighting at St-Malo, Brest, and Lorient prompted Bradley to question whether the Americans had sufficient resources engaged there. In the afternoon, he talked with Montgomery about sending more units westward in order to seize the Breton ports quickly. Montgomery told Bradley to be patient. He advised Bradley to concentrate on capturing each port in turn. Where were they to find additional formations for Brittany?

At eleven P.M., August 9, Hitler issued a new order for another and larger attack to Avranches. His message reached Normandy on the morning of August 10. As Kluge read the paper, he was uncomfortably aware of how events were outrunning Hitler's knowledge and reaction time. It was impossible to carry out Hitler's instructions. Although the Germans had blocked the Canadians on the road to Falaise, they faced another danger in the south. The Americans at Le Mans, Kluge reported to Hitler's headquarters, "unmistakably swerved" from an eastward orientation to a northward course. They were heading for Alençon. The advance threatened the German troops at Mortain with a flank attack and most of the German forces in Normandy with encirclement.

CHAPTER 15

The Stop Order

WITHOUT INTELLIGENCE INFORMATION ON what to expect, Haislip's two armored divisions, followed by two infantry divisions, pushed from Le Mans on August 10. The tanks advanced fifteen miles toward Alençon that day and got halfway to the city. The resistance was light, not enough to matter.

Alençon interested Bradley less than Mortain. To him, the Germans at Mortain still constituted a threat. Why the Germans refused to budge mystified him and made him uneasy. According to his professional judgment, the implicit threat of double envelopment from Falaise and Alençon should have pried them out of the Mortain area. "Either they are crazy," he remarked disparagingly to his aide, "or they don't know what is happening." After his staff briefing that morning of August 10, he set out for Hodges's headquarters. He hoped to discover the German logic.

Shortly after Bradley left, Patton arrived at Bradley's headquarters. He had hoped to talk with Bradley and persuade him to send Hodges eastward to close the wide and unprotected opening on Haislip's left. With Bradley out, Patton spoke with his chief of staff, Leven Allen. He obtained little response or satisfaction. As he recorded in his diary that evening, "The people at army group headquarters did not take any interest because Bradley feels that there is no danger."

It was peculiar for Patton to manifest caution and for Bradley to be unconcerned. Yet Haislip's open left flank, Patton intuitively felt, clamored for German counterattack. If the forces gathered at Mortain turned and sprang at Haislip, they could inflict serious damage on the American column.

Kluge saw the same opportunity that evening. Communicating with Hitler's headquarters, he thought it "worth considering" to hold off the westward effort to Avranches in favor of having the American advance north from Le Mans "smashed by a . . . panzer thrust." He asked for a decision, meaning, would they pass his implicit recommendation to Hitler.

In the next few days, the Ultra Secret intelligence system operating in Bletchley Park, England, intercepted, translated, and disseminated to the top Allied commanders in Normandy several messages relating to a possible German attack against Haislip's corps. The news prompted caution.

Montgomery was writing to Brooke around eleven P.M., on August 10. He too had his eye on Haislip's unprotected left flank, and although he had yet to receive the warning from Ultra, he had vague indications, he said, of German planning to attack there. Like Patton, he had an intuitive sense of dangerous areas.

Continuing his report, he said, "The First Canadian Army made no progress today, but the attack toward Falaise will continue this night. I ordered the Second British Army to put its weight on the left and to push strongly toward Falaise together with the Canadians. I am convinced that we need to take Falaise quickly because I have ordered the Canadian Army to be ready to send, soon afterwards, armored forces toward Trun and Argentan." Argentan lies about thirteen miles south and slightly southeast of Falaise. The small town of Trun is about ten miles east and slightly southeast of Falaise.

This was the first mention of Montgomery's interest in Trun, and it indicated his increasing belief in the necessity of extending the front eastward several miles in order to surround more Germans and also of holding the closing ring more firmly against German reaction. Again like Patton, he was coming to question the efficacy of the short envelopment. Yet he failed to say anything about Trun to Bradley. Had he done so, as he should have out of respect for coalition courtesy and the chain of command, Bradley, knowing what Montgomery had in mind, would have been able to plan his troop dispositions more effectively.

The Canadians, Montgomery wrote, were doing well. "The Poles are still on their start line 1. . . . I have told Harry [Crerar] to give the Poles a kick up the fork."

Crerar's attack registered no gain that evening, and Montgomery suspended further immediate effort. He instructed Crerar to prepare a full-scale assault for August 14.

At midnight of August 10, Hitler was querulous. He had yet to receive Kluge's proposal to smash the flank of the Americans heading for Alençon. All he knew was Kluge's intent to resume the offensive at Mortain on August 20. Why did Kluge have to wait so long? A German push to Avranches would nullify the American thrust to Alençon. But if regaining Avranches was impossible before August 20, obviously something was necessary before then at Alençon.

Kluge resolved the issue. At 3:15 on the morning of August 11, he telephoned a subordinate commander. The strong American defenses at Mortain and the Allied threat of double envelopment by the Canadians heading for Falaise and the Americans moving toward Alençon, he said, made another effort to Avranches impossible. The Germans had stopped the Canadians short of Falaise. Now they had to bar the Americans from Alençon.

An hour and a half later, at 4:45 A.M., Kluge talked on the phone with Hitler, who had by then received Kluge's recommendation to smash the Americans heading toward Alençon. It would take him, Kluge said, two days to prepare his strike. He could deliver the blow on August 13.

Turning the matter over in his mind, Hitler withheld immediate comment.

At noon on August 11, Kluge wired and asked for a decision. The Germans, he repeated, needed to abandon the Avranches counterattack in favor of hitting the Americans around Alençon.

Hitler finally approved in midafternoon. He gave Kluge permission to assemble strong panzer forces for a blow against the left flank of the Americans on the Le Mans–Alençon road. The attack was to cut across the highway in a southeasterly direction. Kluge could have another day to get ready, but he had to launch the venture, Hitler said, no later than August 14.

That evening of August 11 Hitler clarified his intentions. He still wished Avranches, but he recognized the prior need to act in the Alençon area. In the interest of the Alençon maneuver and in consonance with Kluge's insistence on reducing the Mortain salient, Hitler said, "I am agreeable" to what he called "a minor withdrawal" around Mortain.

Kluge immediately ordered the hard-pressed troops to pull back from the town that night.

About that time, the early morning of August 11, Haislip's XV Corps reached the outskirts of Alençon. His swift movement delighted Patton, who had visited Haislip that morning and who had conspicuously inspected and cheered the French armored division. Patton sent a message, saying, "My congratulations on your rapid advance. Continue. Avoid as much as possible confrontation with the enemy [and possible delay]."

Expecting soon to be in Sées and Carrouges, Haislip complied. Before nightfall on August 11, he designated Argentan as the next corps goal. Argentan was across the army group boundary and eight miles into the British-Canadian zone, but that seemed to be of no importance. Haislip instructed Leclerc's and Oliver's French and American armored divisions to fight through the night.

Patton was still concerned about Haislip's open flanks. During most of the day on August 11, he had tried to get Bradley to commit troop units into the large piece of open territory on Haislip's left. The continuing danger at Mortain prevented Bradley from acceding to Patton's wish. The area west of the XV Corps remained inviting to the Germans, and that was precisely where Kluge intended to strike Haislip.

To protect Haislip's right, Patton asked Bradley for two of Hodges' infantry divisions. These, if combined with an armored division newly arrived on the Continent and heading for the front, could go under Walker's XX Corps headquarters and not only cover Haislip's right flank but also strengthen the encirclement. Bradley refused to transfer two infantry divisions from Hodges to Patton so long as the threat persisted at Mortain.

Montgomery on August 11 issued a new directive and set forth his concept of how to encircle the Germans. "The bulk of the enemy forces," he estimated, fought west of the north-south Caen-Falaise-Argentan-Alençon line. If the Canadians reached Falaise and the Americans entered Alençon, only thirty-five miles would separate them. Through this terrain the Germans would have to move—either to bring reinforcements and supplies to the west in order to continue their battle or to escape to the east. By taking both Falaise and Alençon, the Allies would deprive the Germans of two of the three main east-west highways. "Obviously," Montgomery wrote, "if we can close the gap completely, we shall have put the enemy in the most awkward predicament." The Germans would be surrounded.

Because of the nature of the country, Montgomery expected the Germans to mass forces in the south against the Americans around Alençon and Argentan. The Canadians, facing lighter opposition in the north, would have easier going as they drove to the south to Falaise and Argentan. It was "vital," Montgomery said, for Crerar to get to Falaise "quickly," then to hasten south to Argentan. At the same time, Dempsey's British Army was to push eastward to Falaise and Argentan both.

"Clearly," Montgomery concluded in a curious locution, "our intention must be"—this choice of words is puzzling; did Montgomery hesitate to apply his logic or was he rendering an opinion on the virtual impossibility of his Allied troops doing what he wished and expected?—"to destroy the enemy forces between the Seine and the Loire." If somehow the Germans escaped the short hook, Montgomery added, they were to face entrapment at the Seine River, a wider or deeper encirclement.

As Russell Weigley has said, Montgomery reminded his subordinate commanders to return to the Seine River envelopment if the jaws at Falaise and Argentan failed to close the trap or to close it rapidly enough.

Montgomery's statement is peculiar. To some extent he admitted fault in accepting Bradley's short envelopment. Yet even stranger, he presented a summary of options rather than issuing a categorical command to pursue a certain course of action to gain a definite and clearly stated goal. By waffling, by expecting failure in the shallow encirclement, Montgomery virtually assured that result.

At ten forty-five P.M., August 11, Montgomery ran down the situation for Brooke. There were indications of a German withdrawal from Mortain. The Canadians had made no progress. He had ordered Dempsey and Crerar both to get to Falaise in forty-eight hours. He had instructed Bradley to collect a fresh corps of three divisions around Le Mans, the corps to be ready to push toward Chartres. Once again, with respect to the last point, Montgomery and Patton, for somewhat different reasons, were on the same wavelength.

Montgomery's ruminations were soon out of date. On the morning of August 12, while Leclerc's 2nd French Armored Division captured the still-standing bridges over the Sarthe River at Alençon and entered the city, Oliver's 5th U.S. Armored Division pushed ahead and took the town of Sées.

According to Nigel Hamilton, "the speed of Patton's [Haislip's] manoeuvre [to Alençon]" profoundly "surprised" Montgomery. He may also have been uncomfortable, for the advance to Alençon extended the large and unbroken American expansion of the Continental lodgment since the Cobra operation. Quite in contrast, the British and Canadians had made slight progress. Furthermore, the XV U.S. Corps had covered the thirty miles from Le Mans to Alençon in two days, while the Canadians had moved forward eight miles toward Falaise. The strength of the German opposition against the Canadians and the virtual nonexistence of resistance against the XV Corps explained the differences in mileage gained. But to the casual newspaper-reading public, what was immediately apparent was the dissimilarity in the amounts of territory liberated by the two Allied forces.

Among the staff members of Bradley's 12th Army Group, the speed of the movement to Alençon displayed an audacity lacking in the thrust to Falaise. "The British effort," someone wrote, according to Russell Weigley, ". . . appears to have bogged itself in timidity and succumbed to the legendary vice of over-caution." The Americans were riding high.

Ahead of Haislip's XV Corps on August 12 lay Argentan, ripe for the plucking. A German bakery company had abandoned the bread-making ovens in town that morning and the men were digging defensive positions along the southern approaches to the city. Argentan was open to easy capture.

Between Haislip's two armored divisions operating side by side and the bakers preparing for combat at Argentan was a formidable terrain feature. A forest grew on a rugged piece of upland. The steep and thickly wooded slopes offered excellent defensive positions. Still without intelligence information on what was in front of him, Haislip rated the forest as an excellent place for the Germans to delay and stop the XV Corps. With Patton seeking to avoid a direct confrontation with the enemy, Haislip saw his task as getting to Argentan at once. He instructed his armored division commanders to skirt the forest and its potential defenders. The French were to go around the western edge of the woods, the Americans to bypass the height on the eastern side.

In a defiant or thoughtless yet inexcusable gesture of disobedience, Leclerc disregarded Haislip's order. The act was perhaps a sign of what the French call *je m'en foutisme*—I don't give a damn. Perhaps Leclerc's decision was meant to show how daring and invincible the French were. Perhaps it was supposed to indicate a contempt for restraint. It may have been simple inexperience and an inability to control his elements, for Leclerc had never before led an armored division in combat. Whatever it was, Leclerc's action turned out to be a most significant error.

Leclerc sent one third of his division to the west of the barrier, one third through the forest, and one third around the eastern edge. The latter units trespassed on and usurped the highway from Alençon to Argentan, which Haislip had reserved for the American armor. Against spotty resistance, the French advanced steadily and converged on Carrouges.

Unfortunately, it took six hours for Leclerc's troops on the right to clear the Alençon–Argentan road. Only then could trucks with gasoline come forward to replenish the empty American tanks. When Oliver's men headed for Argentan, they found their entrance blocked. What had been defended by a company of bakers digging trenches in the morning was now guarded by three veteran panzer divisions and at least seventy tanks.

The German withdrawal from Mortain during the night of August 11 had enabled Kluge to move the panzer divisions to Argentan on the morning of August 12. Arriving ahead of the Americans, they took firm control of the town. The loss of important stocks of gasoline and other supplies near Alençon inhibited an offensive strike against Haislip's left flank, but the retention of Argentan ensured access to the major east-west highway through the town. If the Germans lost Falaise to the Canadians and Argentan to the Americans, only a narrow gap of thirteen miles, a stretch of territory without good east-west roads, would separate the Allied forces from tightening and buckling a belt around the bulk of the German armies in Normandy.

The German departure from Mortain ended the battle there. During those five days of close and vicious combat, Hodges was unable to exploit the breakout. The result was a temporary setback and 4,000 American casualties. The German costs included one hundred wrecked and abandoned tanks.

The retrograde movement from Mortain, Montgomery believed, was the beginning of the full-scale retirement to the east he had always expected. As he would tell Brooke in his usual evening message on August 12, some German forces, whatever their numbers, had more than likely already escaped the short hook or were about to do so. The Allied task, then, was to block them from crossing the Seine River. Exactly how, Montgomery had yet to decide.

The Germans having gone from Mortain, Hodges, with Bradley's permission, turned the V and XIX Corps loose on August 12. They met surprisingly stiff resistance and made little gain. Collins was unable to join the attack, for he had to reorganize his VII Corps elements, to reassemble them and change them from a defensive posture to an offensive mode. The VII Corps would jump off on the following day.

As a consequence, Haislip's left flank still lay open and insecure. Late in the afternoon of August 12, Haislip's troops crossed the army group boundary drawn by Montgomery five days earlier. Haislip had no idea of the nature or the strength of the Germans defending Argentan. The halt imposed on his advance just south of Argentan, he believed, was merely temporary. He had every expectation of penetrating into the town on the following morning. Thus, at nine-thirty P.M., August 12, and once again twenty minutes later, Haislip pointedly informed Patton of his presence in front of his last designated objective, Argentan. Anticipating his possession of the town no later than noon, August 13, Haislip asked Patton whether further movement to the north beyond Argentan was authorized. If so, that is, if Patton approved, Haislip reminded him of a disagreeable situation. By moving over an ever increasing length of territory, the XV Corps was being stretched and thinned out. Haislip was leaving an ever decreasing number of troops behind his advancing spearheads. If he surrounded the Germans, he was sure to stir up a furious reaction. The Germans were bound to strike to regain control of the roads permitting east-west travel. They would no doubt launch a strong effort to break out of the trap. To contain them in the pocket, Haislip needed more troops. As vital as the need, Haislip thought, to continue through and beyond Argentan was the requirement to block the east-west arteries soon to be behind him, the east-west highways between Alençon and Argentan.

Patton had no intention of stopping Haislip. It was necessary for Haislip to go beyond Argentan and complete the encirclement. That was the whole point of the operation—to create a pocket confining the Germans in Normandy. Patton's only hesitation came from further extending Haislip's corps. With Ultra intercepts warning Allied commanders of a German strike against Haislip's left flank, was it wise to let Haislip go ahead? Or was it better to hold him where he was and let him assume a defensive posture?

As always, Patton opted for audacity, letting Haislip close the pocket. If that course increased the risks, so be it. On the other hand, perhaps the Germans would never be able to attack Haislip's flank. Even if they did, they lacked the strength, Patton surmised, to create more than a fleeting crisis. Either way, the Allies seemed about to eliminate the two German armies west of the Seine River. That goal, firmly in Patton's mind, warranted accepting danger.

Consequently, at 10:17 P.M., August 12, Patton authorized continued advance. After capturing Argentan, Haislip was to go slowly toward Falaise, then beyond if necessary, until he made contact with the Canadians.

Patton then telephoned Bradley to apprise him. Closing the pocket by meeting the Canadians was, after all, Bradley's objective, his original idea, his operation.

"We have troops in Argentan," Patton told Bradley. The statement was exaggerated and untrue, but on Haislip's say-so, Patton confidently expected French and American units to be there soon. They were, Patton said, on their way to Falaise.

In what was to become one of the most controversial decisions of the campaign, Bradley said, "Nothing doing."

As a dumbfounded Patton listened, Bradley spoke of the need to avoid a collision between Americans and Canadians. A meeting might prompt accidental gunfire against each other and produce casualties. "Don't go beyond Argentan," Bradley said. "Stop where you are and build up on that shoulder. Sibert"—Bradley's G-2—"tells me the German is beginning to pull out. You'd better button up and get ready for him."

Startled, profoundly disappointed, Patton complied. At 10:40 P.M., August 12, he rescinded his earlier instruction to Haislip and told him to halt where he was. Haislip was to assemble his troops and keep them well in hand.

Haislip immediately directed his armored divisions to go no farther.

Sometime during the evening of August 12, according to Michel Dufresne, news of Haislip's progress beyond Argentan reached Montgomery. To his chief of staff, Francis de Guingand, Montgomery said, "Tell Bradley they ought to get back." He made the remark presumably in the interest of letting Haislip get ready to repel the German attack indicated by Ultra intercepts.

De Guingand was appalled. To Montgomery's intelligence officer, Edgar Williams, who also heard the comment, de Guingand said, "Monty is too tidy." They and other staff members were scandalized because they believed Montgomery to be determined to block an American advance to Falaise in order to preserve Falaise for a British-Canadian triumph.

When they heard of Bradley's stop order, they supposedly urged Montgomery to overrule Bradley. He refused, probably on the basis of caution and security.

In de Guingand's memoirs, entitled *Operation Victory*, written and published shortly after the war, he stated his belief in the ability of the Americans to have gone beyond Argentan and to have closed the pocket. The blame for the failure to do so, he believed, fell on Montgomery. The Americans, in his opinion, regarded the army group boundary as a firm restriction against further movement. They needed Montgomery's invitation to cross, and Montgomery, de Guingand was sure, should have erased the line on the map and let them proceed. Had he done so, the Americans would have eradicated the Argentan-Falaise gap and shut the Germans into confinement.

For the period of two hours between 10:40 P.M., August 12, when

Patton instructed Haislip to remain in place, and twenty minutes before one A.M., August 13, when Patton canceled that instruction, the records on what transpired at Patton's headquarters are silent. After speaking with Bradley on the telephone and hearing the surprising order to stop Haislip, Patton no doubt conferred with his closest staff officers, his chief of staff, his operations officer, and perhaps one or two others. In accordance with Patton's wish, they immediately transmitted Bradley's desire to Haislip, stopping him.

As the small group around Patton discussed the meaning of Bradley's order and its possible consequences, someone probably noticed the wording of Bradley's message. According to the stenographic record, Bradley had said, "Don't go beyond Argentan." Did that, by inference, authorize Haislip to get to Argentan?

No one seemed to care whether Haislip captured Argentan. To a large extent, it mattered little whether Haislip's troops physically occupied the town. For the east-west highway through the place was already well within range of American artillery, and the road was under severe interdictory shelling. What was at issue was whether Haislip should go beyond Argentan.

Having canceled Haislip's movement toward Falaise at Bradley's bidding, Patton probably phoned Bradley again and somehow wheedled permission for Haislip to continue into Argentan; once there, he might as well go on. Perhaps Bradley seemed to equivocate for an instant after his apparently firm decision. Perhaps he said he would see in the morning. Perhaps he uttered what to Patton sounded like a tentative or qualified okay. Whatever occurred, there must have been something. For Patton, contrary to popular legend, never violated instructions, never deliberately disobeyed orders.

In any event, forty minutes after midnight, early in the morning of August 13, Patton told Haislip to advance. He was, Patton said, to "push on slowly in the direction of Falaise." Once there, he was to "continue to push on slowly until . . . [he made] contact [with] our Allies," the Canadians.

Haislip jumped off on the morning of August 13 and found his way barred. He tried to sideslip to the east and skirt the town. The result was the same. The Germans held and Haislip's offensive effort subsided.

To what extent the contradictory orders inhibited the XV Corps is a matter of conjecture. Had the upper echelons exhibited a firm resolve to close the pocket, Haislip might have defeated the Germans at Argentan. The fragmentation and dissipation of intent, together with the loss of the prior momentum, sapped the enthusiasm and the confidence of the troops.

If Leclerc's men had stayed within their zone of operations, Oliver's troops would certainly have reached and taken Argentan on the morning of August 12, that is, before the panzer divisions arrived. Would Bradley have held Haislip there? There is no clear answer, only speculation.

Yet a controversy was developing on the Allied command levels, and one of the points in the argument was how important the army group boundary line was. Haislip had already crossed Montgomery's tracing on the map. Should he further violate Montgomery's authority by going even farther north?

Bradley provided the answer on the morning of August 13, and in doing so gave credence to the probability of a second conversation with Patton on the previous night. Bradley's chief of staff, Leven Allen, telephoned Patton's chief of staff, Hugh Gaffey, on what appeared to be unfinished business, now about to be firmly concluded. Bradley, Allen said, wanted the XV Corps to halt on the army group boundary. Would Gaffey pass the message to his boss.

Gaffey told Patton, who was upset. Perhaps Allen's mention of the boundary as a limiting feature grated on his nerves. There was no point in having Haislip withdraw several miles to the boundary.

Patton telephoned the army group headquarters. Bradley, he learned, was away, visiting Eisenhower, who was starting to assemble his headquarters on the Continent. Patton tried to reach Bradley there, but was unable to do so, probably because of the distance between his command post and Eisenhower's at Granville on the Cotentin west coast.

Again Patton phoned Allen. He requested, then pled for Bradley to talk with Montgomery. Perhaps Montgomery would rescind his boundary and allow the Americans further incursion into the British-Canadian zone.

Allen said he would check with Bradley.

While Allen was on the phone with Bradley, A. Franklin Kibler, Bradley's G-3, supposedly telephoned de Guingand, Montgomery's chief of staff. Kibler asked permission to send Patton north of Argentan, that is, well beyond the boundary.

"I am sorry," de Guingand replied. He made no offer to consult with Montgomery about a possible alteration.

On the phone with Bradley, Allen passed on Patton's message.

Bradley was adamant. The stop order stood. He had persuaded Eisenhower to his point of view. The Americans had to observe Montgomery's army group boundary in the interest of the coalition and the chain of command.

Allen then reached Patton, who impatiently asked, "Have you talked with Brad?"

"Yes, George," Allen replied. "The answer is always no."

With this, Patton confirmed the order for Haislip to halt at Argentan. He was to "assemble and prepare for further operations in another direction."

At the same time, Patton told Gaffey, "The question why XV Corps halted on the east-west line through Argentan is certain to become of historical importance. I want a stenographic record of this conversation"—presumably with Leven Allen—"included in the History of the Third Army."

That the XV Corps was hardly on an "east-west line through Argentan" was, in Patton's mind, beside the point. So far as he was concerned, Bradley's refusal to let Haislip proceed was additional proof substantiating his belief, as he remarked often enough in his diary, of Eisenhower's and Bradley's influence on each other. When they were together, Patton frequently observed, each reinforced the other's natural timidity.

That evening of August 13, Patton entered into his diary his feelings over Bradley's stop order. Haislip's XV Corps, he wrote, "could easily advance to Falaise and completely close the [Argentan-Falaise] gap [and encircle the Germans], but we have been ordered to halt because the British sowed the area [from the air] with a large number of time bombs [presumably to hinder a German withdrawal]. I am sure that this halt is a great mistake, as I am certain that the British [including the Canadians] will not close on Falaise."

Three days later, he added to this entry, saying, "I told him [Leven Allen] . . . it was perfectly feasible to continue the operation. Allen repeated the order [from Bradley] to halt on the line and consolidate. I believe that the order . . . emanated from the 21st Army Group, and was either due to jealousy of the Americans or to utter ignorance of the situation or to a combination of the two. It is very regrettable that the XV Corps was ordered to halt, because it could have gone on to Falaise and made contact with the Canadians northwest of that point and definitely and positively closed the escape gap."

Patton had not changed his mind by the end of the war. In the immediate aftermath, overwhelmed with bitterness toward all his superiors, British and American alike, all of whom, he felt, had botched the operations consistently, Patton wrote his account of the campaign in northwest Europe. After his death, his wife had the manuscript edited and published under the title *War As I Knew It*. In these pages, Patton considered Bradley's stop order to have been "a monumental error."

Bradley gave his side of the story after the war in his narrative, *A Soldier's Story*. By then bitterly anti-Montgomery because of what had transpired at the battle of the Bulge, Bradley placed responsibility for the halt on Montgomery. For Bradley and Patton, Bradley said, had doubted "Monty's ability to close the gap at Argentan" from the north. They had "waited impatiently" for word from Montgomery to continue Haislip's thrust northward. While waiting, Bradley and Patton watched the Germans reinforce the shoulders of the gap between Argentan and Falaise. They also observed German troops and matériel escaping through the gap.

Dempsey's British army, Bradley said, accelerated the German escape by pushing them out of the open end of the Argentan-Falaise pocket, like, Bradley wrote, squeezing a tube of toothpaste. "If Monty's tactics mystified me," Bradley continued, "they dismayed Eisenhower even more. And . . . a shocked Third Army looked on helplessly as its quarry fled [while] Patton raged at Montgomery's blunder."

The explanation is dishonest and anti-British. Patton was hardly one to "rage" at this kind of activity beyond his control. If Eisenhower was "dismayed," he might have stepped in to rectify the situation. All he said afterwards was to imply that the Allies could have closed the pocket, which, he wrote after the war, "might have won us a complete battle of annihilation."

If this had been clear at the time, Eisenhower or Bradley could have picked up the telephone and called Montgomery to propose sending the XV Corps through and beyond Argentan. If either or both had so recommended, Montgomery would no doubt have consented to a further infringement of the boundary. By refusing to make the suggestion, Eisenhower and Bradley were unwilling to accept the risks involved. Nor could they saddle Montgomery with responsibility for the dangers implicit in this course of action.

Bradley preferred, as he later said, "a solid shoulder at Argentan to a broken neck at Falaise." Ultra, there is no doubt, warned Bradley of Kluge's projected attack against Haislip's open left flank. Although Bradley believed Haislip had the ability to close the gap despite the increasing resistance at Argentan on the morning of August 13, he thought it would be impossible for Haislip to keep the gap closed against the German offensive strike he expected.

Because it was impossible in the immediate postwar years publicly to mention Ultra intelligence, which remained a well-kept secret closely held for three decades, Bradley was unable to acknowledge Ultra's importance in his decision to halt Haislip. To explain his action, he referred to the Germans virtually bottled up around Mortain. Nineteen panic-stricken German divisions, he said, were already stampeding through the Argentan-Falaise gap. These forces were sure to trample Haislip's thin line of troops.

But, of course, Bradley knew better. According to Ultra, the Germans had yet to withdraw. The pullback from Mortain was anything but a full-scale retirement. Hitler had yet to give his permission for the troops to abandon Normandy.

Furthermore, the open ground on Haislip's left, that is, between Haislip and Collins, would have permitted a German attack in that area to gather momentum. It would have been difficult to stop the onrush. Not until August 13 could Collins begin to come up on Haislip's flank. Starting from Mayenne and going toward Carrouges, Collins would fill the ground adjacent to Haislip and cover his flank on the following day, August 14.

Meanwhile, the army group boundary, Bradley later said, inhibited him. With the Americans already across the line, Bradley felt a need for Montgomery's assent to go farther. Bradley made no such request, and, so far as Bradley knew, Montgomery issued no refusal. "Montgomery never prohibited me," Bradley said, "and I never proposed that American troops block the passage between Argentan and Falaise." Both were cautious, for both were aware of the German preparations for the attack to drive southeastward across the Alençon–Argentan highway.

Haislip at Argentan had four divisions—the fifth was protecting Le Mans and Alençon in the rear—already blocking three major exit routes, at Alençon, Sées, and Argentan. To extend fifteen miles farther to Falaise, Bradley believed, would have made it impossible for Haislip to hold the Germans confined. When Bradley halted Haislip, he said, "I had not consulted Montgomery. The decision to stop Patton was mine alone."

As Raymond Callahan has pointed out, "Although still Allied ground commander, Montgomery's authority in fact was fading. . . . Bradley [was] an army group commander and Monty's equal. The swelling tide of American reinforcement and the palpable fact that they were driving forward—at a pace that only a nation in love with the internal combustion engine could contemplate—gave the American commanders mounting confidence and assertiveness. Eisenhower would take over from Montgomery as overall ground commander in barely two weeks. Monty was a realist about professional matters. He could not give orders to Bradley, only make suggestions. Given the history of Monty's relations with Bradley, it is not likely that Bradley was terribly interested in working more closely with Monty than necessity—or Eisenhower—demanded. And Eisenhower, like [Sir Harold] Alexander, tended to let his strong-willed subordinates go their own ways. So Bradley was free to do as he felt best. He felt it best to stop Haislip."

According to Russell Weigley, who quoted Chester Hanson's diary, the journal kept by Bradley's aide, Bradley, as late as March 27, 1945, was still anxious about whether his decision to hold up Haislip's advance had been correct. "By his tone this morning," Hanson wrote, "the General [Bradley] indicated he will not delay in pressing [to capture] a bag [of prisoners] as he did at Falaise when he was told by the British that they would push south to close it [the pocket] and he stopped his forces at Argentan. . . . That is the only decision [of his] he has ever questioned. The burden was not his [but Montgomery's]. But he feels that had he forced the issue and insisted on the advance of our troops, our bag at Falaise might have been considerably more than it was."

The difficulty of resolving the question and the issue remained in Bradley's mind for at least three decades. In June 1974, thirty years after the D day landings, when large national delegations from the Allied nations visited France and commemorated the anniversary at the invasion beaches, General of the Army Omar N. Bradley was the senior American member. At a luncheon served under a huge tent near Ste-Mère-Église, a youngish Frenchman, with great admiration and in utter awe, approached Bradley and, in all sincerity, congratulated him for having closed the pocket and trapped the Germans in Normandy.

Moved by the tribute, touched by the confirmation of what he wanted to believe, full of emotion and close to tears, Bradley, who was hardly sure himself that he had trapped the Germans, took the proffered hand and held it for a long moment. "Thank you," Bradley murmured. "Do you really think so? Yes, yes. Of course. Thank you."

Some years after the war, Brian Horrocks, one of Montgomery's best corps commanders, gave his impression of what had happened. His observation was a curious non sequitur. "Few Germans," he said, "would have escaped if Bradley had not halted Patton's northerly advance. Montgomery, the master of the tactical battle, realized this only too well. To be quite honest, it was because of their lack of battle experience that he had little confidence in the US Commanders."

In actuality, Montgomery's army group boundary was a nonissue. A day or two earlier, Montgomery had asked Bradley to fly to his headquarters for lunch on August 13, in order to ensure coordination, that is, to make certain that British and Americans followed the same course of action. Montgomery also invited Dempsey. The three met at twelve-fifteen and discussed future operations and army group boundaries. Dempsey noted in his journal, "So long as the Northward move of Third Army meets little opposition, the . . . leading Corps [of Patton's army] will disregard inter-army boundaries." Montgomery had no strong feeling against, and certainly no objection to, American progress across and beyond his boundary into the British-Canadian zone.

The working lunch on August 13 produced a new plan of Allied action. "The whole [idea]," Dempsey recorded in his journal, "is to establish [Allied] forces across the enemy's line of communications so as to impede—if not to prevent entirely—his [the German] withdrawal."

Shortly before the Allied meeting on August 13, Josef Dietrich, who commanded the Fifth Panzer Army in Normandy, sent Kluge a report. He stated categorically what all officers later claimed had been on their minds for several days. "If the front . . . is not withdrawn immediately," Dietrich wrote, "and if every effort is not made to move the forces toward the east and out of the threatened encirclement, the Army Group [Kluge's headquarters] will have to write off both [German] armies." In short, it was time to start escaping from the pocket being formed by the Allies.

CHAPTER 16

The Second Stop Order

At lunch on August 13, Montgomery, Bradley, and Dempsey agreed to trap the Germans by the following maneuvers. In twenty-four hours, the Canadians were to attack southeastward, no longer toward Falaise, which they were to sideslip on the east, but rather to Trun and Argentan. Dempsey was to drive to the east and seize Falaise. Hodges was to cover Haislip's left flank with Collins's VII heading northeast toward Argentan. Patton was to bring a corps to Le Mans, send it northeastward to Dreux, and thus fashion a deeper envelopment, this one between Argentan-Falaise and the Seine River.

Facilitating these projected operations was the fine summer weather. Allied aircraft everywhere were harassing the Germans.

Patton had been thinking about what Montgomery and Bradley might ask the Third Army to do. There were three possible missions, he figured: go north and close the Argentan-Falaise pocket, go northeast to Dreux and cut off the Germans from the Seine, go east to the Paris-Orléans gap. Talking with his corps commanders personally or by telephone on the morning of August 13, he told each of them to be alert and flexible, ready for operating in any of three directions, north, northeast, or east. This applied to Haislip's XV Corps around Argentan, Walker's XX Corps getting ready to head for Dreux, and the XII Corps under Gilbert Cook, a World War I veteran, assembling near Le Mans.

Working out these plans lifted Patton's spirits. If he could send

Walker's XX Corps to Dreux and Cook's XII Corps to Chartres, he would be able to pinch off the Germans who would soon, he thought, be escaping through the Argentan-Falaise gap and heading for the Seine. "It should be a very great success," he confided to his diary that evening, "God helping and Monty keeping hands off."

To his wife he wrote, "This [scene] is better and much bigger than [the operations in] Sicily and so far all has gone better than I had a right to expect. L'audace, l'audace, toujours l'audace . . . . It's a great life but very dusty."

About the same time that evening, Montgomery as usual was writing to Brooke to give him a rundown of activities. The circle, he said, was tightening around the Germans. The Canadians, supported by air, were to attack at noon of the following day. He believed the bulk of the Germans to be still inside the pocket. Considerable German movement had taken place that day, but according to his impression, only non-combat elements, that is, supply and administrative organizations, had gone eastward through the gap separating the Canadians near Falaise and Haislip's XV Corps short of Argentan. To block the combat units sure to cross the same ground later, Patton was to get Walker's XX Corps to Dreux as soon as he could.

The Germans had bent their energies on August 13 to consolidate, reinforce, and strengthen their defenses around the line of the pocket being formed and compressed around them. They were working feverishly to prevent the wall from caving in on them and also to keep open the Argentan-Falaise gap, their only avenue of escape.

Dietrich's frank statement of needing to move quickly to avoid encirclement produced an echo on August 14, when Heinrich Eberbach, who headed an army-level panzer group, called for the same action. Kluge could do nothing to implement such a course, because offensive operations still obsessed Hitler.

The unreality of Hitler's outlook continued to be quite apparent to the major battlefield commanders. The Germans in Normandy had suffered about 160,000 casualties since D day; 30,000 men had come to replace them, and another 10,000 were on the way. Probably 250,000 soldiers were fighting in Normandy. In contrast, the Allies had about a million and a half men on the Continent, but they had fewer combat troops than noncombat soldiers. Allied losses numbered approximately 180,000 in the same period of little more than two months, but a steady stream of individual soldiers and of new units arriving in France more than offset the casualties. The Germans were growing weaker, the Allies stronger.

Despite the disparity, Hitler repeated his order to Kluge on the morning of August 14: destroy the enemy near Alençon. He authorized additional retirements in the Mortain area to shorten the defensive line, which would require fewer units, so that additional troops were available for the Alençon effort.

Kluge at once carried out local disengagements and short withdrawals to retract and straighten his front. That evening, he went forward to see personally how best to comply with Hitler's wish and also how best to save his forces from encirclement. He arrived at Dietrich's command post in the Falaise area as the Canadian attack was coming to a halt.

The Canadians, holding a line nine miles long astride the Caen–Falaise highway, had struck at noontime, August 14. Medium bombers dropped a concentrated load to help the troops get started on a narrow front. Smoke and dust hampered coordination between infantry and armor, but two tank columns were making good progress when more than 800 British and Canadian heavy bombers dropped 3,700 tons of bombs. Some fell on Canadian and Polish units, inflicted more than 500 casualties, and temporarily held up the operation. By the end of the day, nonetheless, despite a high number of changes in command personnel because of casualties, a breakdown of communications, a continuing tendency to flounder because of inexperience, and frequent changes in Simonds's orders, the Canadians and Poles had gained almost four miles and were on the approaches to the height above Falaise. They were less than four miles from the town.

Montgomery had that morning again given Crerar, instead of Dempsey, the responsibility for taking Falaise. After that, he told Crerar, the Canadians were to execute another and even more important task. They were to push to the southeast to occupy Trun. Crerar was to make junction with Patton's Third Army approaching from the south.

Seizing Trun as well as Falaise complicated Crerar's problems, but meeting the Americans at Trun was impossible, for Montgomery had, through oversight or on purpose, failed to tell Bradley to get Patton to Trun.

The lure of Falaise on Montgomery was strong and constant. In August he changed his instructions on who was to take it no less than five times. On August 4, he assigned the place to Crerar, on August 6, to Dempsey, on August 11, to Crerar or Dempsey, on August 13, to Dempsey, and finally on August 14, to Crerar. His inconsistency on Falaise paralleled his lack of firm decision on how to trap the Germans in Normandy.

In a letter to Bradley on August 14, he made his thoughts a matter of record. "Dear Brad," he wrote, "It is difficult to say what enemy are inside the ring, and what have got out to the east. A good deal may have escaped. I think your movement of 20 Corps should be N.E. toward Dreux. Also any further stuff you can move round to Le Mans, should go N.E. We want to head off the Germans, and stop them breaking out."

His words revealed Montgomery's reconsideration of the original intention. He favored closing the pocket now, not by the short hook at Argentan and Falaise, but rather by a deeper envelopment somewhere east of Argentan-Falaise and west of the Seine. His instruction to Crerar to meet the Americans at Trun, which he had yet to tell Bradley, and his desire to get the XX Corps to Dreux indicated a fuzzy concept of how and where to spring the trap.

One of the Allied difficulties was the lack of knowledge on August 14 of how many Germans were almost encircled. Sibert, Bradley's G-2, thought about twelve divisions, seven infantry and five panzer, "may be trapped" if the encirclement continued to closure. Those Germans outside the pocket or in good position to escape easily, Sibert figured, totaled about eight infantry and two panzer divisions. Montgomery estimated the bulk of the Germans to be "nearly surrounded." Some saw about 100,000 Germans in the pocket and about to be trapped, while others began to feel the real mass of the German troops to be already outside.

Writing to Brooke on the evening of August 14, Montgomery explained the XX U.S. Corps move to Dreux. "We want to block against the Seine the elements that have escaped us here." Actually, German administrative and logistical formations but no combat troops had passed through the Argentan-Falaise gap. Montgomery was well ahead of reality and anticipating German success.

He continued, "Things seem to have evolved very well. I doubt very much that the enemy will take the risk of maintaining himself on this [the western] side of the Seine. I conferred yesterday with Bradley, Dempsey, and Crerar, and we have carefully established our plans corresponding to all eventualities. Big things could well happen this week."

Writing also that evening to Phyllis Reynolds, an old family friend who was looking after his son in England, Montgomery had, he said, "just about encircled the bulk of the German forces in Northwest Europe." If the Germans escaped through the Argentan-Falaise gap, they would have to get to the Seine River. There, he said confidently, all the bridges below Paris were destroyed. "We shall see what happens."

Actually, all the bridges across the Seine from Paris to the sea were damaged, but a few could still handle traffic. The Germans also had a plethora of ferries, other craft, small boats, and rafts along the river banks to carry troops and matériel across the stream. A good number of German divisions, particularly those coming from the Pas-de-Calais, had crossed the Seine from east to west in June, July, and early August to reinforce the troops in contact with the Allies in Normandy. The flow could just as easily go the other way.

Furthermore, although Montgomery believed that he had prepared for all eventualities, certain contingencies were about to surprise him. Bradley was soon to act on his own initiative.

In an addendum to his report to Brooke, Montgomery gossiped. "Ike is actually here in Normandy, which is too bad. His ignorance of everything about war is total. He is so amiable that it is difficult to be irritated with him. But I am firm on one point: never will I permit him to be at a conference between me, my army commanders, and Bradley."

The statement was so overly defensive as to be antagonistic. Montgomery was trying to make manifest and to sustain British primacy on the operational level. Although the British had had to cede first place to the Americans in strategic matters—for example, to accept the American wish for an invasion of southern France, an event to occur on the following day—Montgomery's position in Normandy guaranteed British leadership on the battlefield. What threatened to upset the status quo was Eisenhower's preparation—he was gathering and setting up his headquarters in Granville on the Cotentin west coast—to take over from Montgomery command of the Allied ground forces and of the campaign in northwest Europe. It was this to which Montgomery objected.

That same evening of August 14, Bradley's aide Chester Hanson wrote a long entry into his journal. "It is clear now," he said, "that our chance to close the German army between Falaise and Argentan has vanished for reasons both clear and difficult to conceive. It is possible that Montgomery has succumbed to his vice of exaggerated precautions. However, it would be folly to criticize Montgomery[,] due to his prestige position among the British. . . . He occupies an almost papal immunity."

All Americans, Hanson said, were anxious for Eisenhower's headquarters to become operational. Eisenhower in command would relieve the Americans from 21 Army Group control. Operations were then bound to speed up. The Germans, Bradley thought, were preparing defensive positions east of Paris along the Marne River, and it was essential to force the Seine quickly. The Americans were always able to generate momentum—he overlooked the battle of the hedgerows—although British restraint held them back.

The results of the breakout, Hanson continued, proved the point. "Patton, exuberant," Hanson wrote, "calls Bradley 'the Eagle,' admits with pride that he [Bradley] is the general of the war and wishes, like everyone else, that we can soon escape the restrictive tactical control by [Montgomery's] 21 Army Group."

Hanson's notation expressed the American wish for domination in the coalition, on the battlefield as on the strategic level. The progress of the Americans during the breakout gave substance to their claim for supremacy. They were just as experienced as the British, and they had come of age. Their record in Normandy outclassed that of their partner.

Patton's outrageous flattery of Bradley resulted from Bradley's acceptance of Patton's operational ideas. As Patton explained in his diary on the evening of August 14, he had flown to visit Haislip that morning. He found Haislip, he said, "quite pepped up," as a matter of fact, raring to go. Patton deplored stopping the XV Corps and keeping it immobile. He told Haislip of "my plan" to send Walker's XX Corps to Dreux and Cook's XII Corps to Chartres. He then flew to Bradley's headquarters "to see Bradley and sell him the plan. He [Bradley] consented and even permitted me to change it" for the better. Instead of putting Walker's XX Corps on the road to Dreux, as Montgomery and Bradley had agreed, Bradley allowed Patton to send half of Haislip's XV Corps to that place. Walker and the XX Corps were instead to head for Chartres. Cook and the XII Corps were to drive to Orléans.

"It is really a great plan, wholly my own, and I made Bradley think he thought of it. 'Oh, what a tangled web we weave when first we practice to deceive.' I am very happy and elated. I got all the corps moving so that if Monty tries to be careful, it will be too late."

Bradley's approval flowed from his self-esteem, which was growing markedly, a result not only of American success in the breakout since Cobra but also of the complimentary remarks from high-ranking American officers on his perspicacity and tactical skill. His decision to permit Patton to remove half of the XV Corps from the Argentan area in favor of going to Dreux, a decision made on the spur of the moment, was inconsistent with his prior actions. Bradley had, as he said, "refrained from lifting a finger to change the interallied boundary" near Argentan, and Montgomery had refrained from altering the boundary on his own initiative: thus both commanders believed that Haislip lacked the strength to close the Argentan-Falaise gap firmly. By giving Patton, who hated standing in place, his head to go eastward, Bradley, without consulting Montgomery—he should have done so out of respect—dispersed his troop elements and further depleted his strength at what had been the focal point of the encirclement that he himself had initiated.

He rationalized his action. "Due to the delay in closing the gap between Argentan and Falaise," he later said, a delay he implicitly blamed on the Canadians, "many of the German divisions which were in the pocket have now escaped." With this apparently the case, Bradley was, by implication, simply following Montgomery's earlier directive to execute a wider envelopment at the Seine. Bradley could not let Patton move the entire XV Corps out of the Argentan area, for he had to maintain the southern jaw. Additionally, if Montgomery got the Canadians or the British to close the Argentan-Falaise gap from the north, some Americans had to be near Argentan to ensure a firm closure.

The expansion of Bradley's self-confidence led him to make decisions in partial disregard of Montgomery's valid claim to Allied leadership. Bradley's intent was to promote American interests. The result benefited Patton, who, on the surface at least, seemed happy enough to work under Bradley's direction.

"Patton's dramatic transformation in less than two months from *bête noire* to hero among Bradley's staff," wrote Russell Weigley, "was a direct function of the correspondingly swift decline of the hero of El Alamein." Even Montgomery's appearance disenchanted some Americans. Chester Hanson, Bradley's aide, described Montgomery in unflattering fashion and spoke of "his sharp beagle like nose, the small grey eyes that dart about quickly like rabbits in a Thurber cartoon." But more than Montgomery's appearance, Weigley said, explained "the amount of poison that had so swiftly seeped into the relationship between the two army groups [in Normandy]. The arrogance and coldness of [Montgomery] . . . his impenetrable self-satisfaction, all formed the nettle around which animosity clung; that that suspicion and dislike had grown so rapidly . . . indicates sources far deeper than Montgomery's unamiable personality, old distrusts between Americans and British far stronger than the rhetoric of the Grand Alliance." Without mutual confidence and trust between Montgomery and Bradley, with both acting on their own and each failing to keep the other informed of his activities, with Americans feeling Montgomery to be overcautious and letting the Germans escape, with the euphoria of the breakout inflaming American egos, the Americans were anxious to get out from 21 Army Group control. The coalition seemed about to fall apart.

Kluge, who spent the night of August 14 at Dietrich's headquarters, found the situation, he said, "most unpleasant." The Canadian penetration on the Caen–Falaise highway was a major blow, but other local successes by the Allies threatened to break the German lines.

On the following morning, Kluge departed Dietrich's command post. He traveled toward the front and into the pocket. Four hours later he vanished. Search parties sent out were unable to find him. No messages came from him.

Hitler was highly suspicious of Kluge's disappearance. There were vague intimations of Kluge's association with some of the conspirators of the July 20 putsch. Also incriminating was the simple timing of Kluge's act. Allied forces had that day come ashore on the French Riviera. Had Kluge dropped out of sight and sound to make contact with Allied authorities? Was Kluge trying to surrender the German forces in Normandy? Was he endeavoring to negotiate some kind of deal? Hitler consulted with two of his field marshals for a possible successor for Kluge.

Shortly before nine A.M., August 15, as Kluge was leaving Dietrich's headquarters, the Allied commanders at army group and army levels in Normandy received two Ultra Secret intercepts of German messages dispatched to Hitler on the previous day. One was a request for permission to withdraw the front to the Falaise–Argentan line. The other made known an intention to attack the Americans near Argentan with five or six panzer divisions. Were the Germans then still bottled up? Were they planning a breakout attack?

Montgomery, Bradley, and Dempsey met at eleven A.M. at the 21 Army Group command post. Crerar's Canadians were still struggling to get to Falaise. Dempsey was heading eastward to take not only Falaise but also Argentan. Whenever Falaise fell, either to the Canadians or to the British, Montgomery said, he would have Crerar strike to Trun for a possible meeting with the Americans to close the pocket.

Learning of Montgomery's intention for juncture at Trun, Bradley informed him of having reduced Patton's forces near Argentan. The 2nd French Armored Division had extended its positions to cover the Argentan exits on the south. The veteran 90th U.S. Infantry Division, which had followed the French to Sées and Carrouges, moved eastward and further extended the line six miles from Argentan to the small town of Le Bourg-St-Léonard, which occupies the crest of a ridge three miles south of Chambois and overlooks the Orne and Dives river valleys. With these adjustments made, Haislip's XV Corps headquarters and two divisions, one armored, the other infantry, had sped off toward the east, toward Dreux.

Startled by Bradley's independent action, Montgomery cautioned him to be alert to the German attack expected across the Alençon–Argentan highway.

Despite the Ultra warning, slackening pressure from the Germans around Argentan seemed to confirm the German passage and escape through the Argentan-Falaise gap. Yet other information pointed to the continuing existence of the pocket. As Bradley tried to reconcile the conflicting data, the easing of German contact, and the notice of the anticipated German assault, he became anxious. Had he made a mistake to let Patton go?

Patton's three corps were galloping side by side to the east. Cook, instructed by Patton to "get started as soon as possible," formed a tank-infantry column from both of his divisions and dispatched the force toward Orleans. By darkness of August 15, he had troops at the edge of the city. Walker's XX Corps switched from the road to Dreux to routes heading eastward in the direction of Chartres and made good progress despite growing resistance. Haislip's XV Corps drove toward Dreux and was within five miles of the place by evening.

That afternoon, Patton wrote in his diary, "Bradley came down to see me suffering from nerves. There is a rumor, which I doubt, that there are five panzer divisions at Argentan, so Bradley wants me to halt my move to the east on the line of Chartres . . . Dreux, and . . . [Orléans]. His motto seems to be, 'In case of doubt, halt.' I am complying with the order and by tomorrow I can probably persuade him to let me advance [farther east]. I wish I were Supreme Commander."

To Patton, the decision to close the pocket and trap the Germans had produced in its wake a string of errors. The initial encirclement had been too shallow. The drive north from Le Mans through Alençon to Argentan had taken place without proper flank protection. The order to halt at Argentan had come at the most inopportune moment. Now with a deeper envelopment well under way, Bradley had suspended Patton's movement to the east. It was his second stop order, and it shut down, once again, a chance to trap the Germans.

No wonder Patton dreamed of being the Supreme Commander. He would take absolute hold of the operations and surround and destroy all the Germans in Normandy with resolution and finality.

There was still no word from Kluge or about him at six P.M., August 15, when Gunther Blumentritt, Kluge's chief of staff at theater headquarters, in the Paris suburb of St-Germain-en-Laye, talked with Hitler's G-3, Alfred Jodl, on the telephone. "The situation west of Argentan," Blumentritt said, "is worsening by the hour." Without directly mentioning the solution required to redress the circumstances, avoiding the disagreeable sound of the option in everyone's mind, Blumentritt continued. "An over-all decision has to be made." Hitler, he meant, needed to permit the forces in Normandy to start escaping.

"If such a decision has to be made as a last resort," Jodl said smoothly, correcting Blumentritt's statement and rephrasing it into language more conventional around Hitler's headquarters, "it could only be to attack toward Sées to gain room so that other intentions"—he too was averse to spelling out the obvious thought—"can be carried out."

"I am duty bound," Blumentritt pressed, "to point out the state of the armored units." They were dwindling in numbers and short of gasoline.

Jodl then got to the point. In order to break out of the encirclement, he said, the Germans had first to attack.

"We must speak frankly," Blumentritt countered. Having all the forces attack to get out of the pocket was sound. But to attack for other purposes was no longer feasible.

Jodl wavered. Hitler was still interested in offensive operations.

"I must emphatically state," Blumentritt said, "that I am in a difficult position as chief of staff when Kluge is not here. I have the most urgent request. As long as Kluge is absent, someone must be appointed by the Führer to take charge." The senior commanders were Paul Hausser at the Seventh Army, Josef Dietrich at the Fifth Panzer Army, and Heinrich Eberbach, who headed an army-level panzer group.

Jodl inclined toward Hausser.

"I'll be most grateful," Blumentritt said, "for the quickest possible decision." He added, "As far as I am concerned, I am as cool as a cucumber." Why not? He was in the outskirts of Paris. "But I must say that the responsible people on the front contemplate the situation as being extremely tense."

Jodl remarked sarcastically on the reports of Eberbach's inability "to do anything," that is, to start an offensive anywhere.

Blumentritt overlooked the comment. "If a new commander is appointed by the Führer," he told Jodl, "he must be given a clearly stated limited mission without any strings attached." What he meant was, the commander had to be able to take quick action when required, without having to wait for approval from higher headquarters. Otherwise, the German divisions in the field were lost. Time was short—"it is," Blumentritt figuratively said with a sigh, "five minutes before midnight."

At seven P.M., an hour after Blumentritt's report, Hitler named Hausser temporary commander of Army Group B. He ordered Hausser to launch an attack near Sées. He was to destroy the American forces there and prevent them from closing the circle around the Germans.

Given up for dead or at best a prisoner of the Allies, Kluge turned up at Dietrich's headquarters around ten P.M. Where had he been? He had spent the day in a ditch. An Allied plane had strafed his vehicle

CHAPTER 17

Closing the Pocket

FIVE HOURS AFTER RETURNING from his harrowing day in a ditch, around two A.M., August 16, Kluge sent a message to Jodl, Hitler's G-3. He recommended an immediate evacuation of the pocket through the still open Argentan-Falaise gap.

There was no response for more than ten hours. Then, at forty-five minutes past noon, Jodl telephoned. He admitted the soundness, even the necessity, of Kluge's suggestion. But, again, he considered a preliminary action to be essential. Kluge, Jodl thought, had to broaden the Argentan-Falaise gap in order to allow the troops to exit more easily.

Kluge understood Jodl's logic. But he simply lacked the troop strength to carry out any sort of offensive operation. What the soldiers had to do, above all, was to maintain the walls of the pocket and prevent them from caving in. They had, first of all, to keep from being crushed. "No matter how many orders are issued," Kluge said firmly, "the troops cannot, are not able to, are not strong enough to defeat the enemy. It would be a fateful error to succumb to a hope that cannot be fulfilled."

Jodl seemed to accept Kluge's outlook. He would now have to persuade Hitler to the validity of the view.

Lacking Hitler's authorization to pull back but expecting to receive permission momentarily, Kluge, two hours later, at 2:40 P.M., August 16, disseminated instructions for a partial withdrawal. In order to deny the Allies observation of German movements and thus accurate bombing and shelling, the Germans would travel through the hours of darkness. Starting that night, the units in the westernmost part of the pocket were to pull back to the Orne River. On the following night, all were to cross the river to the eastern bank. Beyond that, Kluge made no provision for additional movement, although the troops were hardly out of danger on the right bank of the Orne. Yet Kluge, looking ahead, ordered an attack to throw the Americans off the ridge at the village of Le Bourg-St-Léonard, six miles east of Argentan. Eventually, the Germans would have to move over the three miles of ground between Le Bourg-St-Léonard and Chambois. Holding the St-Léonard ridge, the Germans would prevent observation of their escape .

Two hours afterwards, at 4:40 P.M., August 16, Hitler's directive arrived in Normandy. He acquiesced in a withdrawal not only across the Orne River but also over the Dives River.

Hitler's decision flowed from the Allied invasion of southern France on the previous day. The Allies had easily come ashore on the Riviera because relatively few Germans were there to oppose them. The Overlord operation since June 6 had drawn so many units from the south to Normandy that skeleton numbers remained to defend the Atlantic coast below Brittany and the Mediterranean shore between Spain and Italy. Unable to keep the Allies from landing on beaches west of Nice, Hitler wished to hold, as long as possible, the ports of Marseilles and Toulon. Substantial garrisons in these cities guaranteed German retention for some time and the eventual destruction of the harbors. The forces elsewhere were so sparse and dispersed that they were unable even to shut down the extensive French Resistance activities. Widespread sabotage against communications, roads, and railways, as well as almost constant ambush and raids, created uncertainty and eroded German morale throughout the area. Too weak to defeat the quasi-military French Forces of the Interior, how could the Germans hope to block the Allies from the Rhône River valley, the natural route north to Lyon, Dijon, and the provinces of Alsace and Lorraine?

The Führer was therefore considering abandoning southern France and was about to reach that conclusion. By getting his forces out, he could mass them somewhere, perhaps in the foothills of the Vosges Mountains, for a heavy and disabling counterattack, possibly in combination with units coming from Normandy.

Also involved were about 100,000 men in the Bay of Biscay coastal area south of the Loire River. They would soon start marching, mostly on foot, eastward across the interior of France toward Dijon. Harassed by Resistance groups and by Allied aircraft along their routes, many of them would eventually cross the Loire River and surrender to the Americans.

On August 16, Hitler allowed Kluge to retire out of the pocket and toward the Seine. He had intended to defend the Paris-Orléans gap, but the loss of Orleans that day to Patton's army dissipated his hope.

Yet Hitler stipulated two actions as prerequisites to Kluge's retrograde movement. Kluge had to attack near Argentan to widen the escape opening; he had to hold Falaise as a "corner pillar."

That was about the time that Falaise started to slip from German fingers. The Canadians fought their way up the height dominating Falaise, then battled into a corner of the town. The place was a pile of rubble from Allied air bombardment and artillery shelling. Still the German defenders continued to hold out and to resist in the ruins. It would take the Canadians and the Poles the rest of the day and most of the next to clear the opposition and take firm possession of Falaise.

With the Canadian army owning a foothold in Falaise and striving to extend its control, Montgomery phoned Crerar and told him to head for Trun, about ten miles east and slightly southeast of Falaise, and Chambois, four miles farther, even as his men gained Falaise. Crerar was then to push south from these small towns to meet the Americans coming north. Allied juncture would close the pocket. Montgomery also wished Crerar to start advancing his left flank elements about twenty-five miles eastward to Lisieux, an important road hub, and impede German escape movements toward the Seine.

Shortly thereafter, probably around five P.M., Montgomery telephoned Bradley. He spoke about the departure of the XV Corps headquarters and two divisions from Argentan and wondered whether the remaining forces, French and American, would be able to cope with the five or six panzer divisions thought to be preparing to strike nearby.

Bradley remained silent. Had he made a mistake to send the units off? Had he been wrong to listen to Patton's urgings?

Montgomery continued. In addition to safeguarding Argentan, could Bradley push to the northeast for several miles across the gap to Trun and Chambois? If the Americans met the Canadians and Poles, they would cut the passage allowing German escape. What did Bradley think?

"I agree with you, sir," Bradley responded. He was uncomfortable. The focus of his attention was already elsewhere. But he promised to take appropriate action.

Two days earlier, four American divisions and twenty-two artillery battalions under the XV Corps headquarters had held the southern edge of the pocket near Argentan. With the corps headquarters, two divisions, and fifteen artillery battalions gone, two divisions, the 2nd French Armored and the 90th U.S. Infantry, and seven artillery battalions remained. A third division, the inexperienced 80th, was in the Alençon area and available to come up and reinforce the other two.

Like Montgomery, Bradley questioned whether he had enough strength to hold the positions around Argentan and also to go to Trun and Chambois. For on the afternoon of August 16, in compliance with Kluge's order, a German force gathered at Le Bourg-St-Léonard and pushed the 90th Division off the ridge. They thus denied the Americans observation of the Orne and Dives bottomland, territory across which the German troops about to start pulling out of the pocket that night would eventually have to travel.

The Americans counterattacked at once, regained the village, and restored their positions on the high ground. But the contest, they understood, was hardly at an end. The height was important to both sides, and the struggle to possess it would continue.

To Montgomery, indications of what the Germans were up to were less than clear. Had they escaped from the pocket or were they still bottled up? He seemed to have set into motion solutions designed to meet either case. If the Germans remained vulnerable to encirclement in the pocket, closing off the neck near Argentan and Falaise promised to trap them. If they were out and heading for the Seine, the Canadian move to Lisieux and Patton's drive to the east threatened to intercept them.

Having thus provided for either contingency, Montgomery, for the first time on August 16, began seriously to consider what the Allies ought to do once they got beyond the Seine River. Given the importance of overrunning the German rocket bases in the Pas-de-Calais and thereby stopping further flying bombs from falling on London, of gaining the great port of Antwerp just above Brussels, and of taking the shortest distance to the Rhine River, the main route to follow, surely, led to the north, along the Channel coast. Making no decision for the moment, Montgomery pondered the idea.

Patton was in high spirits on August 16. Eisenhower had made a public announcement of Patton's active participation in the campaign. Newspaper correspondents were now free to mention his name and his Third Army and to recount their feats during the past two weeks. They leaped at the opportunity and spread Patton's fame. "I supposed you had guessed," he wrote his wife that evening. "We took Brittany, Nantes, Angers, Le Mans, and Alençon and several other places still secret."

The capture of Orléans, about seventy-five miles south of Paris, by

Cook's XII Corps, also elated Patton. Although Cook had to halt in place temporarily in compliance with Bradley's order, the territorial gain put the Allies in possession of the eastern edge of the Overlord lodgment area. This was of little importance to Patton, but the corps was in a key position for further advance, depending on what the high command decided.

Traveling to Chartres on August 16, Patton met Walker. The XX Corps was heavily engaged with strong German forces in a battle for the city, but the Americans, careful to avoid damaging the cathedral, were slowly taking control. They would own the place on the following day and be about fifty miles southwest of Paris. Walker too had to remain where he was for the moment.

Delighted with the progress of his elements, Patton drove to Dreux, which the XV Corps had seized that afternoon. About forty miles west of Paris, Haislip had also stopped in conformance with Bradley's instruction. Patton told him to reconnoiter northeast in the direction of Mantes-Gassicourt on the Seine River and to move in strength only after receiving explicit orders.

Patton's visits to his two subordinate corps commanders, as well as reports from Cook in Orléans, exhilarated him. Nothing serious barred the advances of his corps. His troops could go in any direction without interference. What possible reasons justified Bradley's order to halt at Dreux, Chartres, and Orléans, the second shutdown of offensive operations?

As he flew back to his headquarters in a small plane—when he visited the front, he traveled in a jeep or other vehicle so that the soldiers always saw him going forward; when he returned home, he rode in, sometimes piloted, his Cub aircraft—he pondered what had prompted Bradley to stop him again: a shortage of gasoline? a concern with the Third Army open left flank? an intent to halt at the Seine in accordance with the Overlord plan? None seemed compelling. Was it simply astonishment over and discomfort with the speed and the seeming recklessless of Patton's advance to the east?

As he wrote to his wife that evening, "At the moment the fear of they"—a favorite expression of Patton's, the phrase meant unnecessary worry over vague conditions unable to be defined exactly but producing paralysis—"has stopped us on what was the best run yet. . . . I feel that if [I were] only unaided [alone and independent] I would win this war." He meant quickly.

"When I returned to Third Army headquarters at 1830 [6:30 P.M.]," Patton recorded in his diary, "Bradley called up and directed that I use the 2nd French, 90th, and 80th Divisions to capture a town called Trun about halfway up in the gap [separating Canadians and Americans]. He said that [Leonard] Gerow of the V Corps [under the First U.S. Army] would arrive in a couple of days to take over the command of these divisions, as his own corps [Gerow's V Corps] had been pinched out. I told him that pending the arrival of Gerow, I would make a temporary corps [headquarters] with Gaffey [Patton's chief of Staff]. Gaffey left at 2000 [8 P.M.] with orders to attack tomorrow morning."

Appointed to form and to head a Provisional Corps headquarters to direct the push to Trun and Chambois, Gaffey was an exceptionally efficient soldier. He had come to North Africa with Patton and had been with him ever since. He had commanded an armored division with distinction in the fighting in Sicily. Patton had complete confidence in Gaffey, and Gaffey always knew what Patton wanted.

He set out for Alençon in a heavy downpour of rain with four officers to assist him. He was thoroughly acquainted with the situation, the terrain, the units in the area, their locations, dispositions, and capacities. Establishing a command post in the largest hotel in town, Gaffey quickly made communications contact with his three divisions, the 2nd French Armored, the 90th and 80th U.S. Infantry. Before long he had drawn a plan for an attack to start anytime after ten A.M. on the following day, August 17.

Sensitive to French aspirations, Gaffey had fashioned his projected thrust to Trun and Chambois in such a way as to place the main burden on the 90th Division. The Americans were to head north from Le Bourg-St-Léonard, go three miles, cross the Dives River, and enter Chambois. They were then to advance on Trun. The French were to commit a small element to cut the Argentan–Falaise road.

Leclerc, Gaffey knew, had no particular interest in the Argentan area and no special wish to close the pocket. He was burning with desire to liberate Paris. At Argentan, he was more than a hundred miles away. Haislip at Dreux, Walker at Chartres, and Cook at Orléans were much closer. Would the force of circumstances compel Patton to send any one of them or all three to Paris before he could call on Leclerc?

As early as August 14, Leclerc had asked Haislip to query Patton on when Leclerc could head for Paris. "It is political," Leclerc explained. Haislip passed the question to the Third Army headquarters, and Gaffey told Leclerc to stay where he was.

Smarting with impatience, fretting over standing idly before Argentan, Leclerc went to Patton's headquarters on the evening of August 15. As Patton recorded the meeting, "Leclerc . . . came in, very much excited. . . . He said, among other things, that if he were not allowed to advance on Paris, he would resign. I told him in my best French that he was a baby, and I would not have division commanders tell me where they could fight, and that anyway I had left him in the most dangerous place. We parted friends."

On August 16, Leclerc wrote to Patton. The situation at Argentan, he pointed out, was quiet. It was probably, he suggested, time for him to start assembling his division for its movement to Paris.

Patton's reaction was direct. "Leclerc cut up again to day," he wrote in his diary, "and Gaffey had to ask him categorically whether he would disobey a written order."

Altogether aware of Leclerc's reservations over becoming involved in operations that might keep him from being available for Paris, Gaffey wrote his instruction with Leclerc's concern in mind. He forwarded his directive to the three divisions. Then he received a telephone call from Patton.

Patton narrated in his diary what happened. "At 2330 [11:30 P.M., August 16], Bradley called up and told me to withhold the attack [to Trun and Chambois] until he, Bradley, ordered it. I delivered this order [to Gaffey]. Life is rather dull."

He was deeply disappointed. No one save himself seemed to understand the need to press advantages home with speed and determination.

Bradley's order to cancel Gaffey's attack stemmed from two events. The Germans were massing at Le Bourg-St-Léonard. And Gerow was arriving to take command.

The Germans in the westernmost part of the pocket retired to the Orne River during the night of August 16, shortening the length of the pocket by about ten miles. They followed a meticulously planned and strictly enforced timetable. The movement occurred smoothly and without hitch. The Allies interfered not at all.

Montgomery wrote to Sir James Grigg, Secretary of State for War, on the evening of August 16. Important things were happening, he said, and great events could well take place. The Allies had partially encircled the bulk of the German forces. Some were undoubtedly going to escape, but he could hardly see how they could maintain themselves and fight seriously on the near side of the Seine River.

To Brooke at 10:45 P.M., he outlined his actions. He had Dempsey and the Canadians both pushing toward Argentan. He had ordered Crerar to advance his right to Trun and his left to Lisieux. The Third Army was in Chartres. He was thinking of having Bradley send units from Dreux toward Mantes on the Seine. He expected the Germans to strike around

Argentan, but the American strength, he estimated, was sufficient to absorb the blow and also to move toward Chambois.

On his way to the Argentan area to start the push across the small lowland basin to Trun and Chambois was Gerow, a commander of impeccable credentials, hardly brilliant but balanced and sound. Like George C. Marshall a graduate of the Virginia Military Institute, Gerow had attended and graduated with distinction from all the army schools required for high rank. At the time of Pearl Harbor, he was chief of Marshall's War Plans Division. Replaced by Eisenhower, who was also a close friend of his, Gerow went on to division command, then corps. His V Corps came ashore at Omaha Beach on D day and fought on the First U.S. Army left flank, adjacent to the British, until August 15. Converging boundaries then pinched his corps out of active operations.

He had been at his headquarters about eighty-five miles from Alençon at ten P.M., August 16, when he received a telephone call. A staff officer at Hodges's First Army command post asked him to take eight or ten key officers and report at once to the army commander.

Traveling in three jeeps through a heavy rain, Gerow and his party arrived at their destination around midnight. The war room, despite the late hour, was humming with activity. More officers than usual were clustered around the large wall map. Hodges was there, and he instructed Gerow to proceed to the vicinity of Argentan, take command of three divisions, and launch an attack without delay to close the pocket by taking Chambois, then Trun, unless the Canadians were already in Trun.

"Where are those divisions?" Gerow asked.

"We do not know," was the response. The units were in the Third Army area, and the First Army had no precise knowledge of their locations. "You will have to find them."

The enemy situation? Gerow asked.

The answer was the same.

Early on August 17, in the midst of a howling rainstorm, Gerow left. Only one of Gerow's jeeps had a radio, but it was out of order. Lacking communications, Gerow picked his way through the dark, rain-swept night. Finally, around daybreak, he reached the 90th Division command post. Informed of Gaffey's provisional corps headquarters in Alençon, Gerow joined Gaffey about seven A.M.

Who was in command? All Gaffey knew was the order from Patton to hold up his attack until further notice. Figuring the area to be in the Third Army zone of operations and believing himself to have been transferred from Hodges's to Patton's control, Gerow telephoned Patton, whose command post was closer than Hodges's and who was consequently easier to reach.

Gerow announced his presence. He was there with a small staff, he told Patton, and ready to take over.

As Patton later wrote in his diary, "Since Gaffey had arranged the attack, which might come off at any moment, [I told him that] Gaffey should run it and he, Gerow, could take over as the opportunity afforded." What Patton was after was speed, getting the push off at once.

Gerow was reluctant to launch Gaffey's operation for several reasons. The Germans had driven the 90th Division off the ridge at Le Bourg-St-Léonard at dawn that morning. Gerow was unacquainted with the terrain and the unit dispositions. He had read Gaffey's directive and was less than enthusiastic about his scheme of maneuver. If Gerow was the responsible commander, he wanted to put on his own show. Besides, the V Corps Artillery was on its way to the area and would arrive later in the day to provide support for the attacking infantry.

At an impasse, Gerow and Gaffey sat at Alençon and waited for someone in authority to tell them who was to command. The Falaise gap remained open.

Why Bradley sent Gerow to take charge of an area and a situation Gerow knew nothing of is difficult to understand. Perhaps Bradley simply lacked confidence in Gaffey, who had commanded a division, never a corps. Gerow, in contrast, was an experienced and competent corps commander who had suddenly become available. By using Gerow, Bradley expected to lose some time. To compensate for this regrettable result, Bradley counted on Marshall's and Eisenhower's pleasure over Gerow's participation in a pivotal action, for Gerow was a favorite of both.

Montgomery flew to Bradley's headquarters on the morning of August 17. They talked about how to trap the Germans. Montgomery thought it would be well to send the troops at Dreux northward to Mantes-Gassicourt on the Seine River. Bradley was receptive.

They also discussed how to develop the campaign beyond the Seine. Bradley agreed with Montgomery on the objective. The Ruhr was the next place on which to set their sights. Whether Bradley actually acquiesced in the route to follow, Montgomery understood him to favor his own preference, an advance to the north, toward Belgium and Luxembourg.

On that morning of August 17, Patton was eager to get something going to Chambois and Trun. He was frustrated, unable to do so. He could neither resolve the command situation nor put pressure on Gerow, because he lacked knowledge of whether Gerow belonged to him or to

Hodges. Only Bradley could say. Patton could reach Bradley by radio, but because the Germans could intercept messages over the air, Patton decided to fly to Bradley's headquarters.

Bad weather prevented his plane from taking off until noon. At the 12th Army Group command post fifty minutes later, he found Hodges. Bradley was in conference with Montgomery.

Hodges straightened Patton out. Bradley had shifted the army boundaries to place the Argentan area and the units there under the First Army. Thus Hodges was in control, Gerow belonged to him, and Gerow was to run the operation.

Before leaving his headquarters that morning, Patton had anticipated this possibility. He had therefore arranged a simple code with his acting chief of staff, Hobart Gay. If command was to switch from Gaffey to Gerow, Patton would call on the radio and let Gay know by saying, "Change horses." Gay was then to notify Gaffey to step aside.

Patton acted on this understanding. Raising Gay on the radio, he announced, "Swap horses." Although he had no further say in the matter, because the operation was under Hodges, he added his wish for speed in the attack. The objective, Patton specified obliquely, still speaking a kind of coded language, was the same, Trun, "thence on."

What did he mean by "thence on"? Gay asked.

"Another Dunkirk," Patton said.

What he was trying to say was, if Gerow found no Canadians at Trun, he was to go on until he made contact with them. But "Another Dunkirk" suggested otherwise. The two words were the origin of a remark attributed to Patton and widely quoted to fuel Anglo-American antagonisms. "Let me continue," Patton was supposed to have said to Bradley, "and I'll drive the limeys into the sea."

Gay telephoned Gaffey and passed on Patton's message. Gaffey put Gerow on, and Gay repeated what he had said.

Tired after driving all night in the rain, Gerow failed to understand. "What do you mean by 'swap horses'?" he asked.

"It means you in place of Gaffey."

Gerow wanted to be sure. Did this come from Eagle 6? he asked, speaking in veiled fashion and referring to Bradley's code name.

"It came from Lucky 6 [Patton], who was at that time with Eagle 6."

Gerow took over. Gaffey returned to the Third Army headquarters.

At the 12th Army Group command post, Montgomery having departed, Bradley met with Hodges and Patton. They discussed "spheres of influence" and "zones of action" for both armies. Bradley removed the halt order holding Patton's forces at Dreux, Chartres, and Orléans.

In keeping with Montgomery's wish, he projected an extension of the lower jaw of the trap. The Americans were now to establish and hold a line stretching from Argentan, through Chambois and Dreux to the Seine. Cook was to remain at Orléans to conserve gasoline pending decision on how to continue the campaign beyond the Overlord lodgment area. Walker was to occupy Chartres and also free Haislip at Dreux. Haislip was to go twenty-five miles to the Seine at Mantes-Gassicourt, thirty miles northwest of and downstream from Paris. To cover Haislip's left flank and the wide expanse of open ground between the American units around Argentan and around Dreux, Hodges was to dispatch the XIX Corps, soon to be pinched out of action, about a hundred miles to the east. Bradley asked Hodges to draw a plan for his movement.

According to the letter of instructions issued by Bradley that day, August 17, Hodges's First Army was to seize Chambois and Trun, then continue north to make contact with the British and Canadians and thus "complete the destruction of the Germans caught in the pocket." As divisions were pinched out on the First Army left, Hodges was to move them east between Argentan and Dreux. Patton's Third Army was to seize Mantes and prevent the enemy from escaping.

The three U.S. commanders in conference considered long-range objectives beyond Normandy. The Ruhr, all agreed, had come into sight. Bradley and Hodges had no strong feeling on how to get there. Patton proposed, if they were about to move beyond the confines of Normandy, an eastward drive to Germany. The Americans, and particularly Patton's forces, were better placed for such movement.

At Alençon, where Gerow was preparing to act, a letter of instructions confirming verbal orders came from Hodges and told Gerow to capture Chambois, then go on to Trun. To Gerow, it was too late to attack that afternoon. Besides, he wanted the 90th Division to drive the Germans from the ridge at Le Bourg-St-Léonard and to secure a good line of departure for the effort to Chambois.

With the Americans unable or unwilling to close the pocket, Montgomery at two forty-five P.M., August 17, telephoned Crerar. It was "absolutely essential," he said, for Crerar to take Trun and go on from there four miles more to Chambois "at all cost."

Both armored divisions, Canadian and Polish, jumped off and found their way bitterly contested. By evening, they were about two miles short of Trun.

On the other side of the pocket, after darkness fell, the 90th Division moved up the long slope to the Le Bourg-St-Léonard ridge and threw the Germans off. At midnight, the Americans again owned the high ground.

Gerow had by then drawn his attack order. The operation to Chambois was to open on the following morning, August 18.

Inserting Gerow into the chain of command had lost the Allies another day in the effort to close the pocket.

Patton, unwilling to instruct Haislip over the radio to advance to Mantes on the Seine, dispatched an armored car with orders to the XV Corps at eight P.M., August 17. Later that evening, Patton noted in his diary what he hoped to do. "I will close [turn] the XX and XII Corps to the north," he wrote, "to support this [XV Corps] movement." He envisaged a broad, all-encompassing sweep by the three corps down both banks of the Seine River to the sea. Moving across the entire German escape area in Normandy, the maneuver would fashion a deep encirclement as well as a strong envelopment.

Of all the notions on how to trap and destroy the Germans west of the Seine River, Patton's idea offered the best chance. It promised to eliminate ruthlessly and permanently the most experienced, the most capable enemy forces opposing the Allies in western Europe. Although other German units elsewhere, those in the Pas-de-Calais, Belgium, and the Netherlands, those south of the Loire River in southern France, those undergoing training in Germany, were outside of Patton's projected net, they hardly possessed the power of the two German field armies battling for their lives in Normandy. With that main enemy army group eradicated, the Allies could steamroller their way into Germany against feeble opposition. The end of the war would be close at hand.

Unfortunately, only Patton had his eyes fixed and focused on the proper military objective, destroying the enemy forces. To Montgomery and Bradley, getting to Germany took precedence over trapping and liquidating the Germans west of the Seine. To them, the Germans in Normandy were no longer important. They were as good as destroyed. They thus rejected Patton's concept. For Patton's projected movement would cut across and block the routes leading the British, Canadian, and Hodges's armies to and across the Seine River. Although the battle of Normandy remained unfinished, the two leading Allied commanders, Montgomery and Bradley, were already ignoring the main chance of ending the war. Prematurely, they looked ahead to a triumphal march to Germany.

Giving credence to their outlook was a remarkable document published by the First U.S. Army on August 17. It was the daily G-2 report, and it received wide distribution. The paper noted the movement of the Germans from their most western positions to the Orne River during the previous night, which was quite correct. The G-2 then jumped to a conclusion. "The main portion of the enemy forces," he reported, inaccurately as well as ungrammatically, "have extricated themselves from the pocket."

Contributing to the mistaken belief of the German escape was an action taken by the tactical air forces on August 17. If much about the land battle seemed to be confusing—for example, how many Germans were trapped—one condition appeared to be in sharp focus to the air commanders: the Allied ground forces compressing the pocket were operating in such close proximity to each other, at such close quarters, that air support became too dangerous. The bomb line, set daily, a boundary to keep pilots from accidentally attacking Allied ground troops, was removed from the pocket that day. As a result, the pocket became off-limits to Allied fliers. Tactical flights against the Germans virtually surrounded ceased. From then on, damage inflicted on the Germans still bottled up would come from Allied artillery pieces and infantry weapons. The tactical aircraft would roam far and wide on subsequent days, attacking targets of opportunity everywhere—everywhere, that is, except in the pocket, where the considerable German forces were about to move across the Orne River and beyond.

Writing to Brooke around eleven P.M. on August 17, Montgomery said, "The best news I can give you tonight is that the gap has now been closed and the Polish Armoured Division has reached Trun and is pushing on to Chambois." The report was wishful thinking. Montgomery was anticipating reality. The Poles and Canadians were still outside Trun. Across the gap, the Americans were still at Le Bourg-St-Léonard.

"The whole area," Montgomery continued, "is covered with burning tanks and MT [motor transport]." The problem was, "It is really impossible to say exactly what is inside the ring and what has escaped so far to the east." Some intelligence officers guessed the greater part of five panzer divisions, together with substantial infantry forces, to be still west of the Falaise–Argentan road. But how accurate the information was was a matter of conjecture.

The Allies, Montgomery said, controlled the principal routes leading to the east but lacked the time to organize barriers across all the exits. "If a major breakout is attempted during tonight," he figured, "it is quite possible that elements will get through and we shall not know what the situation is until later tomorrow."

Montgomery noted that the Germans had openly moved their barges and ferries to the near bank of the Seine and were waiting to transport across the river those who came from the pocket. "Any German formation or units that escape eastwards over the Seine," he ventured, "will be quite unfit to fight for months to come."

To Phyllis Reynolds he wrote in high spirits, "Here everything goes well. I now have troops in Orleans, Chartres, and Dreux. And I have some 100,000 Germans almost surrounded in the pocket. The whole prospect of what may lie ahead is fascinating." Montgomery seemed to be passively observing the unfolding events instead of actively controlling and shaping them.

The slowness in closing the jaws at Argentan and Falaise or to fashion a meeting at Trun and Chambois prompted Eisenhower to explain to Marshall what was happening. "Due to the extraordinary measures taken by the enemy north of Falaise," he wrote, ". . . it is possible that our total bag of prisoners will not be so great as I first anticipated." The blame, Eisenhower implied, lay in the north, with the Canadians and the British. He exempted his own passivity from blame.

Field Marshal Walther Model, who had performed in outstanding fashion on the Eastern Front, arrived in Normandy on the morning of August 17. He was to relieve Kluge as soon as he was familiar with the battlefield situation. He consulted with various officers, visited several headquarters, studied reports of operations, and began to develop a feel for what was happening.

That night the Germans in the pocket withdrew across the Orne River. Road congestion, Allied artillery fire, and shortages of supplies were minor problems. The movement proceeded smoothly. Specially appointed bridge commanders funneled traffic through potential bottle-necks. The troops remained well disciplined. As some high-ranking German officers later said, part of the success was due to the British. They "did not follow up very vigorously from the west."

Very early during the morning hours of darkness on August 18, forty-five cargo planes delivered gasoline to the troops in the pocket. At six A.M., Model conferred with his three senior officers, Hausser, Die-trich, and Eberbach. He had yet to assume formal command, but he assigned them roles in the continuing withdrawal. The Germans planned to move that night from the Orne River across the Argentan–Falaise highway to the high ground immediately east of the road.

Montgomery was concerned with matters outside the Overlord lodg-ment area. Having spoken with Bradley on the previous day and appar-ently having obtained his agreement on what the Allies ought to do beyond the Seine River, Montgomery sent a message to Brooke at eight-thirty A.M., August 18. Both army groups, he wrote, after crossing the river, should, he thought, move north in "a solid mass of some forty divisions," the British and Canadians toward Antwerp, the Americans toward Brussels, Aachen, and Cologne.

Brooke, later that day, signaled his approval. It was the last message he would send Montgomery for about ten days, for he flew to Italy for conferences and inspections. There would be no more nightly letters from Montgomery to Brooke in the immediate future.

On the same morning of August 18, Eisenhower visited Bradley. They discussed how to shape the campaign beyond the Seine. The Ruhr was obviously the ultimate objective. To get there, both officers favored moving eastward across France directly toward Germany. The objectives they saw as immediately pertinent were Karlsruhe, Mannheim, and Wiesbaden, along the Rhine River, 250 miles away.

The armored car dispatched by Patton the night before took much longer than anticipated to reach the XV Corps headquarters. It arrived at six A.M., August 18. Haislip immediately complied with Patton's instructions. His corps rushed to Mantes-Gassicourt and reached the bank of the Seine River. Mantes was just inside the 21 Army Group operational area, but Montgomery had specifically permitted, even encouraged, the American incursion.

Writing to his wife on the evening of August 18, Patton was reflective and somewhat moody. Bradley had failed to listen sympathetically to his advocacy of a broad sweep to the north by his three corps. "The family," he said, meaning the Canadians, "got Falaise. . . . I could have had it a week ago but modesty [Bradley] via destiny [Eisenhower] made me stop." He was referring to Bradley's halt order and using his pet names for his American superiors. Apropos of nothing in particular, Patton remarked, "Courtney [Hodges] is realy [sic] a moron." He failed to elucidate what had prompted the comment. "Omar [Bradley]," he continued, "is O.K. but not dashing." Patton owed him quite a bit, for Bradley had agreed with many of Patton's suggestions. Yet getting his way was always an uphill struggle for Patton. "All that I have to do [I do] over protest. I just [recently] pushed on a lot and will [soon] be warned of over extension"—that is, of moving his forces too fast and too far and thereby assuming unnecessary risks—"when the phone works." The phone at the moment, he was glad to say, was out of order.

Near Argentan, Gerow got his attack off on the morning of August 18. Alerted by Gaffey of Leclerc's indifference to the pocket, Gerow asked little of the 2nd French Armored Division except for firepower to help the 80th Division seize the town of Argentan. In its initial combat, the 80th fumbled and made no progress. The 90th Division advanced north from Le Bourg-St-Léonard toward Chambois and took a barely perceptible mound of earth, a small hill more apparent on maps than on the ground, little more than a mile away, about half the distance to Chambois. The Germans contested vigorously.

On the other side of the gap, the Canadians fought hard on August 18 and against fierce opposition took Trun. Troops tried to continue on to Chambois but could go only halfway, two miles. They battled against extremely heavy resistance, for the Germans were desperately trying to keep their escape passage open. Toward the end of the day, a few Canadians reached the outskirts of St-Lambert-sur-Dives, a village burning and clogged with wreckage and bodies.

Off to the west, the British approached Argentan.

Ignoring the fighting around Trun, St-Lambert, and Chambois, Montgomery wrote to the military authorities in London that evening. "All German formations that cross the Seine," he said, "will be incapable of combat during the months to come."

To Churchill, he promised, "Our aerial strength is such that the enemy cannot escape us."

That night the Germans resumed their withdrawal. As intense Allied artillery fires rained down on them from all sides, they moved eastward from the Orne River, crossed the Falaise–Argentan highway, and occupied high ground immediately to the east. The Germans threatened with encirclement now filled a small area measuring about six by seven miles. The escape gap remained open between the Canadians at St-Lambert, the Americans on the mound about a mile from Chambois, and the Poles a mile or so on the other side of Chambois. The opening was no more than three to five miles across. Through this narrow passage, obstructed by wrecked equipment and dead horses, a substantial number of Germans would have to try to escape.

Replacing Kluge, who, while returning to Germany by automobile, swallowed poison and committed suicide, Model took command of the theater and of Army Group B at midnight, August 18. His task was to extricate as many of his soldiers as he could from their near-encirclement. To that end, he ordered a panzer corps, consisting of two panzer divisions, probably 15,000 to 20,000 men, to cross the Seine River to the west bank. From the Bernay and Vimoutiers area, the twin divisions were to strike to the southwest toward Mount Ormel, Trun, and Chambois. Creating a diversion, threatening to overwhelm the Allies seeking to block German passage out of the pocket, the panzer divisions were to help the bottled-up Germans to escape.

While the Germans bent their energies to get out of the still unclosed pocket, and while the Canadians, Poles, and Americans tried to block the opening, the Allied commanders on August 19 were busy in a variety of places on a variety of other matters.

Quite early that day, Bradley and Hodges met to consider how to set a trap along the lower Seine. While Haislip's XV Corps drove downstream from Mantes to Louviers, the XIX Corps of the First U.S. Army was to shift to Haislip's left and fashion a parallel advance to Elbeuf. Since the terrain belonged to the British and Canadians, the two Americans repaired to the 21 Army Group headquarters for a conference with Montgomery, Dempsey, and Crerar.

The Allied commanders first discussed post-Overlord operations, how to proceed beyond the Seine River. Montgomery outlined his preference—the Canadians to take Le Havre and continue up the Channel coast, the British to go to Calais and into Belgium, the Americans to establish themselves in the Beauvais, Laon, Reims, Châlons-sur-Marne, and Troyes areas, ready to go farther to the east or northeast or both.

To Montgomery's surprise, Bradley spoke of Eisenhower's desire to split the Allied forces. His notion had the British and Canadians going north, the Americans heading east toward Nancy and Metz. Bradley himself, he said, favored Eisenhower's course.

Disappointed because he had counted on Bradley's support of his own plan, Montgomery deferred resolution of the problem. He and Eisenhower would decide what paths to follow beyond the Seine.

The Allied commanders then turned to the more immediate job of cutting off the Germans at the Seine. To avoid an American incursion into British territory along the river north of Mantes, Bradley proposed letting Dempsey send several of his divisions through the American zone of operations to Mantes for the push down the left bank. Dempsey refused with thanks. His resources, he said, were insufficient for such a detour and such a drive. Montgomery then approved Bradley's recommendation. The XV and the XIX Corps, both U.S., were to progress down the Seine and erect "stop lines," as the British said, or barriers. Dempsey's task, he wrote in his diary was: "To drive the birds into the stop lines."

No one mentioned the battle at Trun, St-Lambert, and Chambois.

Afterwards, Bradley saw Eisenhower, who set two objectives. The first was to destroy the enemy west of the Seine. There were, he estimated, 75,000 men and 250 tanks still vulnerable. In actuality, about 115,000 men and an unknown number of tanks remained west of the river. The second task was to prepare for the next move. The Americans were to go eastward to the Rhine River.

There was no discussion of the troops drawing the string shut at the Dives River near Chambois.

Eisenhower that day reached a significant decision. With the Allies about to secure the Overlord lodgment area and thus complete the Overlord operation, with the Germans reeling in defeat, there was little point to halt at the Seine for several weeks. Instead of waiting to transform the lodgment into a base to support a drive beyond the Seine, the Allies were to go into post-Overlord operations immediately. The object was to finish off the Germans by pursuing the disorganized and fleeing forces to Germany.

At the same time, Eisenhower, somewhat reluctantly, resolved another problem. Although he preferred to retain the command arrangements as they were, with Montgomery in charge of the Allied ground forces and responsible for the detailed land operations, Eisenhower could no longer disregard the growing pressure, not only from his American colleagues in the field but also from Washington, to terminate Montgomery's pro tem appointment. It was time for Eisenhower to assume the place he had always reserved for himself, no doubt more as an option than as a definite wish.

Unable to resist the clamor for change, Eisenhower decided to take direct command of the Allied ground armies on or about September 1. He informed Montgomery as a matter of information and courtesy.

As Nigel Hamilton has said, "The American armies in the west had come of age on the beaches and in the bitter bocage fighting in Normandy. They had acquitted themselves with growing confidence and distinction—and in the nature of coalition warfare could no longer be expected to tolerate further tutelage under a Briton." More specifically, in Hamilton's words, "With each passing day . . . Bradley had become less willing to operate under Monty's command. With Allied victory in Normandy, the American army had finally come of age."

Bradley, according to his aide's diary, was hardly interested in Falaise or the Seine. He was looking ahead to an eastward drive to Germany. The Germans, he was sure, were finally unraveling, falling apart. The entry of Allied troops into Germany, he believed, would have such an adverse effect on the enemy as to bring the war to an end quickly.

Patton on August 19 drove "to Mantes, and saw the Seine," he wrote in his diary. He "then flew to" Bradley's headquarters. Bradley "had just returned from a visit to Monty and Ike. He now had a new plan. . . . He wants me to move the 5th Armored Division of the XV Corps north along the west bank of the Seine to Louviers, while the XIX

Corps of the First [U.S.] Army comes up on its left [and heads for Elbeuf, also on the Seine]."

He was hardly interested. Relieved of responsibility for Chambois, he was merely a critical observer. His superiors had failed to fasten the trap shut in an expeditious and firm manner, had let the Germans out, and now wanted, by means of imperfect and inefficient means, to catch them again at the Seine.

His thoughts were elsewhere. "I asked if the 79th [Division] could make a bridgehead [across the Seine] at Mantes, and was given reluctant permission."

In offensive operations, Patton hated to stop on the near bank of a stream, particularly if no opposition was present, as at Mantes. On the basis of Eisenhower's decision to go at once beyond the river, Bradley approved.

A single division on the far side of the Seine could do little more than to establish and maintain a bridgehead, which would provide security for additional units crossing the water. A force built up on the far bank could do at least one of two things: drive downstream and strip away German reception facilities for troops escaping the pocket; or start heading cross-country toward Germany. But Bradley, and presumably Montgomery and Eisenhower, had decided against reinforcing the 79th Division, that is, sending more formations across the river at Mantes. They had opted for the more cautious course, driving down the near bank. That made the 79th crossing a temporary dead end. Yet having the troops across was useful for a future advance in any direction. It was also useful for generating newspaper publicity on the first Allied crossing of the Seine River.

Dispirited over these developments, Patton looked to the east. Perhaps he could salvage something besides the newspaper publicity. "I then asked [Bradley]," Patton continued, "if I could take Melun-Fontainebleau [on the upper Seine] and Sens [on the Yonne River, a tributary of the Seine]. By getting these [large towns], in addition to the crossing at Mantes, the line of the Seine becomes useless to the enemy. Bradley said it was too risky, but eventually I talked him into letting me try Monday, the 21st, if I do not receive a stop order by midnight, Sunday, the 20th."

Meanwhile, in the night and rain of August 19, Haislip sent the 79th Division across the Seine River at Mantes. A regiment walked across a dam in single file, each man touching the one ahead. There was no German interference.

One hundred miles to the west, near Falaise, the Allies finally closed the pocket. Some Americans on the morning of August 19 fought their way to the Dives River beside Chambois. The small group of Canadians just outside of St-Lambert battled strenuously and entered the northwestern corner of the village while Germans held stubbornly to the church in the southeastern part. The Poles, leaving some men to attack toward Chambois, turned to the northeast and ascended the steep slope of Mount Ormel, an imposing height towering above the lowland.

Late in the afternoon, a rifle company of the 90th U.S. Division surged across the Dives River and entered Chambois. The men met a Polish detachment of about the same size coming in from the other side. Their juncture at 7:20 P.M., August 19, in the burning town, where the stench of death was strong and pervasive, completed the encirclement.

"The exits from the pocket," Montgomery signaled London that evening, "are closed and no enemy force will escape me."

"Practically speaking," a German officer admitted, "the pocket was closed."

Canadian, Polish, and American troops formed a fence across the neck of the pocket from Le Bourg-St-Léonard to Chambois and St-Lambert. But the barrier they represented was porous and less than sturdy. Germans continued to flow through what was in effect a sieve for at least two more days.

For instead of concentrating an overwhelming mass of soldiers to block and turn back the Germans, the Allies could muster merely a handful of men. Perhaps two hundred in all at Chambois, probably two hundred more at St-Lambert fulfilled what had promised, since August 8, eleven days earlier, to be the climactic event of the Normandy campaign.

PART V

THE
AFTERMATH

THE DEVELOPING POCKET

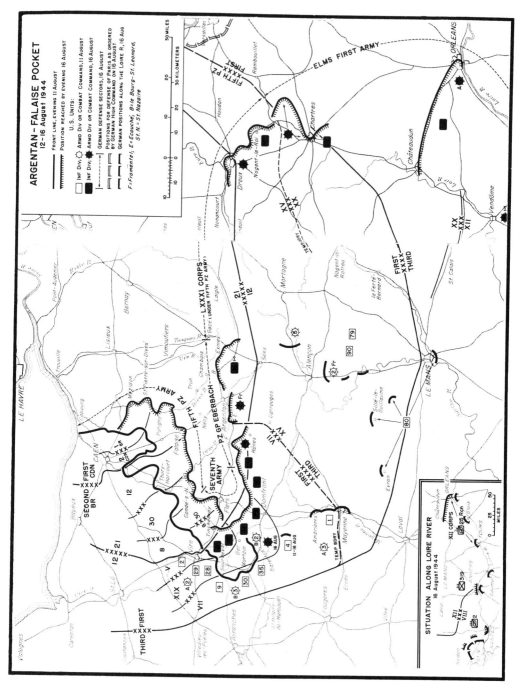

ARGENTAN-FALAISE POCKET
12-16 August 1944

Front Line, Evening 11 August

Position Reached by Evening 16 August

U.S. Units:

Inf Div; Armd Div or Combat Command, 11 August

Inf Div; Armd Div or Combat Command, 16 August

German Defense Sectors, 16 August

Positions for Defense of Paris as Ordered
by German High Command on 16 August

German Positions Along the Loire R., 16 Aug

F=Frometel; E=Ecouché; B=le Bourg-St. Leonard;
St. N.=St. Nazaire

SITUATION ALONG LOIRE RIVER
16 August 1944

CHAPTER 18

The Seine River Crossings

WHERE WERE THE ALLIED FORCES? In Brittany, not quite three hundred miles west of Paris, about 50,000 men were about to start a month-long battle to capture Brest. Along a rough north-south line from Mantes through Dreux and Chartres to Orléans, about 150,000 soldiers waited for orders to go north, northeast, or east. Making a wide swing to the south and east, another 50,000 were moving into position for a thrust down the left bank of the Seine. Near Argentan, around 15,000 French troops stood idly for more than a week and abstained from helping to close the pocket.

The armies of Crerar, Dempsey, Hodges, and Patton were badly coordinated and seemed to be going separate ways. The campaign had become fragmented, split into mutually exclusive segments having little relation to each other or to a single overriding goal. No coherent leadership bound all the parts together to form a unified whole.

The Allied commanders at the top, Eisenhower, Montgomery, and Bradley, had failed to grasp an efficacious method, to enunciate a clear course, and to implement a firm execution of how to destroy the Germans in Normandy. They were unable to do so in large part because they pursued conflicting objectives. Gaining the Overlord lodgment area, providing security along the Loire River flank, seizing the ports in Brittany, and driving to the Rhine River and Germany competed with what should have been the aim of sweeping the Germans entirely from the field. The multiplicity of goals diverted commanders' attention from the principal task and diluted battlefield resources at the climactic point.

All the while, national rivalries, Anglo-American as well as Polish, French, and Canadian, exerted their malevolent effects.

"The final battle of Normandy," said George Kitching, who commanded the 4th Canadian Armoured Division, started on the night of August 19, as the Germans "fought to withdraw through the gap between Trun and Chambois . . . [in] an area four miles by four miles of lovely rolling countryside interspersed by small villages, farms and woods." The German soldiers were desperate to pass through the narrow opening, "the only way to get back to Germany." Kitching estimated about 70,000 Germans on the move, most of them on foot, supported by a small number—perhaps twenty, he judged—of tanks.

Pounded by incessant Allied artillery fires from all sides of the pocket, German troops who had been compressed for the most part into the forest of Gouffern streamed across the bottomland toward Trun, St-Lambert, and Chambois. Those who were able to squeeze through small apertures in the line held by Polish, Canadian, and American soldiers hurried out of the trap.

A drizzling rain out of overcast skies turned into a downpour on the night of August 19, and torrents of water streamed from the sky all day on August 20, hampering Allied artillery observers. The few Allied tactical aircraft flying that day were elsewhere over France. No planes harassed the Germans who had fought at St-Lambert and Chambois to keep a path open and who now marched to the east toward the Seine.

The Germans having abandoned Argentan during the night, the 80th Division finally entered and took the town on August 20. British troops came up from the west.

At Mantes, the 79th Division was crossing the Seine River. One regiment having marched across a dam in single file during the previous night, a second regiment paddled over starting at daybreak of August 20. Early in the afternoon, engineers installed a treadway bridge for vehicular traffic, and the third regiment crossed. Establishing a strong bridgehead on the far bank, the division sent a small group to La Roche-Guyon and seized the Army Group B command post while German headquarters personnel scurried off. Then the 79th sat tight, waiting for orders.

Early that morning, Haislip committed the 5th Armored Division to sweep down the left bank of the river. The ground was difficult. Heavy fog and rain, mud and poor visibility impaired progress. The going was extremely slow.

Two divisions of the XIX Corps came up on Haislip's left, and on the morning of August 20, they attacked abreast to the north, complementing the XV Corps push down the near bank of the Seine River. Progress here was also slow and painful. Stubborn resistance held up the Americans.

On that day too, Eisenhower initiated a series of conferences, at first with Montgomery's chief of staff, de Guingand, later with Montgomery himself, always involving Bradley, on how to shape the operations on the other side of the Seine. The discussions eventually became known as the broad front versus narrow front controversy. At issue were the routes to be followed by the four Allied armies as they pursued the Germans across northern and northeastern France and also the extent of the American assistance Montgomery claimed he needed and Eisenhower was willing to give. The debate, conducted for the most part in polite and diplomatic language, covered the antagonisms between the partners and exposed the divergent desires of both.

On top of Mount Ormel, as the Poles looked out over the lowland on the morning of August 20, they saw the plain crawling with Germans, some in vehicles, some on foot. A long column of miscellaneous transports drove in orderly fashion to the northeast. The Poles opened fire, dispersed and destroyed the formation, drove individual Germans to cover. In so doing, they brought down on themselves wrath and retribution.

Escaping Germans held up their withdrawal, gathered in combat units, then turned on the Poles to suppress their fire and to keep their own escape routes open. At the same time, the two panzer divisions, having crossed the Seine to the west bank and proceeding toward Mount Ormel, struck the Poles on the height.

Buffeted from both sides, threatened with being surrounded and overwhelmed, the Poles withdrew from the southern knob of Mount Ormel to the northern part. Out of contact with the main Allied forces, isolated, in a precarious position, the Poles established a defensive perimeter, fought off and turned back serious assaults against their lines, fired against escaping Germans when they could, and awaited help.

A German commander later spoke derisively of the Poles on Mount Ormel. Accompanying his division headquarters, an artillery battalion, about sixty infantrymen, and some miscellaneous elements, he traveled out of the pocket by way of St-Lambert and Mount Ormel. "The Poles," he said, "were hiding."

The remark was unjustified. Nowhere was the fighting heavier than at Mount Ormel. Kitching, who had no particular admiration for the

Poles, lauded them. "In spite of being attacked from front and rear," Kitching said, "the Poles hung on and fought a great defensive battle."

The Poles were in such bad straits that Simonds ordered Kitching on August 20 to go to their rescue. Kitching, tired from his exertions during the battle, replied, "To hell with them. They have run out of food and ammunition because of the inefficiency of their organization." Simonds peremptorily ordered Kitching to do as he was told. Kitching then tried to reach the Poles but was unable to do so.

Montgomery issued another directive on August 20. "This is no time," he announced, "to relax or to sit back and congratulate our-selves. . . . Let us finish off the business in record time." Presumably "the business" was bringing the war to an end.

Patton that day had to relieve Cook from command of the XII Corps. Cook was ill, and Manton Eddy, an infantry officer who had directed the 9th Division in North Africa, Sicily, and Normandy and who was a good friend of Bradley, replaced him.

As Patton noted in his journal that evening, "Had in Walker of the XX and Eddy of the XII and told them to get ready to move out at daylight Monday [the 21st], the XX [oriented] on Melun and Montereau, and the XII on Sens. I gave them one code word, 'Proset,' which means 'halt in place,' to be used in case Bradley loses his nerve at the last moment."

To his wife he wrote, "Unless I get a stop order in the next two hours, we are jumping again. On paper it looks very risky, but I don't think it is. Manton Eddy who took over Doc [Cook]'s corps asked me when I told him his job: 'How much shall I have to worry about my flank?' I told him that depended on how nervous he was. He has been thinking a mile a day good going. I told him to go fifty and he turned pale."

Patton had mixed emotions. The main business, so far as he was concerned, still lay north of the Argentan-Dreux-Mantes line. The princi-pal task was still to encircle and trap and destroy as many Germans as remained west of the Seine River. But his superiors had let the opportu-nity to eliminate the Germans slip from their fingers. The V Corps, closing the pocket around Argentan with one division, was hardly strong enough to be effective. The XV Corps with one division and the XIX with two divisions were proceeding downstream from Mantes, but they lacked the numbers and the force to be decisive. A total of four divisions, a very small proportion of the Allied troops on the Continent, was all that the High Command could marshal against the Germans escaping out of the Falaise gap and heading for passage over the Seine River.

Marveling at the absence of insight among his bosses, Patton regretted their failure to let him reinforce the 79th Division across the Seine. A substantial force plowing down the right bank of the river would have dealt the Germans a lethal blow. Montgomery and Bradley were uninterested, and Eisenhower, as usual, was keeping his hands off.

Disgusted with the way the closing of the pocket was turning out, Patton set his sights on Germany. Striking eastward, he would gain mileage and newspaper headlines. He would run wild until the enemy surrendered. He might even get to Berlin.

On the following day, August 21, Montgomery published a "Personal message from the C-in-C To be Read to all Troops." He was exceedingly optimistic. "On the 11th of August," he wrote, "I spoke to the officers and men of the Allied Armies in N. W. France. I said we must 'write off' the powerful German force that was causing us so much trouble; we must finish it, once and for all, and so hasten the end of the war. . . . And today, ten days later, it has been done. The German armies in north-west France have suffered a decisive defeat; the destruction of enemy personnel and equipment in and about the so-called 'Normandy pocket' has been terrific, and it is still going on; any enemy units that manage to get away will not be in a fit condition to fight again for months; there are still many surprises in store for the fleeing remnants. The victory has been definite, complete, and decisive. . . . The victory in N.W. France, south of the Seine, marks the beginning of the end of German military domination of France. Much still remains to be done, but it will now be done the more easily. . . . The end of the war is in sight; let us finish off the business in record time."

Montgomery then became caught up in the post-Overlord discussions. Between August 22 and September 3, critical days in the campaign, Montgomery did not see Bradley at all.

Leigh-Mallory flew to the Continent on August 21 and conferred with Montgomery. They reached a remarkable conclusion. Believing the Seine River bridges to be altogether destroyed, forgetting the large-scale German movements across the river throughout the Normandy campaign, they decided to stop aerial attacks on the Seine structures, and Leigh-Mallory so ordered. The Germans, they were certain, were as good as blocked from escaping across the water. And soon the Allies would need to repair and to use the spans to hurry toward Germany. So instead of concentrating their attacks in the Seine River valley, tactical aircraft worked over targets beyond that region. Bombing and strafing far to the north and east, the planes were supposed to hinder the Germans as they sought to establish new defensive lines at the Somme and Marne rivers.

The actuality was quite different. The Germans were in full flight over the Seine.

On August 21, Bradley was to meet with a large number of war correspondents who awaited his briefing of successes accomplished and projects planned. When he appeared, the newspapermen applauded him heartily. There was some talk of a "Bradley for President" movement. Immensely flattered by the warm admiration of this supposedly hard-boiled and cynical group of reporters, Bradley spoke at some length on the psychological effects of the operations. The imminent liberation of Paris, to be followed sometime soon by an Allied violation of the German border, spelled, in Bradley's mind, nothing less than quick German capitulation.

Meanwhile the fighting at Trun, St-Lambert, Chambois, and Mount Ormel on August 21 was violent. The pressure from opposite sides—the two panzer divisions outside the pocket and the Germans trying to get out—came close to crushing the Allied defenders. St-Lambert was the storm center, and in Colonel Stacey's somewhat exaggerated words, it became "the graveyard of the flower of the German army." At noontime the village was finally in Canadian hands.

The battle around Mount Ormel was also fierce. Allied planes dropped ammunition and medical supplies to the Polish units on the mountain. Kitching's Canadian division made contact with them in the early afternoon. The Poles, Kitching attested, were "in desperate shape with many hundreds of wounded on their hands and hundreds of prisoners." The Poles suffered 325 men killed, 114 soldiers missing, and more than a thousand wounded. Montgomery extolled their courage and called them the cork in the bottle preventing the German escape.

That was when Richard McAdoo revisited the field of battle. A forward observer on a height overlooking the Gouffern-Chambois bottomland, he had called the fires of his big guns down on the fleeing Germans. He had added his battalion's shells to the carnage inflicted. His mission having ended, his party having returned to the headquarters near Mortrée, he drove back to the stone house, then descended the steep slope to the valley. The destruction and death he saw were sickening. What he could not see were the thousands of men who had escaped.

Late that afternoon, the German retirement across the lower slopes of Mount Ormel came to an end. Those who had managed to get out of the pocket were gone. Strung out over the countryside east of Mount Ormel, they headed for the Seine River. No Allied troops hindered their march. No Allied units pursued.

Patton's men were speeding eastward. On the morning of August 21, Walker's XX Corps raced, against little opposition, from Dreux and Chartres to Melun and Montereau, both on the upper Seine River, crossed the stream there and also at Fontainebleau, and headed to the east. Eddy's XII Corps jumped from Orléans to Sens on the Yonne River, crossed the water and headed for Troyes, forty miles away.

Around noontime, Patton wrote to his son, a cadet at West Point. "We have been having a swell time, and I trust that good fortune continues to attend our efforts. . . . We are having another try this morning which is the most audacious we have yet attempted, but I am quite sure it will work." That evening, greatly excited, Patton added a handwritten note: "It worked! We got the bridge at Sens before he [the German] blew it. That is worth a week." What he meant was, capture of the intact span at Sens brought the end of the war a week closer.

To his wife, he wrote, "We jumped seventy miles to day and took Sens, Montereau, and Melun so fast the bridges were not blown. . . . My only worries are my relations [Eisenhower, Montgomery, and Bradley], not my enemies."

In his diary, he recorded, "We have, at this time, the greatest chance to win the war ever presented. If they will let me move on with three corps, two up and one back, on the line of Metz-Nancy-Épinal, we can be in Germany in ten days. There are plenty of roads and railroads to support the operation. It can be done with three armored and six infantry divisions. . . . It is such a sure thing that I fear these blind moles don't see it."

To try to make Bradley see, Patton flew to his command post on the following day, August 22. Patton had no luck, for Bradley was out, conferring with Eisenhower and Montgomery.

On the following day, still thinking of his plan to go eastward, Patton decided that he needed two more divisions. Again on August 23, he flew to Bradley's headquarters. "Bradley," Patton later wrote, "was waiting for me on his way to see Ike and Monty. . . ." They talked for a few minutes, not about Patton's concern but rather what was on Bradley's mind. He was concerned about Eisenhower's lack of backbone. Instead of standing up to Montgomery, Eisenhower, Bradley feared, was about to cave in to Montgomery's arguments on how to conduct operations beyond the Seine. Instead of driving eastward, the Americans, Bradley felt, as Patton recorded the conversation, "will have to turn north in whole or in part" in order to support the British. "Bradley was madder than I have ever seen him and wondered aloud 'what the Supreme Commander amounted to.' . . ."

The subject of Patton's concern remained unaddressed.

After Bradley had gone, "It occurred to me," Patton wrote, "that we must go north [rather than east]." Despite his long-held wish to head east toward the Saar, he saw the chance to put the finishing touches on the Germans, another opportunity to trap and destroy them. In a kind of shorthand, he continued, "The XX Corps from Melun and Montereau and the XII Corps from Sens can do it faster than anyone else." The XV Corps too, by reinforcing the Mantes crossing, could join the others. By heading toward Beauvais, all three corps could sweep cross-country to the sea, catch and block and ruin the escaping Germans. The Third Army in a grand wheeling movement toward Beauvais would cross the Seine, Marne, and Oise rivers and cut off the Germans fleeing Crerar's, Dempsey's, and Hodges's armies.

"This is the best strategical idea I have ever had," Patton wrote. "I sold it to Allen."

Leven Allen, Bradley's chief of staff, was impressed with Patton's recital of his concept. When Patton finished his explanation, Allen said in an understated manner, "Seems fine to me, General."

"Tell it to Brad when he comes back," Patton said.

In his diary, Patton said, "If Bradley approves, he has only to wire me, 'Plan A,' by 1000 [ten o'clock] tomorrow. If I do not hear anything by that time, I shall then move east as already decided in 'Plan B.' I am having the staff put both plans in concrete form. This may well be a momentous day."

Like the short hook from Le Mans to Argentan, like the deeper envelopment envisioned at the Seine, Plan A projected a third encirclement. Still thinking of surrounding the German troops in France, Patton was ready to abandon his long-cherished drive to Metz if he could fashion a proper trap at Beauvais. The disadvantage of Patton's idea was the same: his men would move across and athwart the expected paths of advance of the three other armies after they crossed the Seine.

On the following day, August 24, when Bradley returned from spending the night at Eisenhower's command post, where they presumably discussed post-Overlord routes, Bradley found Patton's plan. Leven Allen explained Patton's intention. Bradley's response was negative. The lines of the future campaign were being hammered out. Patton's project was an eccentricity, out of place, not worth considering.

At noontime, Bradley sent instructions. Patton was to continue executing Plan B with the XII and XX Corps, both heading eastward to the Saar.

Bradley formalized his orders on the following day, August 25. The

general objective was the Rhine River. Hodges's First U.S. Army, with
nine divisions, was to advance from Mantes and Melun toward Lille.
Patton's Third Army, with seven divisions, was to go toward Metz and
Strasbourg.

The only problem was a growing shortage of gasoline. Two days
later, Bradley advised his army commanders to "go as far as practicable
and then wait until the supply system in rear will permit further advance."
The hope was to get through the West Wall before the Germans could
repair and man these fortifications protecting the approaches to the Rhine
River. But this was not to be.

Hardly anyone was thinking of the Germans who had escaped the
Falaise pocket and were making their way to and beyond the Seine. The
British and Canadians pursued them, but, according to the Germans,
not very hard. The U.S. XV and XIX Corps compressed them, but not
very much.

Starting to push down the left bank of the Seine on August 20, the
single division of the XV Corps met firm and stubborn resistance. As
the Germans protected crossing sites and put up a spirited defense in
country excellent for delaying action, the Americans fought hard for five
days to cover the twenty-some miles to Louviers and to capture the town.

On the XV Corps left, two divisions of the XIX Corps battled for four
days to move forty miles to the outskirts of Elbeuf. There, the Germans
were especially tough, for they were covering important crossing sites. After
a prodigious effort, the Americans entered the city on August 25.

On the following day, August 26, in accordance with prior arrangements, the Americans in Louviers turned the town over to British troops
marching in from the west, and the Americans in Elbeuf welcomed
Canadian soldiers into the city. British and Canadians then proceeded
to the Seine River at those places.

How effective was the drive down the left bank of the Seine by
the three American divisions directed by two corps headquarters? The
advance inflicted casualties on the Germans, swept some prisoners up,
and denied the Germans the crossing sites along that part of the Seine
between Mantes and Elbeuf, a distance of about sixty miles. But the
overall effect was minor. Interference with the Germans who were travers-
ing the river in wholesale fashion was minimal.

What the Germans feared was an immediate and ruthless drive
down the right bank of the river, as Patton had wished to initiate. Such
an advance would have completely destroyed the German armies that
had fought in Normandy. Further resistance in France would have been
futile. The path to Germany would have been undefended and open to

the invading Allied forces. The Germans were unable to fathom why the Allies failed to pursue this course of action. After the war, Eberbach said, "I still don't understand why the Allies did not crush us at the Seine."

Along the lower reaches of the Seine River, the British and Canadians fought brutally to get to the stream. Montgomery informed the military authorities in London of the problem. The Germans, he said on August 24, were "trying desperately to stop our approach to the river at Elbeuf and Rouen." Two days later, after the Americans turned over Louviers and Elbeuf to their allies, Montgomery was more cheerful. "The enemy forces," he said on August 26, "are very stretched and disorganized; they are in no fit condition to stand and fight us." The time had come to "cripple his [the German] power to continue in the war."

The Canadians, after crossing the Touques River on August 22, needed four days to approach the Seine between Elbeuf and Rouen, then had great trouble on August 27 to get through eight miles of thick woodland where the Germans made a stand in order to let others escape across the stream. Not until August 30 did the Canadians finally clear the wooded area. They reached the near bank on the last day of the month.

Like them, the British engaged in what was called "bitter fighting" around Lisieux and Pont l'Évêque before they could sweep the left bank of the Seine clear of German troops. Although Brooke, returned from the Mediterranean, believed, as he wrote Montgomery on August 28, "the Germans cannot last much longer," the Germans organized a remarkable effort at the Seine.

Early in September, a contretemps marred Anglo-American relations. The London *Daily Telegraph and Morning Post* cited on September 5 an interview with Dempsey and complained of American high-handedness as the reason why the British troops took so long to get to the Seine. Whether Dempsey actually made the remark or whether a reporter ascribed an imaginary comment to Dempsey, the newspaper blamed the Americans for getting in the way of the British advance and thereby delaying the movement of British troops to the river.

Friction and frustration no doubt spawned the bulletin. Eisenhower had, on the first of the month, displaced Montgomery in command of the Allied ground forces. Furthermore, more realistic appraisals of the German escape dissipated visions of the war's quick end.

The story brought to Bradley's attention by his public relations officer, Bradley recalled his offer to let Dempsey's men go through the American zone. Feeling insulted, Bradley took the matter up with Eisenhower, who soothed ruffled feathers on both sides of the coalition.

As the war continued, even Montgomery had to admit how well the Germans had succeeded in escaping the Allied trap. They got, he said, "a very considerable proportion [of their forces] . . . away to the north of the river."

To find out how the Germans had managed to cross what the Allies considered to be a virtually impassable barrier, Montgomery requested the RAF Analysis Group to study and to render a detailed report of the German retreat across the Seine. The British research included interviews with inhabitants along both banks of the river who had witnessed the German escape. This document, published early in 1945 and located recently by Michel Dufresne, revealed the German achievement.

On August 19, according to the RAF analysis, the Germans in the pocket and on the road to the Seine totaled 270,000 men. Adding 50,000 soldiers who were located elsewhere west of the Seine gave a grand total of 320,000. About 80,000 of these troops were lost during the last twelve days of August, between the 19th and 31st. During that period of time about 240,000 arrived at the Seine. The same number, 240,000 troops, crossed, together with 28,000 vehicles and several hundred tanks.

Most of the men traversed the Seine by means of sixty ferry-and boat-crossing sites, all of which the Germans identified and numbered and closely coordinated. A good many crossed over three pontoon bridges, at Louviers, at Elbeuf, and near Rouen—one of these structures handled 100,000 men and 16,000 vehicles. Quite a few Germans traveled across the partially destroyed railroad bridge at Rouen. Many more crossed on a multitude of small boats and rafts found by chance along the river banks.

The bulk of the crossings occurred at night. By far the greatest number of soldiers got out on August 26 and 27. Forests and wooded patches along the river on both banks served as places of concealment. By September 1, the effort was complete, the Germans were over.

The Allies offered no serious interference with the German movements to and across the Seine. Bad weather prevented most of the Allied planes from flying; the few in the air were far from the Seine River valley. Had reconnaissance pilots been directed to the area, they might have discovered the German crossings.

Meanwhile, during the last week in August, the Allies embarked on a spectacularly fast and motorized rush, nobody walking, everybody riding some kind of vehicle on the main roads toward distant objectives in Belgium, Luxembourg, and Germany. The immense clearing operation liberated thousands of square miles of territory before gasoline supplies diminished, dwindled, and finally ran out, thereby bringing what was called the pursuit to an end. Fuel was plentiful on the invasion beaches, but the Allies were unable to transport sufficient quantities to the front quickly enough to keep the momentum going. Patton's forward movement ended on August 31, Crerar's, Dempsey's, and Hodges's during the second week of September. Winter set in early, and as bad weather hampered operations increasingly static in nature, the Allies found themselves up against German resistance crystallizing and growing stronger.

Using back roads and traveling at night, most of the Germans avoided the Allied columns. By mid-September, the Germans had a continuous, if not completely solid, defensive line stretching for more than 125 miles in length from the North Sea to the Swiss border. With Model commanding Army Group B, Rundstedt returned from retirement to take command once again of the theater. A surge of hope, called by the Germans the Miracle in the West, reinvigorated the German military organization.

Allied miscalculation had allowed Hitler's luck to hold. The Allies had gained their invasion objective, the Overlord lodgment area, within the time allotted, three months. But they had failed to grasp the more important opportunity of eliminating the Germans in Normandy. Dislodging them from the region was hardly enough. The German continuing combat efficiency in post-Overlord operations on the approaches to Germany and beyond ensured the endurance of the struggle. The fighting in Europe would last for eight more months.

CHAPTER 19

Reflections

A SMALL TOWN IN the Calvados region, Falaise had been the capital of Duke William of Normandy, called the Bastard, who in 1066 crossed the Channel, defeated Harold at Hastings, became King of England, and was thereafter known as the Conqueror.

Almost nine hundred years later, Falaise was the place where the Allied invasion of Normandy code-named Overlord reached a climax in August 1944 and promised to bring Hitler down quickly and the war in Europe to a close.

The expectation remained unfulfilled during the summer, fall, and winter months of that year, and the reasons stem from the three basic conditions of the Allied campaign: the undue weight of the invasion plan, the tensions within the coalition, and the less than adequate abilities of the leaders at the top.

From the Allied perspective, despite occasional setbacks, the developments in Normandy from D day to the Seine River gave every indication of success and produced a growing confidence. Overcoming the immense task of battling ashore over the beaches dissipated prior anxieties of potential disaster. As early as mid-June, little more than a week after the landings, Churchill predicted final triumph in 1944. The attempted assassination of Hitler in July heightened belief in the approaching end. The explosion of the Allied forces in the breakout and their spread over the designated lodgment area created the prospect of winning quickly. The apparent German collapse west of the Seine River gave hope of concluding the conflict at least by Christmas. The easy invasion of southern France in August enhanced sensations of satisfaction. In September, the Combined Chiefs of Staff met with the president and the prime minister in Quebec and diverted resources from Europe to the Pacific because they judged the war to be as good as won.

A rising tide of optimism engulfed the Allied leaders during the less than three months of Overlord's existence. Carried away by their euphoria, the top Allied commanders, Eisenhower, Montgomery, and Bradley, anticipated reality and set about laying future plans. Raising their eyes from what was actually happening and looking ahead into the distant time to come, they simply took for granted, before the event, the outcomes they desired. The result was tactical and operational carelessness and negligence, together with a misreading of what was required to vanquish the enemy.

The ultimate mistake was to dismiss the fate of the Germans almost trapped in the Falaise pocket. Because the war seemed to be on the verge of being over, Eisenhower, Montgomery, and Bradley cared little whether the Germans escaped. To them, the Germans appeared to be uprooted and fleeing, incapable of further resistance, no longer important.

During the bitterest fighting around Trun, St-Lambert, Chambois, and Mount Ormel, the principal Allied commanders had their minds fixed elsewhere, far from closing the pocket. They were already pondering post-Overlord ventures, figuring how to get to the Rhine River, thinking of overrunning Germany. In verity, their delay in springing the trap, their pursuit of other goals, and the weakness of their encirclements at Falaise and at the Seine prevented them from properly finishing the invasion, the Overlord operation, the Normandy campaign.

Conditioned by the Overlord planning, which established possession of the lodgment area as the objective, the three Allied leaders forgot the basic precept of warfare. They believed the capture of terrain instead of the destruction of the enemy to be the correct way to win the war.

Even Patton was lured astray, to some extent by the company he kept, his superiors. In addition, his disgust over the manner in which they were trying to surround the Germans led him to wash his hands of the maneuvers. He wheedled permission to strike eastward and gain territory on the road to Germany. Soon thereafter, Patton recorded his contradictory feelings of power and emptiness. "Really," he wrote to his wife on September 1, 1944, "I am amazed at the amount of ground the Third Army has taken"—to no avail, he might have added, so far as the end of the war was concerned. The liberation of occupied and captive localities and people produced a series of triumphs, along with elation and gratitude among those freed, but left the enemy his cohesion and power.

So long as the German military forces remained strong, that is, organized and effective, and so long as the political regime sustained its belief in a victory of some sort, the war continued. The German loss in Normandy was tactical and operational. It had no strategic significance. Had the Allied triumph encompassed the strategic dimension, the Nazi government would have had to concede defeat. Instead, the Ardennes counteroffensive three months later, in December, clearly indicated Hitler's still unshakable vision of his ability to win the war or at least to bring about a conclusion favorable to Germany.

The fighting in Normandy was "as much a German success as an Anglo-American failure," Raymond Callahan has said. "In the end, the Falaise pocket gave the Allies a great, if an incomplete victory."

Callahan goes on. "In theory, of course, the pocket could have been sealed off more quickly. In fact, given the problems of coordination in coalition warfare, the personal feelings that affected vision at the top, the inexperience of the Canadians, and the quality of the German army, the failure to do so more quickly becomes, if not inevitable, at least unsurprising."

The summary is excellent, but the words are too charitable. The Allied generals in charge of the campaign were the best of the available professionals. Despite their expertise, the three at the top fumbled badly.

Eisenhower's major fault was to allow his two army group commanders, Montgomery and Bradley, to drift apart. Each pursued his own course at critical moments, and a single firm direction of the operations never emerged. Although Eisenhower had the power to rectify the situation, he permitted the pocket to remain open too long and let the Seine River envelopment unfold haphazardly. Had he been more perceptive and more forthright, he could have insisted on behavior in conformance with what was his forte, coalition cooperation and coordination. Instead, he pursued his traditional hands-off policy, and the result was unsatisfactory for all save the Germans, who took advantage of the loose Allied reins.

When Eisenhower assumed from Montgomery command of the Allied ground forces on September 1, he was hardly seeking to eliminate hesitation from the direction of the war on land, hardly trying to establish a decisive impetus of his own making. The fact is, Eisenhower replaced Montgomery most reluctantly. Eisenhower preferred to distance himself from the operational details, to avoid exercising direct command, to keep the Normandy arrangements in effect, with Montgomery—or anyone else, for that matter—running the battlefield show. What forced Eisenhower to step in, for there was no one on hand except himself, was the widespread dissatisfaction with Montgomery's performance during Overlord.

Montgomery seemed to have lost the firm grasp, the master's touch, the flamelike leadership he had heretofore displayed, particularly in North Africa. Of the verve and arrogance formerly characteristic of him, only the arrogance was visible. He seemed tired and dispirited in Normandy. Perhaps the campaign in June and July did him in. Perhaps the developments in August overwhelmed him. Perhaps the task on the Continent was always beyond him.

The situation west of the Seine in August begged for Allied audacity. Yet Montgomery, Harold Deutsch has written, "has never been credited with a rich imagination." He was, therefore, "bound to miss opportunities that called for daring exploitation." Deutsch continues, "Actually with the sole exception of Patton, there usually was small urge toward risk-taking among Allied military leaders." Closing the pocket at Falaise and again at the Seine River was hazardous, and Montgomery, like Bradley, preferred to be safe.

Furthermore, coalition warfare was never Montgomery's strong suit. He was superb in command of British troops during the withdrawal to Dunkirk in 1940. He was outstanding in Egypt and Libya, where he commanded British and Commonwealth forces. Entering the Allied command structure in Tunisia, he maintained his firm control over the same national units and demonstrated his flair. He was at ease in Sicily at the head of British and Canadian formations. His British Eighth Army in Italy engaged in virtually independent combat, separated as it was from the Fifth U.S. Army by the Apennine mountain wall.

In Normandy, Montgomery held an overtly Allied command position over British and American contingents, and he seemed uncomfortable. As always, he kept his concentration fixed exclusively on the battlefield, as was his habit. But the post demanded other considerations also, those of a political or coalition nature, and although he tried to dismiss them, they pulled at him and exasperated him. Whether the operational course he set was working successfully and producing glory for him and the Allied cause, as he and his admirers have claimed ever since, he displeased some very important persons, political and military both, who lost confidence in him. Despite Eisenhower's deepest inclinations against depriving Montgomery of his Allied post, he was unable to resist the pressures building among his American colleagues, a variety of British officials, and authorities in Washington. They compelled Eisenhower to act.

The shift from Montgomery to Eisenhower at the head of the Allied ground forces, some have maintained, was a perfectly natural succession. For the United States was contributing a greater number of troops to the campaign in northwestern Europe. That superiority in resources dictated, or at least suggested, the desirability of having an American in Montgomery's place. The British army had reached the limit of its growth in May 1944 with under three million men, while the U.S. Army by then totaled almost six million and was still short of its potential maximum. Facing up to these figures, Max Hastings has said, British leaders were "despondently conscious of America's dominance of the Grand Alliance and its strategy."

Sadly, Nigel Hamilton has written, "The days when Britain was the preponderant power in numbers of men, in arms, in naval and in air strength, were over." The Americans were more powerful and consequently more important, and they deserved to command in the field. Therefore, according to this polemic, Montgomery's loss of control over the Allied ground battle was, Hamilton has said, "inevitable." Unfortunately, Montgomery was "unable to understand the imperative." Because he failed to comprehend, he gave way to Eisenhower with, in Hamilton's words, "bitter frustration, disappointment and chagrin."

The argument just enunciated seeks to protect and to enhance Montgomery's reputation. It is, in fact, a rationalization, an alibi after the event. For, according to Max Hastings, the British disregarded, paid no attention to, the discrepancy between the dissimilar amounts of resources furnished by the allies. The difference between the American and British assets in the struggle mattered to the British not at all. "Until the very end of the war," Hastings has acknowledged, "the British demanded that they should be treated as equal partners in the alliance."

For, as William McNeill has remarked, there is deeply ingrained in the British psyche a belief in the natural right of the British to lead. The leaders were a select group, prepared by birth and education, augmented over the generations by newly recruited talent, and imbued with the obligation to guide the people of the world, the duty to use their gift of leadership for the benefit of all.

The conviction sometimes bred snobbery, arrogance, and condescension. Toward the Americans the British often showed at least traces of assumed superiority. The British, as Alun Chalfont has noted, tended to gaze down on Americans with amused contempt.

The Americans felt and disliked the attitude. "This is the last day," Patton recorded in his diary on August 31, "that Montgomery commands the U.S. troops, for which we all thank God!" On September 1, when Montgomery was promoted to field marshal to counter the thought of his demotion as Eisenhower took command, Patton wrote to his wife, "The Field Marshal thing made us sick, that is Bradley and me."

If the preponderance of American resources in reality provoked the requirement for the primacy of American leadership, Eisenhower as Supreme Allied Commander already possessed and displayed, in fact embodied, the notion. There was no need to supplant Montgomery on a lower echelon for that reason. The objections leading to his removal centered not only on Montgomery's smugness and narrowness but also on his operational mediocrity in an Allied setting. It was that which made him ineligible to command a sizable number of American divisions.

Was any other British officer of high rank capable of meeting the demands of the job? Only Alexander comes to mind. It is difficult to conceive of his exercising firm control over the battle. Most likely, he would have let British and American operations develop largely on their own. Perhaps, in the end, much the same results would have occurred. Yet Alexander, by virtue of his personal grace and coalition experience, would have avoided the discomfort over Montgomery that almost everyone on both sides of the alliance tried to conceal.

And so the inter-Allied frictions and resentments went on for the rest of the war. With Eisenhower both Supreme Allied Commander and the Allied ground forces commander, in the latter capacity having Montgomery and Bradley directly under him at the head of army groups, and with Dempsey, Crerar, Hodges, and Patton functioning as before, the command system installed on September 1 remained in place, unchanged during the remainder of the struggle. Yet Montgomery never abandoned his hope of reassuming his former position as director of the land battle. From time to time, he sought to reascend the single step to that level. During the battle of the Bulge, when the German penetration made it difficult for Bradley to be in contact with Hodges, Eisenhower asked Montgomery to look after the First U.S. Army temporarily, that is, until the German threat could be erased. In an unfortunate conference with war correspondents, Montgomery exacerbated the Allied tensions by obliquely running down Eisenhower and the Americans. They had been unable, he intimated, by virtue of their lack of operational savoir faire, to avoid the crisis in the Ardennes. Only Montgomery's messiahlike intervention had saved the Allies from complete disaster.

Since then, there have been two competing theses, one generally

British and pro-Montgomery, the other usually American and pro-Eisenhower, endeavoring to explain the course of events in wartime Europe. According to the pro-Montgomery or anti-Eisenhower claim, Montgomery, as the Allied ground forces commander, performed brilliantly and directed the Allies to victory in Normandy even though Eisenhower never understood his strategy. When the inept Eisenhower took over, everything went sour. He misinterpreted, then turned a deaf ear to Montgomery's plea for a single and massive advance to Berlin in the fall of 1944. He allowed Hodges's First U.S. Army to become bogged down in the morass of the Huertgen forest. He was responsible for permitting the Germans to build up strength and to counterattack in the Ardennes, then was unable to turn back the German thrust until Montgomery took charge again. Finally, Eisenhower drew back from capturing Berlin and thereby lost the Allies the initiative in the postwar world.

According to the opposing view, Montgomery botched the Normandy campaign. He erred badly at Antwerp—his failure to take the seaward approaches to Antwerp rendered the port unusable. He made a mess of the airborne-armored Market Garden operation designed to cross the Rhine River by capturing the "bridge too far" at Arnhem in the Netherlands. Eisenhower's broad-front strategy ensured an Anglo-American victory for both nations together instead of a triumph by either the British or the Americans alone.

These diametrically opposite perceptions are still hotly debated. They seem no closer to reconciliation now than they were in 1944 and 1945.

Since those years, criticism of Bradley has been subdued, anything but widely voiced. Yet whispers of bad judgment on his part have scratched the surface of his modest portrait.

Catapulted over Patton to prominence, Bradley worked free of his dependence on, sometimes subservience to, Montgomery and Patton both. Tunisia had been his introduction to corps command in combat, and Normandy served as his entrance into battle at the head of an army. During his two months in the latter post, Bradley had his ups and downs.

Although the landings on Utah Beach went well, the difficulties at Omaha, for a moment, sickened him with dread. He gained confidence in June as Joe Collins dashed to Cherbourg and captured the port. The battle of the hedgerows started in July with great hope, but as the offensive dragged on in seemingly endless fashion, it reduced Bradley to frustration. The sudden success of Cobra, with Joe Collins carrying the ball, abruptly turned Bradley's head.

As he rose to direct an army group in combat in August, Bradley manifested inconsistent behavior, fluctuating between flaming independence and depressing doubt. He initiated the short hook to Argentan, then apparently lost confidence in Montgomery and Patton as well as in himself. What he should have executed with speed and élan and in conjunction with Montgomery became, on his side of the enclosure, complicated and ponderous. Abandoning his idea of closing the pocket at Falaise because of the inherent risks, he stopped Haislip at Argentan. With misplaced decisiveness, he dismissed the hazards at Argentan and sent half of Haislip's corps toward the Seine, thereby weakening his southern jaw and increasing the dangers there.

He transferred command at Argentan from Patton to Hodges, inserted Gerow into the chain of command, and wasted several days as a result. He halted Patton's movement to the Seine River at Dreux, Chartres, and Orléans and thereby slowed the tempo of achievement. He permitted Patton to gain a bridgehead over the Seine River at Mantes, then forbade him to reap the benefits of the action, nullifying Patton's wish to fashion a potent pincer. Finally, he let Patton charge off toward Germany even though the main work lay west of the Seine.

Bradley attempted to play the role of the bold leader, then was troubled by doubt. He made instant decisions, then second-guessed himself and wondered whether his quick-trigger timing was little more than ill-considered impulse. He initiated potentially brilliant maneuvers, then aborted them because he lacked confidence in his ability to see them through to completion. As a consequence, he backed and filled, and in the end mismanaged the affairs on the southern side of the pocket from Argentan to the Seine.

The failure of the Americans to close from the south put the weight of closure on the Canadians, and they floundered. "There was considerable dissatisfaction," Raymond Callahan has said, "with the performance of the Canadian units." John A. English has given the best explanation of why they faltered. The neglect of the military in prewar preparation, the rapid expansion of the ground forces upon the outbreak of war, an "unbounded enthusiasm and amateurism" as well as "serious inadequacies at the high command level," all these "seriously impaired Canadian fighting performance. The Canadian field force was from its inception compromised by a military leadership that had for too long concentrated on bureaucratic, political, and stratego-diplomatic pursuits to the neglect of the operational and tactical quintessence." Inefficient, unlucky, manifesting "a traditional artillerist and technological bent . . . [instead of] a more manoeuvre-oriented approach to warfare," the First Canadian Army, by failing to achieve its objectives quickly along the road to

Falaise, provoked profound disappointment and helped to prolong the existence of the Falaise gap, the German escape route.

Montgomery knew the Canadians very well and was aware of their strengths and weaknesses. He had trained them in England, brought them up militarily, put them on the right track. Yet his inability to judge what they were capable of as they struck repeatedly toward Falaise prevented him from reinforcing Crerar and Simonds.

Simonds also held back units he might have committed. Instead, they remained in the rear and useless, perhaps because of road congestion or supply shortages, perhaps because the Allied focus had shifted to the Seine, perhaps because Simonds was saving these elements for post-Overlord advances.

According to Jean Pariseau, Anglo-Canadian relations were not always smooth despite the Commonwealth connection. The British believed there was only one way to fight, and that was the British way. Far too easily they ascribed incapacity or mediocrity to troops who were non-British. Far too often they mistrusted people who, like the Canadians, except Guy Simonds, lacked an Oxford accent.

The location near Argentan of Leclerc and his 2nd French Armored Division was unfortunate for the unfolding Normandy operations, particularly for the shallow envelopment, and also for the liberation of Paris. The French were uninterested in the Falaise pocket and refrained from participating in a significant manner. From August 12, when they arrived near Argentan, they did little except to look with yearning toward Paris. Leclerc's mission, political in nature, was to enter Paris quickly, not only to prevent left-wing elements from seizing power but also to facilitate the accession of de Gaulle's supporters to the seats of government. Because Leclerc was integrated into the Allied chain of command, he needed his superiors' permission to set off for Paris. Because his troops near Argentan were important in helping to coop up the Germans and prevent them from breaking out at that point, exactly where Ultra warned to expect a German strike, Leclerc's superiors were unable to release him for the run to the capital.

According to General de Langlade, a principal subordinate, Leclerc from the first made plain his hands-off policy at Argentan. The division, Leclerc said, had nothing to do there. The Allies were so well equipped with tanks that they had no need of the French. The essential French aim was eventually, and the quicker the better, to head for Paris.

On August 18, the critical time of closure at St-Lambert and Chambois, Leclerc specifically forbade the division from making what he called a "real intervention" in the battle. If the French became involved in the action, they might be so heavily drawn in as to be unable to disengage for Paris.

Three days later, as British troops coming from the west moved across the V Corps front and through Argentan, Gerow pulled his divisions, including the French, out of the British zone and assembled them well south of the town. Having understood the need to keep the French division near Argentan to guard the southern jaw of the pocket, Leclerc saw absolutely no further reason to remain in the area and so far from his ultimate objective. He became understandably impatient, particularly since American troops at Mantes, Chartres, and Orléans were much closer to the capital than he.

Learning of de Gaulle's arrival in France, Leclerc wrote him a hasty letter, telling him what had happened to the French soldiers on the Continent. They had made an "acrobatic march from Avranches to Le Mans," then had fought to the Argentan outskirts. "The outcome of this attack," he said, "could have been splendid if it had been decided to close the Argentan-Falaise buckle. The [Allied] High Command formally opposed it, history will judge. . . . For 8 days the [High] Command has had us mark time. They made good and wise decisions but generally 4 or 5 days too late. They have assured us that my division's objective was Paris. But given such paralysis, I have taken the following decision."

Without authorization from his immediate superior, Gerow, Leclerc had sent a small detachment of 150 men to Versailles. They were to be ready, if the situation compelled the Allies to enter Paris suddenly without being able to call on Leclerc, to join and accompany the liberating columns into the capital and thus ensure a French presence.

The action had no importance except to stir up Gerow's and Leclerc's tempers. Eisenhower decided to liberate Paris, Bradley sent Leclerc on his way, and the French division arrived in time to accomplish what de Gaulle wished.

The point is, respecting Leclerc's task, Gerow, Hodges, and Bradley requested that he furnish only artillery fire at Argentan to help close the pocket, and he complied. If the division had been American, the soldiers would have participated actively in the closure and would have thus strengthened the trap. What was unfortunate was the mismanagement that dispersed American assets across the Overlord lodgment area in pursuit of other less essential goals. As a consequence of the shortage of resources, no American division was available to replace the French at Argentan and thereby to add force, weight, and authority to the closing of the southern jaw.

In retrospect, Langlade understood the lost opportunity at Argentan.

Closing the pocket and eliminating the Germans expeditiously had been more important than liberating Paris and ensuring its fall into de Gaulle's hands. Langlade admitted the soundness of meeting the Canadians, and he tried to justify the 2nd French Armored Division's passivity at Argentan. "We [the French]," he said, "had the impression of slowness" on the part of the Americans, who showed little of the "ardor and will . . . necessary for a rapid conclusion" of the maneuver. Not the French but the Americans, by hesitating, were to blame for the continued existence of the German escape hatch, the Falaise gap.

And what of Patton? From the first, he understood the need for dispatch in whatever his bosses decided to do west of the Seine River. Willing to take chances in order to terminate the warfare, he was the single commander who grasped what needed to be done and how to do it. He had more than enough self-confidence to be sure of his capacity to react quickly and correctly to any crisis arising.

Harold Deutsch has put it succinctly. "Patton was obsessed with speed and surprise. He became impatient in static situations and was always anxious to start moving. He was an ideal commander for fluid situations, being completely flexible in responding to a sudden turn of events. Nothing could have appealed to him more than the idea of instantly responding to unexpected opportunities."

More specific are the few lines written by General de Langlade. "Only General Patton, who has the sense of maneuver," Langlade wrote, "possesses enough ardor and faith to execute the closing [of the pocket]. He is an offensive warrior of high class who seems to have no equal among his compatriots for exploitation warfare. One wonders even if he is appreciated or even understood."

It took some years after the war for the fullness of Patton's stature to emerge. Unlike most of his contemporaries, whose reputations have steadily declined since the war, Patton's has continued to rise. This phenomenon has occurred despite the relatively lowly role he held in the chain of command.

Bound to execute the plans formulated by his superiors, Patton suffered from his helplessness. After September 1, he had no contact, no official relationship with Montgomery, but Eisenhower and Bradley and their customary caution tormented him throughout the war. He was able to maintain an outward equanimity by blowing off steam in the privacy of his office or his quarters. He rid himself of frustration and resentment in his diary and in his letters to his wife by castigating his bosses for their inability to think big and brilliantly.

By late August 1944, Patton had settled into an acceptance of his fate. He learned to curb his tongue. He made peace with his inner turmoil. He obeyed orders cheerfully, did all that was asked of him, and contributed more than enough to final victory, all the while retaining his unique personality and point of view. Yet the bitterness built up within him.

His darkest thoughts were borne out on May 10, 1945, two days after the end of the war in Europe, when Eisenhower had his four American army commanders, Patton included, to lunch. The reason for the gathering was hardly to celebrate the victory they had achieved. Rather it was something shocking to Patton.

Eisenhower held forth, Patton wrote in his journal that evening, "very confidentially on the necessity for solidarity" among them if any of them was called to testify before a congressional committee looking into the conduct of the war. "It is my opinion," Patton said, "that this talking cooperation [by Eisenhower] is for the purpose of covering up probable criticism of strategical blunders which he unquestionably committed during the campaign. Whether or not these were his own or due to too much cooperation with the British, I don't know. I am inclined to think that he over-cooperated."

The sentiment came out skewed, somewhat off the mark. What Patton was trying to express was his contempt toward those who had delayed final victory because of their mediocrity. Like P Wood, Patton believed his superiors had won the war the wrong way. They had been much too slow.

The Allied gamble to win the war in 1944 by sprinting toward Germany without first sweeping the German forces from the field turned out badly. Bradley was optimistic about getting quickly through the German West Wall to the Rhine. Eisenhower was gazing beyond the Rhine River. Montgomery had his eyes fixed on Berlin. Only Patton was out of step, concerned by the mistake being made, unable to make his genius felt.

"The remarkable resurgence of the German army in the autumn [of 1944]," Raymond Callahan has pointed out, "obviously owes something forever unquantifiable to the imperfect Allied victory of Falaise."

In the make-believe world of might-have-been, it is easy enough to visualize Patton in Bradley's place. Had the slapping incidents in Sicily not occurred, Eisenhower would most certainly have named Patton to go to England in the fall of 1943 to prepare the American side of the invasion. As the top American field commander, Patton would have been Eisenhower's closest military adviser. They had been close friends since their meeting in 1919, when both had been in the Tank Corps. Eisenhower then returned to the infantry, Patton to the cavalry, but they maintained contact by correspondence, and their mutual liking deepened. Their military thinking was much the same. They trusted each other. If Patton had run the American part of the enterprise in Normandy, Eisenhower would have been easy in his mind and free to be himself, interested, encouraging, and supportive of his field soldiers, and disinclined to meddle. In this case, there would have been no need to remove Montgomery.

For as the American army group commander, as the most experienced American battlefield general, as the most senior American soldier who had proved without a shadow of doubt his combat expertise, Patton could meet Montgomery as an equal. They would have worked closely and effectively together. For they respected each other. Their interests were professional and tied to the operational scene. Their strengths were complementary. The thrust of Patton and the balance of Montgomery would have produced a perfectly matched team.

In the finely spun reveries of speculation, it is easy enough to imagine the Eisenhower-Montgomery-Patton relationship as producing a less discordant Normandy campaign, a happier resolution of Overlord, a firm entrapment of the Germans west of the Seine, and a much earlier end of the war in Europe.

Author's Note

I AM INDEBTED ESPECIALLY and I wish to express my particular thanks to Samuel S. Vaughan, my editor, for helping me to define the problem of my book and to sharpen the focus of my research; and to Michel Dufresne of Vimoutiers, France, for facilitating my understanding both of the terrain and the events around Falaise.

Others have helped me enormously during the course of my work, and I am glad to acknowledge with thanks their contributions and support: John J.-G. Blumenson, Jean Delmas, John A. English, Mary Lou Evans, the late Joseph R. Friedman, Dominick Graham, Blanche Gregory, the late Charles B. MacDonald, Andre Martel, Millicent Neusner, Reginald Roy, Richard Hart Sinnreich, and Marge Melun Thompson.

As always, I thank my wife for her constant collaboration.

I alone am responsible for all the errors, misstatements, and faults in the text.

M.B.

Select Bibliography

Bedarida, François. *Normandie 44: du débarquement à la libération*. Paris, 1987.

Benamou, J. P. "18–22 août 1944: La lre DB polonaise clot la Poche de Falaise." *39–45 Magazine*, October 1987.

Blumenson, Martin. *Breakout and Pursuit*. Washington, 1963.

———. *The Patton Papers*, 2 vols. Boston, 1972, 1974.

Bradley, Omar N. *A Soldier's Story*. New York, 1951.

Bradley, Omar N., and Clay Blair. *A General's Life*. New York, 1983.

Callahan, Raymond A. "Imperfect Victory Assured." *World War II*, May 1989, pp. 26–33.

Carver, Michael. "La Stratégie anglo-américaine," in Bedarida, *Normandie 44*.

Chalfont, Alun. *Montgomery of Alamein*. New York, 1976.

Dallek, Robert. *Franklin D. Roosevelt and American Foreign Policy, 1932–1945*. New York, 1979.

D'Este, Carlo. *Bitter Victory: The Battle for Sicily, 1943*. New York, 1988.

———. *Decision in Normandy*. New York, 1983.

Deutsch, Harold C. "Commanding Generals and the Uses of Intelligence." *Intelligence and National Security*, Vol. 3, No. 3 (July 1988), pp. 194–260.

Dufresne, Michel. "Normandie Août 1944: Heurs et Malheurs d'une fin de Campagne." *Revue Historique des Armées*, No. 168 (September 1987), pp. 96–122.

———. "Le Succès Allemand sur la Seine." *Revue Historique des Armées*, No. 176 (September 1989), pp. 48–60.

Eisenhower, John S. D. *Allies: Pearl Harbor to D-Day*. New York, 1982.

Eisenhower, Dwight D. *Crusade in Europe*. New York, 1948.

Ellis, L. F. *Victory in the West*, Vol. I: *The Battle of Normandy*. London, 1962.

English, J. A. *The Casting of an Army: Being a Treatise on the Basis and Conduct of Canadian Army Operations Beyond the Normandy Bridgehead to the Closure of the Falaise Gap*. Unpublished manuscript 1989.

Graham, Dominick. Letter to author, May 31, 1988.

Hamilton, Nigel. *Master of the Battlefield: Monty's War Years, 1942–1944*. New York, 1983.

———. *Montgomery: The Making of a General, 1887–1942*. New York, 1981.

Harris, Stephen. "The Canadian General Staff and the Higher Organization of Defence, 1919–1939." *War and Society*, Vol. 3, No. 1 (May 1985), pp. 83–98.

Hastings, Max. *Overlord: D-Day and the Battle for Normandy*. New York, 1984.

Keegan, John. *The Mask of Command*. New York, 1987.

Kitching, George. *Mud and Green Fields*. Langley, British Columbia, 1986.

Langlade, General de. *En Suivant Leclerc*. Paris, 1964.

Lucas, James, and James Barker. *The Killing Ground: The Battle of the Falaise Gap, August 1944*. London, 1978.

Maule, Henry. *Normandy Breakout*. New York, 1979.

McAdoo, Richard B. "The Guns at Falaise Gap." *Harper's Magazine*, Vol. 216 (May 1958), pp. 36–45.

McMahon, J. S. *Professional Soldier: A Memoir of General Guy Simonds, CB, CBE, DSO, CD*. Winnipeg, Manitoba, 1985.

McNeill, William Hardy. *America, Britain, and Russia: Their Co-operation and Conflict, 1941–1946*. New York, 1953.

Miller, Merle. *Ike the Soldier: As They Knew Him*. New York, 1987.

Pariseau, Jean. "Les Canadiens dans la bataille," in Bedarida, *Normandie 44*.

Patton, George S., Jr. *War as I Knew It*. Boston, 1947.

Roy, R. H. "The Canadian Military Tradition," in Hector J. Massey, ed., *The Canadian Military: A Profile*. Canada (n.p.), 1972.

Skibinski, Franciszek. "La Participation polonaise à la bataille de Normandie," in Bedarida, *Normandie 44*.

Stacey, C. P. *Canada's Battle in Normandy (The Canadian Army at War)*. Ottawa, 1946.

———. *The Canadian Army, 1939–1945*. Ottawa, 1948.

Sullivan, John J. "The Botched Air Support of Operation Cobra," *Parameters*, March 1988.

Weigley, Russell F. *Eisenhower's Lieutenants: The Campaign of France and Germany, 1944–1945*. Bloomington, Indiana, 1981.

Index

Air Defense Command, British, 133
air support, 239, 253
Alençon, 168, 175, 191, 199, 205, 212, 223, 237
  Corps drive on, xv
Alexander, Harold, 29, 30, 56, 64, 72, 73, 111, 213, 266
  Italian campaign and, 62, 63
  Sicilian campaign and, 60–61
  Tunisian campaign and, 58–59
  on U.S. performance at Kasserine Pass, 57
Angers, 167, 168, 189, 191
Antwerp, 267
Algeria, 54, 55
Allen, Leven, 199, 209–210, 256
Allied Expeditionary Air Forces, 133, 136, 137
American Expeditionary Force, 76
Analysis Group, RAF, 259
Anders, Wladyslaw, 185
Anderson, Fred, 137
Anglo-American alliance, 73, 221, 250
  American dominance in, 265–266
  Anzio landings and, 65–67
  British media and, 258
  Casablanca Conference and, 56–57
  chain of command and, 48
  Eisenhower and, 42, 63
  Europe First strategy and, 47–48
friction within, 41–42, 57–58
  Kasserine Pass Battle and, 57–58
  leadership and, 50–51
  post-Overlord operations and, 251
  postwar theories of, 266–267
  Roosevelt-Churchill relationship and, 42–44
  Sicilian campaign and, 61–62
  strategy conflict in, 53–55
  Tehran Conference and, 64–65
  World War I influence on, 48
Anvil, Operation, 64, 65–66, 67
Anzio, Battle of, 65–67
Argentan, 202, 203, 204, 205, 206–209, 211, 212, 215, 222–223, 232, 233–234, 242, 250, 268, 269–271
Armed Forces Netherlands, 93
Army Group B, German, 92, 93, 94, 224, 242, 250, 260
Army Group G, German, 93, 96
"Army Group Patton," 96, 157
Atlantic Charter, 46
Atlantic Wall, 91, 92
Austria, 89
Avranches, 129, 131, 145–146, 147, 148, 149, 155, 156, 161, 166, 174–175, 177, 187, 188, 192, 193, 197, 201
Avranches counterattack, see Mortain counterattack
Azores, 46

Belgium, 89, 91, 92, 93, 235, 238, 243
Blumentritt, Gunther, 223–224
Bradley, Omar N., 22, 28, 39, 59, 61, 72,
    84, 113, 124, 155, 166, 169, 187,
    196, 203, 219, 229, 230, 240, 252,
    253, 264, 266, 270, 271, 272
  assessment of, 267–268
  background of, 31–32
  Brittany campaign and, 145, 160–161,
    162, 163, 197
  Cobra ended by, 145, 149
  Cobra Operation and, 120, 129–140, 143,
    145, 149, 150, 151
  Cobra's success and, 150, 151
  Eisenhower's correspondence with, 150
  encirclement concept and, 188, 189–190,
    191, 192
  enemy situation misread by, 244, 249, 262
  on Falaise Operation, 20
  as First Army commander, 33–34,
    114–115
  first stop order of, 206–212, 213, 225
  Gerow assignment and, 234–236, 268
  Leigh-Mallory's correspondence with, 136
  Le Mans drive and, 167–168
  London newspaper story and, 258–259
  Mantes bridgehead and, 244–245
  Marshall and, 31–32, 34–35
  memoirs of, 140
  military career of, 31–32
  Montgomery's correspondence with,
    217–218
  Montgomery's meetings with, 118,
    213–214, 215, 235–236, 243
  Montgomery's relationship with, 41,
    146–147, 213, 263
  Montgomery's view of, 81–82, 107
  Mortain counterattack and, 167, 177, 199,
    202, 205
  Overlord and, 33–34, 80
  Patton's "over-caution" comment and, 159
  Patton's relationship with, 32–33, 34,
    36–38, 114, 157, 158–159
  personality of, 26–27, 31–32
  post-Overload operations and, 241, 251,
    255, 256–257
  second stop order of, 220–221, 222, 223,
    231
  self-confidence of, 220–221
  Stanmore Conference and, 132–133
  Third Army activated by, 145–146
  Trun attack and, 217, 231–232, 233
  12th Army Group assignment of, 33–34
Brereton, Lewis, 134, 138
Brest, 164, 174, 197, 249
Britain, Battle of, 45, 90
British Broadcasting Corporation (BBC),
    61–62
British Expeditionary Force, 29

Brittany campaign, 145–150, 155–165, 166,
    168, 197, 249
  allied command structure and, 145–147
  Bradley and, 145, 160–161, 162, 163,
    197
  British attacks and, 147–148
  diminished value of, 160
  Eisenhower and, 160–161, 163
  Montgomery and, 146, 147, 150, 160–161,
    163
  Overlord plans and, 155–156, 160, 161
  Patton and, 146, 147, 155–158, 160
  port cities and, 164, 174, 197, 249
  resistance and, 165, 166
  as strategic failure, 164–165
  U.S. attacks in, 148–150
  Wood and, 161–164
Brooke, Alan F., 58, 59, 65, 71–72, 77, 79,
    122, 123, 147, 180
  on Casablanca Conference, 57
  Churchill and, 49
  Marshall's relationship with, 50
  military career of, 49
  Montgomery's correspondence with, 74, 82,
    105, 108, 115, 121, 160, 181, 183,
    196–197, 200, 203, 205, 216, 218,
    219, 225, 233, 239, 240–241, 258
  on Quebec Conference, 62
Bulge, Battle of the, 22, 211, 266
Butcher, Harry, 110, 122

Caen, 103–104, 106, 108, 109, 117,
    118–119, 129, 131, 174, 182, 184
Callahan, Raymond, 76, 212, 263, 268, 272
Canada, military preparedness of, 179–180,
    268
Cannae, Battle of, 20
Carver, Lord, 124
Casablanca Conference:
  Anglo-American alliance and, 56–57
  Brooke on, 57
Chalfont, Alun, 76, 78, 79, 147, 265
Chamberlain, Neville, 44
Chambois, 229, 232, 234, 235, 237–238,
    240, 242, 243–244, 245, 246, 250,
    262
Chartres, 220, 231, 232, 233, 236, 237
Cherbourg, 106–107, 108, 113, 267
Chiefs of Staff, British, 49, 83
China, Nationalist, 47
Churchill, Winston, 22, 33, 48, 72, 73, 81,
    115, 117, 242, 261
  Anzio as brainchild of, 65–66
  Atlantic Charter and, 46
  Brooke and, 49
  Casablanca Conference and, 56–57
  North Africa campaign and, 54
  Overlord opposed by, 69–70
  Overlord planning and, 74–75, 83

Quebec Conference and, 62
Roosevelt's relationship with, 42–43, 44, 45
Tehran Conference and, 64–65
Trident Conference and, 59–60
U.S. visited by, 47, 54
Clark, Mark, 29–32, 33, 34, 65, 67, 194
    Italian campaign and, 62–63
    Montgomery and, 63–64
Cobra, Operation, 120–122, 129–169, 184, 267
    Air Force's misunderstanding of, 135–137
    Army–Air Force relationship and, 140
    bombardment in, 129–141
    Bradley and, 120, 129–140, 143, 145, 149, 150, 151
    Bradley's ending of, 145, 149
    breakthrough in, 144–151
    Canadian units and, 182
    Collins and, 130, 143–144, 147
    doctrinal arguments and, 133–134
    effect of bombardment, on enemy, 144
    Eisenhower and, 133, 134, 140, 141
    failure of, 137–139
    Kluge and, 144–145, 151
    Leigh-Mallory and, 134–136, 137, 138, 139, 141
    Montgomery's status and, 150
    Overlord and, 119–121, 123, 155–156
    Pyle on meaning of, 150–151
    Spaatz and, 133, 134, 137
    Stanmore Conference and, 132–135
    target area of, 131–132
    Tedder and, 134, 140–141
    U.S. ground casualties in, 137–138, 139
Collins, J. Lawton, 106–107, 108, 138, 139, 158, 175, 177, 187, 193, 205, 212, 215, 267
    Cobra Operation and, 130, 143–144, 147, 150
    at Stanhope Conference, 132
Combined Chiefs of Staff, 48, 49, 50, 56, 59, 62, 64, 134, 262
    Overlord plans and, 71
Congress, U.S., 45
Cook, Gilbert, 215–216, 220, 230–231, 232, 237, 252
Corsica, 59
Coutances, 113, 118, 120, 129, 131, 143–144, 145, 147
Crerar, Henry, 39, 81, 83, 84, 107, 108, 111, 146, 166, 168, 185, 200–203, 217, 218, 222, 229, 233, 237, 243, 249, 256, 266, 269
    background of, 181
    First Army command and, 181–182
    first combat of, 182–183, 197
    McNaughton replaced by, 181
    Montgomery and, 182–183
    Simonds's relationship with, 181–182

Crocker, J. T., 182–183, 197
Cunningham, John, 56
Czechoslovakia, 89

Daily Telegraph and Morning Post (London), 258
Dallek, Robert, 45
Darlan Deal, 32
D-Day, see Overlord, Operation
de Gaulle, Charles, 193, 194, 251, 269, 270, 271
    Bradley's stop order and, 207, 209
de Guingand, Francis, 84, 115, 207
Dempsey, Miles, 39, 82, 84, 104, 105, 108, 109–112, 116, 117, 136, 146, 147–148, 166, 168, 182, 183, 190, 203, 211, 214, 215, 217, 218, 222, 226, 233, 243, 249, 256, 260, 266
    Goodwood Operation and, 118–119, 121, 123, 133
    Montgomery on, 107
    Patton's view of, 83
Denmark, 44, 89, 96
D'Este, Carlo, 110, 181
Deutsch, Harold, 264, 271
Dieppe raid, 29, 69, 91, 180–181
Dietrich, Josef, 214, 216, 217, 221, 224, 240
Dollmann, Friedrich, 95–96, 98, 99
Doolittle, James H., 134, 137, 138
Dreux, 216, 218, 232, 233, 235, 236, 237
    XV Corps drive on, 222, 223, 231
Dufresne, Michel, 190–191, 207, 259
Dunkirk evacuation, 29, 89, 264

Eberbach, Heinrich, 216, 224, 240, 258
Eddy, Manton, 252, 255
Egypt, 54, 55, 264
Eighth Air Force, U.S., 134, 136, 137, 138, 139
Eighth Army, British, 74, 107, 181, 185, 194
    Casablanca Conference and, 56
    Italian campaign and, 62, 64, 65, 264
    Leese as commander of, 82–83
    Montgomery's transformation of, 30
    Sicilian campaign and, 60
8 Corps, British, 119–120, 122
VIII Corps, U.S., 162, 164
    Brittany campaign and, 158, 159, 160, 165, 169
    Cobra Operation and, 130–131, 146, 147
    Middleton as commander of, 156–157
80th Infantry Division, U.S., 230, 232, 241, 250
Eisenhower, Dwight D., 22, 33, 34, 37, 38, 53, 59, 60, 62, 65, 66, 67, 106, 114, 146, 155, 157, 159, 196, 219, 234, 235, 240, 243, 253, 259, 262

Eisenhower, Dwight D. (*cont.*)
  Anglo-American alliance, 42, 63
  appointed Supreme Commander, 72
  assessment of, 263–265
  BBC's remarks and, 61–62
  Bradley's correspondence with, 150
  Bradley's stop order and, 209, 210, 211
  British scorn for, 72–73, 74
  Brittany campaign and, 160–161, 163
  Cobra bombardment and, 133, 134, 140,
    141
  command style of, 27–28, 111–112
  Darlan Deal and, 32
  encirclement and, 187–188, 190
  "killing ground" viewed by, 19
  and liberation of Paris, 270
  as Marshall's subordinate, 49
  in Montgomery-Brooke correspondence, 58
  Montgomery's command arrangement with,
    111, 212–213, 244, 258, 263–264,
    265
  Montgomery's correspondence with,
    115–116, 121, 122, 123
  Montgomery's first encounter with, 29–30
  North African campaign and, 55
  Overlord and, 71, 75, 82, 83, 84–85,
    110–112
  on Patton, 147
  personality of, 26–27, 29, 30
  post-Cobra blueprint and, 165
  post-Overlord operations and, 241, 251,
    255, 256
  postwar perception of, 266–267
  Sicilian campaign and, 60, 62
  Third Army activation and, 146
Eisenhower, John, 66
El Alamein, Battle of, 30, 55, 150
Elbeuf, 257, 258
election of 1940, U.S., 46
Ellis, L. F., 43, 103, 147
English, John A., 179, 182, 183, 268
Europe First strategy, 55
  Anglo-American alliance and, 47–48
  Marshall and, 53, 54

Falaise pocket:
  Anglo-American alliance and, 250
  Anglo-Canadian relationship and, 269
  Canadian attack and, 166, 179–186, 188,
    190, 192, 200–203, 217–218, 229
  closing of, 245–246
  final Allied rush and, 259–260
  French non-participation in, 195,
    232–233, 241, 249, 265–271
  German withdrawal and escape from,
    227–228, 233, 240, 242–243, 250,
    252, 253–254, 259
  and invasion of southern France, 225, 226,
    228

  Mantes bridgehead and, 238, 241,
    244–245, 256
  Montgomery's preoccupation with, 217–218
  Mount Ormel engagement and, 251–252
  Orne River and, 240
  Poles and, 251–252
  post-Overlord operations and, 262
  tactical air support and, 239, 253
Fifteenth Army, German, 93, 96, 157, 192
XV Corps, U.S., 158, 159, 215, 216, 220,
    221, 229–230, 257
  Alençon area and, 201–204
  Dreux movement and, 222, 223, 231
  French contingent of, 194–195
  Le Mans drive by, 166–167, 168, 169,
    191, 192
  Mantes bridgehead and, 238, 241, 256
  Seine River drive and, 243, 244, 252, 256
  stop order and, 208, 210, 211
  thinning out of, 206
5th Armored Division, U.S., 193, 203, 244,
    250
Fifth Army, U.S., 33, 62, 63–64, 65, 67,
    194, 264
V Corps, U.S., 146, 205, 232, 234, 252,
    270
5th Infantry Division, U.S., 168, 189, 191
Fifth Panzer Army, German, 214, 224
Finland, 44, 93, 173
1st Armored Division, Polish, 185, 239
First Army, Canadian, 82, 107, 111, 146
  Crerar in command of, 181–182
  Falaise offensive and, 166, 168, 200,
    268–269
  Overlord plans and, 81, 83
First Army, U.S., 105, 111, 123, 129, 232,
    234, 236, 237, 243, 245, 257, 266,
    267
  activation of, 145–146
  Bradley as commander of, 33–34, 114–115
  casualties sustained by, 120
  Cobra bombardment and, 131, 132, 137,
    138, 139, 140
  Cobra breakthrough and, 147, 150, 165
  Coutances drive and, 113, 118, 120
  G-2 reports of, 154, 238–239
  Hodges assumes command of, 165
  Mortain counterattack and, 177
  Overlord plans and, 80–81, 83–84
  prisoners of war taken by, 150
  St-Lô captured by, 133
I Corps, Canadian, 181
Foch, Ferdinand, 48
Forces of the Interior, French, *see* Resistance,
  French
Fortitude deception, 85, 96
4th Armored Division, U.S., 156, 161
4th Armoured Division, Canadian, 185, 250
47th (London) Division, British, 28

Franco, Francisco, 90
France, 27, 34, 35, 44, 45, 47, 48, 55, 56,
  59, 62, 67, 70, 89, 91, 92, 93, 173,
  180
  Italy's invasion of, 90
  southern invasion of, 225, 226, 228
Free French Forces, 193
French Expeditionary Corps, 194
French Morocco, 54
French Northwest Africa, 54, 55

Gaffey, Hugh, 162–163, 191, 209, 210, 232,
  233, 234–235, 236, 241
  Patton's memo to, 191
Gallipoli landings, 69
Gay, Hobart, 236
George VI, king of England, 30, 83
Germany, Nazi, 43–44, 45, 48, 50, 53,
  89–90, 93, 263
  declares war on U.S., 47
  Soviet pact with, 89
  Soviet Union invaded by, 46
Gerow, Leonard, 232, 233, 237, 238, 241,
  268, 270
  background of, 234
  Patton and, 234–235, 236
Gold Beach, 95, 103
Goodwood, Operation, 133, 136, 182, 184
  Montgomery and, 119–120, 121–124
Göring, Hermann, 90
Gort, Lord, 72
Graham, Dominick, 182
Grand Alliance, see Anglo-American alliance
Great Britain, 42, 43, 44, 53, 54–55, 66,
  89, 91
  Anglo-American leadership and, 50–51
  Europe First strategy and, 47–48
  Lend-Lease and, 46
  manpower shortage of, 27
  U.S. aid to, 45
  World War I and, 27
  see also Anglo-American alliance
Greece, 90
Greenland, 46
Grigg, James, 119
  Montgomery's correspondence with, 233
Guadalcanal, Battle of, 107
Gustav Line, 116, 194

Haislip, Wade, 158, 159–160, 168, 169,
  175, 199–200, 202, 204, 215, 216,
  220, 222, 223, 231, 232, 237, 238,
  241, 245, 250, 251, 268
  Alençon maneuver of, 203
  Argentan as objective of, 205–226
  background of, 167
  Bradley's stop order and, 207, 208, 209,
    210, 211, 212

Le Mans drive and, 166–167, 188,
  189–190, 195, 196
  Patton's instructions to, 191–192
  see also XV Corps, U.S.
Hamilton, Nigel, 54, 79, 81, 190, 203, 244,
  265
Hannibal, 20
Hanson, Chester, 213, 219–220
  Montgomery described by, 221
Harold II, king of England, 261
Harris, Arthur "Bomber," 133, 134
Harris, Stephen, 180
Hastings, Battle of, 261
Hastings, Max, 73, 81, 110, 115, 121–122,
  123, 163, 265
Hausser, Paul, 224, 240
Hautecloque, Philippe François Marie de, see
  Leclerc, Jacques
Heavy Bomber Command, RAF, 134
Hill 317, 175, 176, 177
Hindenburg, Paul von, 20, 89
Hitler, Adolf, 22, 29, 45, 90, 95, 117, 263
  attempted assassination of, 124, 154, 173,
    261
  Avranches attack orders of, 192–193, 197
  Dunkirk evacuation and, 89
  fortress cities concept of, 174
  Italian campaign and, 65
  Kluge's disappearance and, 222, 223, 224,
    225
  Mortain counterattack and, 173–174, 175,
    177, 178
  Overlord and, 96–101
  proposed Alençon counterattack and,
    200–201, 212
  as supreme military commander, 92–93
  unreal outlook of, 216–217
  western defenses and, 91–92, 94
  withdrawal ordered by, 228, 229
Hobbs, Leland, 145, 176–177, 187, 193
Hodges, Courtney, 38, 39, 146, 168, 177,
  187–188, 190, 192, 199, 202, 205,
  215, 226, 234, 237, 238, 241, 243,
  249, 256, 257, 260, 266, 267, 268,
  270
  background and personality of, 34
  First Army command assumed by, 165
  Gerow and, 235–236
  Montgomery's pique at, 114–115
Holocaust, 44
Hopkins, Harry, 54
Horrocks, Brian, 213
Hughes, Everett, 190–191
Hungary, 185

Iceland, 46
Imperial General Staff, British, 49
India, 47
Irwin, Le Roy, 189

isolationism, 44, 47, 180
Italy, 30, 33, 45, 47, 55, 59, 74, 93, 116,
　　173, 181, 185, 194, 228, 264
　allied invasion of, 62
　Anzio landings in, 65–67
　capitulation of, 62
　France invaded by, 90
　Montgomery and campaign in, 63–64, 65
　Salerno battles in, 33, 62, 63

Japan, 47, 49, 53
Jodl, Alfred, 223–224, 225, 227
Joint Chiefs of Staff, U.S., 48, 110
　Marshall and, 49
Joyce, Kenyon, 169
Juin, Alphonse, 194
Juno Beach, 95, 103, 182

Kasserine Pass, Battle of, 32, 92, 189
　Anglo-American alliance and, 57–58
Keegan, John, 28
Kibler, A. Franklin, 209
King, Mackenzie, 180
Kitching, George, 185, 186, 250, 251–252,
　　254
Kluge, Hans von, 117, 124–125, 147, 186,
　　192, 193, 197, 202, 205, 217
　Cobra breakthrough and, 144–145, 151
　death of, 242
　Dietrich's report to, 214
　disappearance of, 221–222, 223, 224–225
　German withdrawal begun by, 227–228, 229
　Model's replacement of, 240, 242
　Mortain counterattack and, 174–175,
　　177–178
　proposed Alençon counterattack and,
　　200–201, 211
Korean War, 42

Langlade, General de, 194, 195, 269,
　　270–271
Lattre de Tassigny, Jean de, 194
Laval, 166, 167
Leclerc, Jacques, 39, 202, 241, 269
　allies resented by, 196
　background and personality of, 193–194
　Haislip's orders disregarded by, 204–205,
　　209
　Paris preoccupation of, 232–233, 270
　Patton's meetings with, 195, 232–233
Leese, Oliver, 82–83
　Montgomery's correspondence with, 107–108
Leigh-Mallory, Trafford, 73, 133, 253
　air support discontinued by, 225–226
　Bradley's correspondence with, 136
　Cobra bombardment and, 134–136, 137,
　　138, 139, 141
　at Stanhope Conference, 134–135

Le Mans, 175, 188, 193, 195, 197, 199,
　　200, 203, 212, 215, 223
　Bradley and drive on, 167–168
　XV Corps drive on, 166–167, 168, 169,
　　189–190, 191, 192
　Patton and, 166–167
Lend-Lease, 46
Libya, 30, 54, 56, 78, 194, 264
Lorient, 162, 164–165, 174, 197
Ludendorff, Erich von, 20
Luftwaffe, 90, 94
Luxembourg, 89, 92, 235

MacArthur, Douglas, 35, 42
McAdoo, Richard, 15–18, 254
McMahon, J. S., 182
McNaughton, Andrew G. L., 180–181, 182
McNeill, William H., 43, 70, 265
Maczek, Stanislaw, 185
Mantes bridgehead, 238, 241, 244–245, 256
Market Garden, Operation, 22, 267
Marshall, George C., 27, 30, 33, 38, 56, 58,
　　59, 160, 234, 235, 240
　Bradley and, 31–32, 34–35
　Brooke's relationship with, 50
　Eisenhower as subordinate of, 49
　Europe First strategy and, 53, 54
　Joint Chiefs of Staff and, 49
　military career of, 48–49
　Patton and, 34–35
　personality of, 49
Mayenne, 166, 167
Mexico, 34, 35
Middle East Forces, British, 29
Middleton, Troy, 130–131, 146, 147, 158,
　　160, 165, 168
　background of, 156–157
　Wood's Brittany campaign and, 162–164
Miller, Merle, 75, 150
Miracle in the West, 260
Model, Walther, 240, 260
Monte Cassino, 116, 185
Montgomery, Bernard L., 20, 22, 39, 41, 58,
　　155, 157, 166, 173, 205, 230, 252,
　　254, 259, 268, 272, 273
　Alençon maneuver and, 203
　allied coalition and, 219–220
　American commanders as regarded by,
　　81–82
　assessment of, 264, 269
　Bradley as viewed by, 81–82, 107
　Bradley's correspondence with, 217–218
　Bradley's meetings with, 118, 213–214,
　　215, 235–236, 243
　Bradley's relationship with, 41, 146–147,
　　213, 263
　Bradley's stop order and, 207, 209–210,
　　211, 212

Brittany campaign and, 146, 147, 150,
  160–161, 163
Brooke's correspondence with, 74, 82, 105,
  108, 115, 121, 160, 181, 183,
  196–197, 200, 203, 205, 216, 218,
  219, 225, 233, 239, 240–241, 258
Caen-Cherbourg strategy and, 107–110,
  111
Canadian troops misjudged by, 269
Clark and, 63–64
Cobra Operation and, 129, 150
command structure altered by, 146
Crerar and, 182–183
Eighth Army and, 30
Eisenhower's command arrangement and,
  111, 212–213, 244, 258, 263–264,
  265
Eisenhower's correspondence with, 108,
  115–116, 121, 122, 123
Eisenhower's first encounter with, 29–30
encirclement concept and, 167, 190,
  196–197, 200, 202–203
enemy situation misread by, 239–240,
  242, 246, 249, 262
German withdrawal as perceived by, 166,
  205
Goodwood Operation and, 119–120,
  121–124
Grigg's correspondence with, 233
Hanson's description of, 221
Hodges and, 114–115
Italian campaign and, 63–64, 65
Leese's correspondence with, 107–108
McNaughton and, 180
media and, 115, 266
military career of, 28–30
North Africa campaign and, 30, 55, 56, 78
Overlord leadership and, 73–74, 104–105,
  110
Overlord planning and, 74–75, 77–81
Patton as seen by, 81–82, 108
personality of, 26–27, 30–31, 78–79
personal message of, to troops, 253
political realities and, 115
post-Cobra planning and, 165–166, 168
post-Overlord operations and, 243, 251,
  253, 255
postwar perception of, 266–267
St-Léonard ridge objective and, 237, 238
St. Paul's School meetings and, 80–81,
  83–84
second stop order and, 225
Sicilian campaign and, 60–61
temperament of, 78–79
Trun objective and, 217, 229
21 Army Group appointment of, 72
U.S. troops disdained by, 57
Morgan, Frederick, 56, 71, 74, 75

Morgenthau, Henry, Jr., 190
Morocco, 32, 55
Mortain counterattack, 173–178
  Bradley and, 167, 177, 199, 202, 205
  Falaise area and, 178
  Hitler and, 173–174, 175, 177, 178
  Kluge and, 174–175, 177–178
  onset of, 175
Mortain salient, 187, 190, 193, 201, 202,
  203
  encirclement and, 188, 197, 199–200
  German withdrawal and, 205, 212, 217
Mount Ormel, 251, 254, 262
Mussolini, Benito, 45, 90
  removed from power, 62

Nantes, 164, 168, 189
Napoleon I, emperor of France, 28, 70–71
National Guard, U.S., 45
Navy, U.S., 47–48, 49
Netherlands, 89, 91, 92, 93, 238, 267
neutrality acts, U.S., 44, 45
XIX Corps, U.S., 146, 205, 237, 243,
  244–245, 250, 252, 257
90th Infantry Division, U.S., 222, 230,
  231–232, 234, 235, 237, 241–242,
  246
Ninth Air Force, U.S., 133, 134, 138
9th Division, U.S., 252
IX Tactical Air Command, U.S., 132, 134
North African campaign, 29, 31, 33, 36, 58,
  90, 91, 92, 150, 194
  allied landings in, 55
  Casablanca Conference and, 56–57
  Churchill and, 54
  Eisenhower and, 55
  Montgomery and, 30, 55, 56, 78
Norway, 44, 45, 89, 96, 180, 185

Oliver, Lunsford, 193, 202, 203, 205, 209
Omaha Beach, 95, 104, 234, 267
Operation Victory (de Guingand), 207
Orléans, 188, 220, 229, 230–231, 232, 236
Overlord, Operation, 56, 59, 62, 64, 65–66,
  67, 69–86, 145, 262
  air superiority in, 94, 100
  allied casualties in, 109, 120, 121, 122
  basic plans of, 71–72
  beaches in, 95, 103–104
  Bradley and, 33–34, 80
  Brittany in plans of, 155–156, 160, 161
  Canadian units in, 182
  Churchill and planning of, 74–75, 83
  Churchill's opposition to, 69–70
  Cobra Operation in, 119–121, 123,
    155–156
  Combined Chiefs of Staff and, 71
  commanders in, 73, 81–83

Overlord, Operation (*cont.*)
  Eisenhower and, 71, 75, 82, 83, 84–85,
    110–112
  Eisenhower-Montgomery meetings and,
    106, 111
  Fortitude deception and, 85, 96
  German casualties in, 118
  Goodwood Operation in, 121–124
  logistics and, 85–86
  Loire River in plans of, 188
  media and, 115
  "Montgomery Plan" of, 74–75, 77–81
  Montgomery's leadership in, 73–74,
    104–105, 110
  Morgan plan for, 75–77
  Norfolk House meeting and, 75
  onset of, 95–96
  Rommel and, 94–100
  Rundstedt and, 96–97, 98, 99–100
  St-Lô taken in, 120
  St. Paul's School meetings and, 80–81,
    83–84
  Seine River ports and, 160
  strategic bombers used in, 116–117
  Villers Bocage incident and, 105
  weather and, 113

Panzer Group West, German, 96, 98–99
Pariseau, Jean, 269
Patton, George S., Jr., 20, 22, 28, 29, 30,
  31, 39, 41, 42, 55, 79, 84, 104, 107,
  111, 145, 151, 193, 199–200, 201,
  202, 204, 215–216, 221, 225, 231,
  237, 238, 249, 260, 262–263, 264,
  266, 267, 268
  "another Dunkirk" comment of, 236
  assessment of, 271–273
  background of, 35–36
  Bradley's relationship with, 32–33, 34,
    36–38, 114, 157, 158–159
  Bradley's stop order and, 206–211
  Brittany campaign and, 146, 147,
    155–158, 160
  chain of command and, 159
  demeanor of, 36
  Dempsey as seen by, 83
  Eisenhower on, 147
  encirclement concept of, 167–168,
    188–189, 190–192, 196, 197,
    202–203, 238, 252–253, 255–256
  Gaffey memo of, 191
  Gerow and, 234–235, 236
  Haislip as instructed by, 191–192
  Hanson's observation of, 219–220
  Joyce's correspondence with, 169
  Leclerc's meetings with, 195, 232–233
  Le Mans drive and, 166–167
  Mantes bridgehead and, 241, 244–245
  Marshall and, 34–35

  media and, 230
  Montgomery's view of, 81–82, 108
  "over-caution" comment of, 159
  personality of, 26–27
  postwar reputation of, 271
  press censorship and, 157
  second stop order and, 223, 231
  Sicilian campaign and, 60–61
  slapping incident and, 34, 38, 157, 163,
    272
  Tunisian campaign and, 58–59
  Wood's operation and, 162–164
Paulus, Friedrich, 20
Pearl Harbor bombing, 47, 90–91
Periodic Report, 153–154
Pershing, John J., 34, 35, 48, 181
Phoney War, 29, 44
Poland, 44, 89, 91, 185
Portugal, 44
Pyle, Ernie, 31, 150–151
  on Cobra breakout, 150–151

Quebec Conference, 62
Quesada, Elwood "Pete," 132–133, 134,
  135, 138

Ramsay, Bertram, 73
Rennes, 161–162
Resistance, French, 53, 95, 96
  Brittany campaign and, 165, 166
  and invasion of southern France, 228
Reynolds, Phyllis, 218, 240
Rhineland, 89
Rokossovsky, Konstantin, 20
Rommel, Erwin, 30, 54–57, 78, 90, 108, 117
  death of, 124
  Overlord and, 94–100
  western defenses and, 92–94
Roosevelt, Franklin D., 47, 48, 49, 54, 66,
  110
  Atlantic Charter and, 46
  Casablanca Conference and, 56
  Churchill's relationship with, 42–43, 44,
    45
  Eisenhower appointed Supreme Commander
    by, 72
  Lend-Lease and, 46
  neutrality laws and, 45
  Quebec Conference and, 62
  Tehran Conference and, 64
  Trident Conference and, 59
Rouen, 258
Roy, R. H., 179
Rundstedt, Gerd von, 91, 108, 117, 260
  Overlord and, 96–97, 98, 99–101
  western defenses and, 93, 94

St-Léonard ridge, 228, 230, 235, 237, 242,
  246

St-Lô, 120, 133
St-Malo, 157, 164, 174, 197
St-Nazaire raid, 91
Salerno, 33, 62, 63
Samsonov, Aleksandr, 20
Sardinia, 59
2nd Armored Division, French, 193, 194,
    203, 222, 230, 231–232, 241, 269,
    271
Second Army, British, 80, 82, 83, 105, 111,
    121, 123, 166, 168, 182, 183, 200
II Corps, Canadian, 182, 183
II Corps, U.S., 32, 33, 36, 58–59
2nd Tactical Force, RAF, 133, 134
Seine River, 230, 239, 243, 252, 257–258,
    262
  bridges of, 218–219, 253–254
  Mantes bridgehead on, 238, 241,
      244–245, 256
  Overlord and, 160
Seventh Army, German, 93, 95–96, 98,
    224
Seventh Army, U.S., 33, 60
VII Corps, U.S., 107, 130, 146, 158, 159,
    175, 177, 205, 215
7th Panzer Division, German, 92
79th Infantry Division, U.S., 245, 250,
    253
Shaw, George Bernard, 41
Sibert (Bradley's G-2 officer), 207, 218
Sicily, 30, 32, 33, 37, 55, 56–57, 59, 74,
    181, 264
  Anglo-American alliance and, 61–62
  Patton-Montgomery rivalry in, 60–61
Siegfried Line (West Wall), 174, 257, 272
Simonds, Guy, 82, 217, 252, 269
  background of, 182
  Crerar's relationship with, 181–182
  Falaise attack and, 183, 184–185, 186
6th Armored Division, U.S., 156, 164
Smith, Walter Bedell, 71, 75, 140
Soldier's Story, A (Bradley), 211
Soviet Union, 44, 50, 91, 92
  German invasion of, 46, 90
  German pact with, 89
  Tehran Conference and, 64
Spaatz, Carl A. "Tooey," 133, 134, 137
Spain, 45, 90, 228
Stacey, Charles P., 180, 254
Stalin, Joseph, 64, 89
Stalingrad, Battle of, 20
Stanmore Conference, 132–135
stop order, 206–212
Strategic Air Forces, U.S., 133, 137
Sullivan, John J., 42, 133, 135, 139, 140
Summersby, Kay, 75
Switzerland, 174
Sword Beach, 95, 103
Syria, 55

Tannenburg, Battle of, 20
Tedder, Arthur, 56, 73, 105–106, 110, 121,
    122, 123
  Cobra bombardment and, 134, 140–141
Tehran Conference, 64–65
Third Army, U.S., 34, 114, 162, 168, 177,
    191, 192, 210, 215, 217, 232, 233,
    234, 237, 262
  activation of, 145–146
  in allied order of battle, 111
  Brittany campaign and, 156, 160, 169
  Overlord role of, 81, 84, 160
  in post-Overlord planning, 256, 257
  secrecy and, 157, 230
3rd Division, Canadian, 182
30th Division, U.S., 145, 175–177, 187
Tobruk, fall of, 54
Trident Conference, 59–60
Trun, 200, 215, 217, 222, 229, 231–232,
    233, 234, 235, 236, 237, 240, 242,
    243, 250, 262
Tunisia, 30, 32, 36, 37, 54, 55, 56, 57–58,
    267
12th Army Group, U.S., 112, 114, 168, 191,
    236
  activation of, 146
  Alençon advance and, 204
  Bradley's assignment to, 33–34
  operational boundaries and, 83
  order of battle and, 111
  Wood's maneuver and, 162, 163
XII Corps, U.S., 215–216, 220, 238, 252,
    255, 256
  Orléans captured by, 230–231
XX Corps, U.S., 167–168, 169, 189,
    191–192, 196, 202, 215–216, 218,
    220, 223, 231, 238, 252, 255, 256
21st Army Group, British, 114, 146, 210,
    222, 243
  control of U.S. units and, 219–220, 221
  Montgomery appointed to, 72
  operational boundaries and, 83
  order of battle and, 111

Ultra intercepts, 78, 85, 222, 269
  German counterattack and, 200, 206, 207,
      211–212
United Nations, 42
Utah Beach, 95, 103–104, 105, 106, 193,
    267

Vandenberg, Hoyt, 136–137
Varro, 20
Versailles, Treaty of, 89
Vichy government, 32
Victor Emmanuel III, king of Italy, 62
Villers Bocage incident, 105
V-Rockets, 92, 97

Walker, Walton, 189, 191, 192, 202,
    215–216, 220, 223, 231, 232, 237,
    252, 255
War As I Knew It (Patton), 210–211
War Cabinet, British, 72
War Department, U.S., 31, 49
War Plans Division, U.S., 234
Weigley, Russell, 189–190, 203, 204, 213,
    221
West Wall (Siegfried Line), 174, 257, 272
William I (the Conqueror), king of England,
    261
Williams, Edgar, 207
Wilmot, Chester, 186

Wilson, Henry Maitland, 66
Wilson, Woodrow, 46
Wood, John Shirley, 161–164, 165, 168,
    189, 190, 272
World War I, 27, 28, 35, 44, 76, 110, 180
    Anglo-American alliance and, 48
    Canadian forces in, 129
    Gallipoli landings in, 69
World War II, 27, 29, 43
    Canadian forces in, 179–180
    isolationism and, 44, 47
    onset of, 44
    *see also specific battles, commanders and
        units*